THE
ENIGMA
OF
ANGER

ESSAYS ON A
SOMETIMES DEADLY SIN

Garret Keizer

JOSSEY-BASS
A Wiley Company
www.josseybass.com

Published by

JOSSEY-BASS
A Wiley Company
989 Market Street
San Francisco, CA 94103-1741

www.josseybass.com

Copyright © 2002 by Garret Keizer.

Jossey-Bass is a registered trademark of John Wiley & Sons, Inc.

Jossey-Bass books and products are available through most bookstores. To contact Jossey-Bass directly, call (888) 378-2537, fax to (800) 605-2665, or visit our website at www.josseybass.com.

Substantial discounts on bulk quantities of Jossey-Bass books are available to corporations, professional associations, and other organizations. For details and discount information, contact the special sales department at Jossey-Bass.

We at Jossey-Bass strive to use the most environmentally sensitive paper stocks available to us. Our publications are printed on acid-free recycled stock whenever possible, and our paper always meets or exceeds minimum GPO and EPA requirements.

Credits appear on page 364.

The Scripture quotations contained herein (unless otherwise noted) are from the New Revised Standard Version Bible, copyright 1989, by the Division of Christian Education of the National Council of the Churches of Christ in the U.S.A. Used by permission. All rights reserved.

Jossey-Bass also publishes its books in a variety of electronic formats. Some content that appears in print may not be available in electronic books.

Interior design and composition by Valerie Brewster, Scribe Typography.

LIBRARY OF CONGRESS CATALOGING-IN-PUBLICATION DATA

Keizer, Garret.

The enigma of anger : essays on a sometimes deadly sin / Garret Keizer.

    p. cm.

ISBN 0-7879-5728-3 (alk. paper)

    1. Anger—Religious aspects—Christianity. I. Title.

BV4627.A5 K45 2002

241'.3—DC21

                      2002003806

FIRST EDITION

HB Printing 10 9 8 7 6 5 4 3 2 1

CONTENTS

For Kathy & Sarah

PREFACE

The aims of this book are perhaps as difficult to reconcile as
are the kindest of our motives with the most volatile of our
emotions. Putting the best face on things, one might say this
is a very human book.

First of all, I wanted to write about anger in a way that
would be genuinely helpful without resorting to the glibness
of the self-help movement. In other words, I wanted to eschew
solutions but not to eschew hope. I also wanted to face what
was ugliest about human history and about myself without
resorting to the creation of further ugliness.

Finally, I wanted to find common ground with my reader
through the only means I know for finding common ground,
which is to dig as deeply as possible into the ground of one's
own particularity, which often includes one's peculiarity too.
This meant that I was often writing as a man, a resident of a
small town, and a Christian, though I never felt as though I
were writing exclusively for men in churches in small towns.
The approach may strike some as restrictive, but to my mind
there is nothing more restrictive than trying to speak for
everyone. The best we can do is to speak as one person among
many, and hope that many—or at least a handful—will find
some good use for what we say. That's what I tried to do.

I had help. I want to thank Sheryl Fullerton, my editor;
Peter Matson, my agent; Jill Chaffee, my typist; James Doyle,
my friend; Kathy Keizer, my dearest partner in everything;

also Lisa VonKann and the staff of the St. Johnsbury Athenaeum; and, finally, every person alive or dead who made me angry enough to write this book.

Garret Keizer

Sutton, Vermont

May 2002

THE ENIGMA
OF ANGER

And when he had made a scourge of small cords, he drove them all out of the temple, and the sheep, and the oxen; and poured out the changers' money, and overthrew the tables; and said unto them that sold doves, take these things hence; make not my Father's house an house of merchandise. And his disciples remembered that it was written, The zeal of thine house hath eaten me up.

John 2:15–17

A covetous person who is now truly converted to God, he will exercise a spiritual covetousness still. . . . So will a voluptuous man who is turned to God find plenty and deliciousness enough in him to feed his soul. . . . And so an angry and passionate man will find zeal enough in the House of God to eat him up.

John Donne

ANGER
IN THE
LORD

"Be not too hasty," said Imlac, "to trust, or to admire, the teachers of morality: they discourse like angels, but they live like men."

Samuel Johnson, *Rasselas*

WHERE I
COME FROM

O nly three limbs of a sugar maple tree, none thicker than
my arm but each broad enough to shade a horse, lay in
a sprinkling of sawdust by the side of the road. On the trunk
above them, three pathetic stumps oozed sap. This was my
tree, one of the beautiful ancient maples that line our rural
Vermont property where it meets the road. Those trees had
caught our eye even before my wife and I had seen the "For
Sale" sign on what is now our home. I love to walk past those
maples on afternoons when I finish work, and evenings before turning again to more work; I had especially longed to
do so on that cloudy June day before unbuckling a briefcase
full of final exams that would keep me up for much of the
night. Mine was a smug little joy, I realized even then, as
much the pride of ownership as the appreciation of nature,
but I didn't care. We want our joys to be harmless; we don't

need them to be noble. But now even that small joy was cut short by the sight of those sawn-off limbs, enigmatic and almost insulting at my feet.

The town road crew had cut them off the tree; I was sure of that. The men had been grading that section of road in the afternoon just before I came home. I was less sure as to why they had cut them. The limbs had not hung out over the road. They had not been near any telephone or power lines. They had not been rotten or in danger of falling off. The only plausible reason I could imagine was that the road crew had cut off the limbs to make it easier to turn the grader, though there was an access to a hay field where they might have done the same thing less than a hundred feet away. Could they really have been so lazy?

But then, there didn't have to be a plausible reason, did there? Maybe one of the men had just felt like sawing off a few limbs—no different, really, from a kid in my classroom feeling in the mood to toss a rumpled wad of paper over my shoulder and into the trash can or to stick out his foot when another student walked by—except that no kid in my classroom would dare do such a thing. Well, some of the men around here (I muttered to myself) believe that nothing grows out of the earth or slips through a birth canal for any purpose better than to be cut down or shot. Today the limbs, tomorrow the whole damn tree, what the heck. If there's dynamite available, so much the better. And I did not think it irrational to suppose that there was a message intended by the gratuitous sawing off of those limbs, something like the message I'd found soaped on my car windows on the first Halloween after we'd moved in: "Fuck you" plus "Ain't Vermont great?"—a message to the flatlanders lest they get too cozy in their precious little farmhouse and forget who was really in charge around here. We had scarcely lived in town long enough to strike up a conversation, let alone to make an enemy.

That was going to change. Tomorrow morning at 7:00, or whenever the town garage opened, I was going to deliver a little message of my own, which is that if you want to touch something that belongs to me, you'd better talk to me first or be prepared to talk to me afterward; and talking to me afterward, as I was fully prepared to demonstrate, is never a good way to start your day. And nobody had better give me any regulatory drivel about "right of way" either; you want to pull out your little rule books, I might show you a few rules you never heard of. Three healthy limbs sawn off a tree—*for absolutely no reason.* And I knew how this stuff worked—you don't teach school without learning how these things work: It's a matter of incremental aggression, beginning with something so deliberately small that you'll look like a fool if you complain and ending with something so outrageously nasty that you'll feel like a fool that you didn't. So much for that bit about choosing your battles. The battle I choose is every single battle that chooses me, and I fight to win every last one. Go on, tell me it's only three limbs off a tree. I want somebody to tell me it's only three limbs off a tree. How about if I break only three limbs on an idiot? God, was I mad!

God . . . was I mad?

⌒

I am a descendant of angry men. My father had a temper. I used to help him work on his cars, and it was rare that we could finish a job without at least one minor flare-up. It was just as rare that we closed the hood with hard feelings. My father once confided to my mother, who wisely shared his confidence with me: "Gary could tell me to go screw myself, but I would still know he loved me." It was the truth. It had been the truth for men in our family before either of us was born.

My great-grandfather, a Dutch Reformed minister, is said to have cursed his Heavenly Father following the deaths of his wife and two young daughters from tuberculosis. He is also said to have refused to sign a doctrinal confession affirming the damnation of all heathen souls. Though after long wanderings he returned to the pulpit (first crossing the Atlantic to the United States) and though it's doubtful he ever lost his faith (one doesn't curse what one doesn't believe to exist), the image of his clenched fist shaken in the face of heaven, and perhaps in the faces of his seminary too, has long been with me.

So have the stories of his son, my grandfather and namesake, another angry ancestor I never knew. One day he came home from work to discover that a neighbor had conveniently emptied the contents of his cesspool next to the sand pile where his son and daughter played across the street. My grandfather threatened to hoist the neighbor up by his ankles if every trace of filth was not removed within twenty-four hours. "And when you're finished, you cheap Holland bastard," roared the minister's son, "you get on your knees and pray."

The phrase "Dutch temper" and the phrase "cheap Holland bastard"—uttered by a Hollander no less—are two signifiers of my heritage, a patrimony passed with fiery love from father to son. They are not the only signifiers, however. Life would be too easy if they were. My first reading of the Gospels was from a New Testament presented by my great-grandfather to my father when my parents were first married. That too was part of the same heritage, and it ensured that my Dutch temper could seldom exist without Christian remorse, nor Christian meekness without some inner resistance. The story of my journey in faith has often amounted to the story of my struggle with anger. This book is a reflection based on those two stories.

⌒

I am writing about anger for at least three specific reasons. All of them are vividly personal, though I trust that they are no less common than anger itself.

1. My anger has often seemed out of proportion—that is, too great or too little, but more often too great—for the occasion that gave rise to it.

2. My anger has more often distressed those I love and who love me than it has afflicted those at whom I was angry.

3. My anger has not carried me far enough toward changing what legitimately enrages me. In fact, the anger often saps the conviction.

It's fair to say that I am writing not only *about* anger, but also *in* anger. In other words, anger is in some ways my inspiration as well as my subject. I can give three reasons for that as well.

First, I have grown increasingly impatient with the blithe reductionism of the so-called self-help movement. I have grown impatient at seeing the laudable idea that life is a series of struggles to be undertaken—or questions to be asked, or burdens to be borne—replaced with the idea that life is essentially a set of problems to be solved by the adoption of the right program (spiritual or electronic) or the purchase of the right product (pharmaceutical or electronic).

I have also grown increasingly angry at our full-bellied acquiescence to social and economic injustice. I'm referring to the notion that everything other than the perfectible self is too vast and complex to admit to any remedy whatsoever, and that our best course of (in)action lies in ironical detachment or in the cultivation of an abrasive attitude that delivers some of the release, but packs none of the punch, of well-aimed rage. Our advertising and even our arts convey the idea that we as a society are brash, irreverent, and free of all constraint, when the best available evidence would suggest that we are in fact tame, spayed, and easily brought to heel.

And finally, I am writing in petulant resistance to the idea that anger is an emotion with no rightful place in the life of a Christian or in the emotional repertoire of any evolved human being. Darwinian evolution I can buy; most of the other forms, however, I can neither buy nor stomach. Darwin saw us linked with the animals, and therefore to the material creation as a whole; so do the Old and New Testaments. But the popular theology (most of it Gnostic) that portrays perfection as the shedding of every primitive instinct, and portrays God as an impersonal sanitizing spirit, is to my mind evidence of a satanic spirit. The Lord my God is a jealous God and an angry God, as well as a loving God and a merciful God. I am unable to imagine one without the other. I am unable to commit to any messiah who doesn't knock over tables.

A few years ago I told a dear friend of mine that I was going to write a book someday for angry men and women. "I think there need to be more of them," he quipped. I'm inclined to agree. But if he's right, if more of us need to be angry, then it follows that we shall require a more careful application of anger and a finer discernment of when anger applies. That is the challenge of this book and one of the main challenges of the man who presumes to write it.

⌒

I never did go to the town garage the morning after I found those three severed tree limbs. That night as I sat at the kitchen table correcting final exams, I began to hear a noise "as of a rushing wind" but of such an immediate and dreadful intensity that I could not at first be certain it was the wind. I remember fixing my eyes on one of the dark window-panes, which seemed about to shatter at any second, and thinking that the force outside could not possibly increase. It increased. I did not think I was dying, but the unreal sensation of those moments must be what it is like suddenly to realize that you are about to die. The rain was falling too hard. The next crack of thunder might be louder than we could bear. The lights snapped off. The roof sounded as though it were being ripped from the house.

I rushed my wife and our year-old daughter into the basement and then foolishly went upstairs to see what was happening and what I could do, which of course was nothing. Within a few minutes, the worst of the storm had passed. The rain subsided enough for me to see through the windows. One of the maple trees in our yard was snapped in two. Moving to the front windows, I saw to my horror that half the roof of our large barn across the road was gone, rafters and steel together.

For the next three days we were without electric power. Two-hundred-year-old maple trees and limbs the size of telephone poles lay across the road for more than a mile. The central path of the storm—and there is still disagreement more than a decade later as to whether it was a small tornado or simply a thunderstorm with a terrific downdraft—crossed the road about a quarter mile from our house and cut a swath of toppled trees and peeled roofs that extended through an entire county and beyond. In spite of the commotion we had heard, our house roof was spared. But twenty-foot-square sections of steel and beam from the barn lay hundreds of yards behind our house in a hay field. They had been torn from the barn and blown over the house. They might just as easily have been blown through it.

How puny my three limbs seemed in comparison to such carnage. And how puny my anger seemed in comparison to such fury. It was difficult for me not to think of them as related in some way, as temptation and warning, as sin and punishment, even as the psychological cause of a meteorological effect. Or as I've since come to think of them, as a man's paltry anger defused by God's tremendous mercy.

I took my chain saw out to the road and began to cut one of the massive limbs that lay across it. One of the road crew drove up, rolled down his window, and thanked me for saving him some work. Had he gotten out of his car, I would have thrown my arms around him.

For the Lord thy God is a consuming fire.

Deuteronomy

THE WRATH
OF GOD

I wonder when I first became aware of anger. Was it as my own reaction or as someone else's that I first knew what it meant to be upset, a word we use for our emotions and also for objects turned over, knocked off their feet.

I can imagine either possibility. I can imagine that I first knew anger as my own inborn emotion. Before anyone allowed himself to be angry in my infant presence, I would have experienced some frustration that led to rage. Don't we sometimes see the spectacle of a baby with his face purple from bawling, his back stiffened, his clenched fists beating the air and say, "Oh, he's mad now!" But is he? Is the baby feeling what I know as anger, or is he merely feeling an extreme form of distress, of enormous helpless need? This may indeed be anger, but only in an embryonic form.

However congenital our capacities for rage, I'm inclined to think that we learn to be angry, and that this learning comes along with other things we learn: with skills, strengths, and possibilities. We could take a step further and say that the fullest experience of anger is not even possible apart from a knowledge of skills, strengths, and possibilities. We may liken an adult's temper tantrum to that of "a big baby," but even a very big baby does not yet know what it truly means to be angry. I say this because I define *anger* as an emotion of extreme frustration (something a baby knows) poised at the possibility of action (something a baby cannot know, or cannot fully know). If we think of our emotions as having purposes—that is, if we think of them as having been created or as having evolved for a reason—might the purpose of anger be to enable us to break loose, to struggle free, and at the most basic level to survive?

I can picture one of our ancestors fighting some ferocious beast, with much at stake, her own life not least of all, and though she is fully conscious of what might be gained or lost, and conscious too of her wounds bleeding and even of her own adrenaline rushing, she is not yet angry. She has not yet attained to the inspiration that our language figuratively describes as being "mad," that is, out of one's everyday mind. But then something changes; suddenly she is no longer locked in a mortal struggle—she has broken the lock. She has reached some place where her own survival and that of her children may mean less to her than giving full vent to the force now welling up inside. And even when the beast is dead under her feet, she continues to strike against its bloody carcass. Her rage is a form of glory, like that of a conductor at the crescendo, whose wand may be little more than the most

refined form of any flailing blunt instrument, Samson's jawbone of an ass in the fist of a maestro and the Philistines laid
out heap upon heap.

⌒

But if that ancestor did indeed learn to be angry, how did she
learn? Very likely anger has prehuman origins—the beast she
killed may have been angry too—though this tells us little
about our own anger. My testicles also have prehuman origins, but that knowledge goes only a little way toward helping
me understand my sexuality. My eyes were once the eyes of
fishes, but I am still a fish out of water when I attempt to
reckon with Cézanne.

Perhaps our ancestors learned their anger from the sky.
Before language there was no one to tell them that the thunder had always thundered; it was new in every generation, in
every single life. Even *with* language that continues to be true:
Who can say that he has gotten used to thunder and lightning? But how tremendous it must have been to hear the
thunder, having never heard *of* the thunder, to hear the rain
—which even the simplest creature must sense in its mostly
liquid body to be good and necessary—accompanied by such
flashing and crashing, to see the tree cloven to the root and
burst into flame. What was this phenomenon if not the primal revelation of anger? And we may wonder: Which came
first to human comprehension, the angry god or the sense of
cosmic anger itself? Did people believe in divinity and then,
seeing the storm, imagine that the divinity was angry? Or did
they first know only anger, perhaps learning it from the
storm and projecting it onto the storm, and did they then

come to conceive of divinity as a force capable of such emotion and commotion?

Whichever came first, the anger of the god was, like human anger, an active power. A part of nature, it also seemed to defy nature. It broke the spokes of predictable cycles. It broke the trees. Even an ape must know where the sun rises, but not even a wizard can tell you where the lightning will strike. The storm manifested the power of the divine to shape nature and even destroy nature—just as our own inner storms may have evolved as the impetus to move beyond the frustration and helplessness of naturally occurring predicaments. The thunder was the fist of the god striking the table, turning it upside down. Before the psalmist spoke of Christ, the thunder did.

The revelation of Yahweh to the children of Israel in the thunder and lightning of Mount Sinai set him apart from the gods of Egypt and the other nations. Those gods were the rhythmic dancers, the weavers of order, the rising and dying overseers of the ever-changing-but-also-never-changing universe, and of its mirror image in static imperial society. Yahweh, on the other hand, was a God of history and of slaves, of order overturned, of thunder and lightning. Many Christians like to think of the references to his wrath in the Hebrew Bible as a primitive anthropomorphism, as something they have outgrown. But the wrath of the Old Testament God is of a piece with the resurrection of the New: It is the will and the power to change the normal or customary course of things. Furthermore, it is the source of, and in some cases the sanction for, our human power to do the same.

I once saw a film clip in which a militant black student at the time of the civil rights movement made this proclamation:

"We're going to have a place at the table or we're going to kick the [censor's bleep] legs off the table." Typically he would have been classified as an angry young man because of his coarse language or his violent figure of speech. But I would also call him angry because, in the image of Yahweh and according to my own definition of anger, he is poised at the place where frustration is ready to become action. He will not be deterred; unlike the gods of the nations, he will not be pacified by ritual magic or the repetition of old formulas. Like someone before him who also kicked over tables, he has become a consuming fire.

⌒

The problem of God's anger is not a new one. Even in the Old Testament we find people of faith attempting to refine the image, to mitigate its force. In the story of Elijah—an angry God's prophet, if ever there was such a thing—we see that mitigating influence extend to the stormy symbols themselves: The prophet learns that God's voice is not in the thunder or the lightning, but in something still and small within. Similarly, more than one biblical writer assures us that the Lord is "slow to anger." Not without anger, exactly, but slow to it. For many, this remains too small a comfort. The seventeenth-century poet George Herbert, himself a man capable of anger, speaks for these tender hearts when he writes:

> Throw away Thy rod,
> Throw away Thy wrath:
>   O my God,
> Take the gentle path.

Implicit in the desire for a God without wrath is the assumption that we ought to have no wrath ourselves. If even God forgoes such a thing, surely we can have no rightful claim to it. You will notice that people who proclaim a God without anger tend to pride themselves on the same attribute. "But I didn't raise my voice," they'll say. The activist Saul Alinsky once defined a liberal as someone who leaves the room when an argument turns into a fight. Presumably a liberal would walk out of heaven for the same reason.

In times past the problem of the angry God was associated mainly with the tenderness of conscience. The guilty sinner winced at its force. Today that problem has increasingly come to be associated with the wounds of abuse. Victims of abuse have typically been victims of anger; for them the image of an angry God can be about as consoling as that of a black-and-blue Madonna. Thus, there are compelling reasons for describing a better path than that of the angry Father God on the wings of the storm. After all, probably every emotion we ascribe to God—with the possible exception of love—is a figure of speech. So we might do well to offer better figures, and to remind those wounded by abusive anger that God's wrath is partly, even mostly, figurative.

And yet there is a zeal for healing that kills. There is indeed such a thing as killing someone with kindness. The thoroughly gentle God, the unceasingly kind God, the God of the unalterable smile is also the fairy God, the clown God, the stuffed animal God—perhaps not a great deal more helpful than the threadbare little giraffe that a child clutches in his dark room as he winces with every cry from his battered mother's throat. The God who never gets mad for fear of offending the abused must sooner or later be construed as the God who never gets mad at the abuser.

Certainly that construction makes some sense within a Christian universe. God's love is not restricted to a certain class of sinner and withheld from another: God loves the abused and the abuser both. It can also be argued that what I have presented so slightingly as a "stuffed animal God" is none other than the Christ who suffers with and in every victim. But to divest God of wrath out of deference for those abused by anger is ultimately to salve their wounds with despair. It is to describe a God so benign as to be indifferent, so slow to anger that he is always late to save. It is to remember the Christ who suffered the little children to come to him, while we forget the Christ who said that their oppressors would be better off drowned with a millstone tied to their necks.

What is more, if we divest God of his anger but not of his righteousness, and if we continue to aspire to "be perfect as our heavenly Father is perfect," then we are compelled to proclaim that perfect righteousness for the oppressed consists of suffering passively without hope of recourse or retribution. We have heard that counsel before. Some would retort that we have indeed heard it before, and where we have heard it is in the Sermon on the Mount. Yet the most uncompromising practitioners of that sermon, Mahatma Gandhi and Martin Luther King Jr. among them, seemed to think differently. Gandhi, for example, eschewed the term *passive resistor.* Like King he saw nothing passive in nonviolent civil disobedience. The actions of Christ himself were hardly passive either. His cleansing of the temple was not even nonviolent.

Perhaps what the abused and oppressed require is not so much a change in metaphor as a change in identification. The wrath of God is not the wrath of the abusive parent or of power abused. It is the absolute claim of personhood asserting itself in the face of power and chaos alike. The voice that

speaks from the burning bush says, "I have heard the cry of my people." The voice that speaks from the fire says, "I Am Who I Am." By implication we are who we are too. Our being is a value worthy of anger.

⌐

The wrath of God is hardest to accept in those biblical passages where it breaks forth in seemingly irrational destructiveness. With some reservations we can accept the wrath that slays the worshippers of Baal or gives those who "sell the poor for a pair of shoes" into the hands of the conquering Assyrians. We are less easy with those passages where divine wrath seems to strike out at those who have not so much been wicked or unfaithful as they have been careless or curious. The Israelites are told not to venture onto Mount Sinai "lest [the Lord] break forth upon them." Adam and Eve are cursed in all their labors for exercising a healthy curiosity in the matter of fruit. A man who reaches out to steady the ark of the covenant as it's carted over rough terrain receives sudden death for his trouble.

The rational reader will say that the man was probably startled to realize the taboo he'd violated and died of a heart attack—surely not from the wrath of God. Yahweh's wrath is simply a poetic expression for his majesty and mystery. From one perspective this adjusted reading makes perfect sense. I'd rather not worship a God who is in the details to such an extent that he'll strike me dead for failing to take account of even one of them. In such a universe my doom is a foregone conclusion.

But here too the wrath of God might best be seen as the sanctity of personhood. By extension it bespeaks the sanctity of all personhood. Perhaps the assumed masculinity of the biblical God coupled with the greater vulnerability of women in a sexist culture prevents us from making that association. In some ways the God whose wrath consumes the presumptuous and irreverent is not far removed from the goddess who angrily metamorphoses the hunter who has discovered her nakedness. To "recover the Goddess" is to recover, among other things, a sense of that divine modesty that abhors violation. It is possible to see much of the Old Testament as a story about violation: from the people of Babel, whose approach to God is that of sophomoric boys climbing a drainpipe to see into a girl's bedroom, to King David fulfilling his own voyeuristic fantasies with command-performance adultery and murder. Add to these Noah's leering son, Susanna's leering elders, Lot's expendable daughters, the rape of Dinah, Absalom going in to his father's concubines, the knife about to plunge into Isaac's heart—and, on another level, the insinuations of Job's friends plunging into his heart. We see the violation of privacy, the violation of flesh, the violation of trust, home, and conscience—all juxtaposed with the wrath of the inviolable God. By the time Jesus cleanses the temple—which in the New Testament is frequently equated with his body and with our bodies (the "temples of the Holy Spirit") —we cannot escape the powerful impression, which nearly amounts to a second definition, that anger is an emotion arising from a refusal to suffer or to permit violation.

In one of the eucharistic liturgies in the Book of Common Prayer, the celebrant prays, "Deliver us from the presumption of coming to this Table for solace only, and not for strength." Deliver us from the presumption, it might read, of seeking God's gentleness without God's wrath. Deliver us from the folly of protecting the victims of abuse from beholding the stormy face of their Redeemer.

He had a terrible temper, you
know, undoubtedly inherited
from His Father.

Robertson Davies, *Fifth Business*

CHRIST
THE TIGER

G od, said Gandhi, could only come to the starving masses
of India as bread; he sometimes seems to have come to
the barbarians of Europe as paint. The Word was made flesh,
and the flesh was made art. For many of us, even now, Jesus is
known not so much by a set of sayings or a body of beliefs,
nor even by a series of stories, as by a display of images—the
stained glass windows and crayon-colored parchment of our
personal and historical childhood.

The most dominant of these images are probably the
crèche and the cross, with good reason. The intersection of
divinity and humanity is most awesome there. Less dominant,
but hardly less important, are those of the Good Shepherd,
the host at the Last Supper, the suppliant in the garden of
Gethsemane, the risen victor in that other garden. Sometimes

one or another of these pictures becomes more prominent. The early church, for example, seems to have been especially fond of the image of Christ raising Lazarus; in the case of certain well-known frescoes, he actually brandishes a little wand before calling his friend, like a dazed rabbit, out of death's black hat. More recently the image of Christ with the Samaritan woman, or with virtually any woman besides his virginal mother, has served as an icon, if not for our devotion, then of a certain ideological emphasis.

Among these lesser images in the Christian gallery is that of Jesus cleansing the temple. Perhaps the best-known example is El Greco's painting, a postcard reproduction of which used to hang over my desk. Clothed in otherworldly blue, like the storm god come down to earth, Jesus scourges his way through the money changers, whose postures alone reflect his fury; his own face remains serene. I don't know of many other presentations of this image. It seems not to have captured the imaginations of painters so much as, say, the flagellation, which also features a whip. No doubt there are reasons for this proportion of emphasis, some perverse, and others merely realistic: The Son of man, with upper- or lowercase *S*, is much more likely to be found flogged than flogging in this world.

Nevertheless, as minor as it may be, the image of Christ driving the money changers from the temple, especially if interpreted as an image of anger, is both beautiful and provocative.

For one thing, his is the zeal of an ego identified with something larger than itself. He is not incensed over some personal insult, but by a communal sacrilege, which he feels bound to take personally. Smite his cheek, and he turns you the other; slap the dignity of the house of prayer, however, and he turns over a table. Perhaps for that very reason, his anger appears at first as an absurd kind of indignation. The cleansing of the temple is as if a mother were to enter a school and begin overturning VCR cabinets and tearing up workbooks all in the sacred name of education. She would have a point, we would grant her that, but the action would be deemed "over the top"—or to use a phrase that has come to mean almost the same thing, "too idealistic." But as with many other actions judged to be too idealistic, it is the unflinching realism of Christ's attack that impresses one most. What is a temple really for? Who, really, is God? What is the only real response to a sacrilege? If not outrage, then how can sacrilege be deemed outrageous?

And yet there is also something mercifully restrained in Jesus' violence. We read that tables were overturned; we do not read that people were knocked down or knocked out. His weapon is a small scourge, not a staff or a cudgel, and of the four evangelists, only John puts any weapon into his hand. I wouldn't be surprised to learn that no one actually felt the lash, that Jesus mostly beat the air. I don't imagine the merchants of the temple courtyard to have been a particularly valiant lot, but if one had been stupid or stubborn enough to hold his ground, he might have received a few welts. If so, it would be hard to feel sorry for him. This was one of those cases where a fool and his money were not parted soon enough.

Of course, there are those who argue that Christ is not angry when he cleanses the temple. His action is calculatingly symbolic, they would say, not the result of his being "mad." He only seems mad. Such a view strikes me as very close to the beliefs of certain Gnostic sects, who held that Christ only seemed to suffer on the cross. On the orthodox side, it also reminds me of those medieval Scholastics who maintained that while Adam and Eve were sexual prior to the fall (since to suggest otherwise was flagrantly heretical), the erectile tissue of Adam's prelapsarian penis had been thoroughly subject to his reason. Sexually speaking, Adam could be resolved to have intercourse, but never aroused to it. So as a theological precedent to the Christ without anger, we can pose an Adam without ardor: the completely "symbolic" scourge prefigured by the utterly voluntary erection. In such a scheme of sacred history, Moses begins to read a bit like Noel Coward. "Eve, old girl, would you mind awfully if we were to reproduce?" Destroy Adam and Eve's passion, and inevitably you must find another name for Christ's passion.

Still we can go to the other extreme, which is the perennial temptation of those who want a more gallant messiah, a temptation probably as old as Judas Iscariot. In this frame of mind one reads the gospel like a Hollywood director, with an action tag that has the temple money changers going down like mobsters on St. Valentine's Day. American Protestantism especially has often seemed to regard Christ like an ex-Marine father regarding his overly bookish son, hoping he'll bloody someone's nose just once, wishing his appeal among women has some other, earthier explanation besides his appeal to them as human beings. But the gesture in the temple is all the more poignant and prophetic when we imagine it executed by a man too slight to carry his own cross without assistance, a man whose idea of a workout is a forty-day fast.

Even after we account for the misinterpretations of this story, however, we can still learn from those misinterpretations. If we go back to the Scholastic concept of Adam as the perfectly reasonable lover: It is ridiculous only because it banishes passion, not because it makes a place for reason. Passion without reason is close to violence, close to rape. The same can be said for righteous indignation that lacks all restraint. That Christ cleansing the temple—"Christ the tiger," to use Eliot's phrase—can simultaneously seem mad and yet admit to the interpretation that he is not mad, that his anger and his purpose can coexist without either subsuming the other, makes for a powerful image. It will seem especially powerful for us less-balanced souls, who can never seem to decide if we wish we were less acquiescent, or less explosive.

In only one place in the Gospels is Jesus explicitly said to be angry. Not surprisingly this occurs in Mark, the evangelist least likely to edit Christ's emotions. A man with a withered hand has approached Jesus on the Sabbath day; his critics wait to see if he will violate the commandment by healing the man. Mark says that Jesus "looked at them with anger" before making the man whole. Here too his anger seems larger than his own ego, identified not with the temple this time, but with a suffering man. To be fair, we must grant that the anger of his critics, assuming they are angry, is also grounded in something beyond the ego. Christ saw the temple violated by money changers; the Pharisees saw the Sabbath violated by Christ. The difference is that for Christ the needs of the human sufferer must come before the letter of the law. From this sole place in the Gospels, where Christ is explicitly said to be angry, grows every consideration of his ability to feel that emotion.

The cleansing of the temple is perhaps the most appealing of these inferences. Christ's cursing of the fig tree is probably the least. Both Matthew and Mark tell us how Jesus came to a fig tree looking for fruit. When he found none, he cursed the tree, and it withered. Here, the anger of Christ is not only personal in the smallest sense, but seemingly irrational and childish as well. The apparent lack of fury only increases the negative impression. The excesses of the roaring mad are in some ways more acceptable than those of the merely irritated. To argue, as some have argued, and as the Gospel writers seem to imply, that the cursing of the fig tree is a dramatized parable about God's judgment or about the power of faith simply does not work for me. This is rationalization after the fact: It is a father pontificating about the harsh blows of life and the need to get used to them and a parent's duty to help that acclimation come about—all delivered in the aftermath of a furious spanking that has appalled even him. Christ doesn't appear to have taken his disciples into a grove of fig trees in order to demonstrate an eschatological idea or a metaphysical truth. He goes there looking for figs. Both of the evangelists make a point of noting that Jesus was hungry. Mark adds that "it was not the season for figs."

And still Jesus curses the tree. At least *curse* sounds like the best word for what he does. "May no one ever eat fruit from you again." Had the tree only become barren as a result, we might have made our peace with the story. We might have concluded that *curse* is too strong a word. After all, can a tree care about bearing fruit, even if it can care at all? If there's such a thing as a happy tree, perhaps a tree is happiest without the encumbrance of fruit, which does nothing but invite ravaging birds and men. But the tree withers. The words reach deeper than the pit, to the very pith of the limbs and branches.

Of course, we shouldn't be too sentimental. If you're reading this book and I'm writing it, then neither of us can be too squeamish about the death of trees. This very minute I am writing these words with the warmth of a wood fire at my back. And the trees that made my woodpile were not, for the most part, what a logger friend of mine calls "volunteers." They did not fall of their own accord. They were felled. But they were not cursed, either. Nor, like the Gerasene swine on the cliff, were they given over to the devils. They were sacrificed, as it were, to the logger's need and to mine. Most of us can accept that. The cursing of the fig tree, on the other hand, appalls us.

When faced with a passage in the Gospels that troubles us in this way, we have basically three possible explanations. We can say that the text is unreliable, that Jesus is unreliable, or that our dismay is unreliable. The first is the route of scholarship; the second, that of the skeptic. Both routes are increasingly popular. And although the third is typically the one most favored by dogmatists and neurotics, it can also be the route that leads to the freshest and most useful understanding. That is because questioning our dismay sooner or later comes down to the question of who we are and why things strike us as they do. At one point Jesus is supposed to have asked his disciples "Who do you say that I am?" The gospel asks the same question of us, and not only of us, but also about us.

⌒

Stepping back from the doomed tree and aside from our dismay, we might look at the road that Jesus is traveling, at where it goes, and at where it will be once our own feet step onto it. The way that Jesus taught has absorbed or been conflated with a number of influences. Some of them, most notably Judaism, are so central to his message that the word *influence* hardly does them justice. Others are more subtle. Each in its own way has made Christianity what it is, but with the wrong emphasis can unmake it. We must never forget that the holy is greater than the sum of its parts.

The job of Christian theology, an enterprise in which every thoughtful Christian has a role, is to identify those diverse influences, to honor them where they deserve to be honored, but never to be intimidated or unduly led by them. The task is not unlike that of recognizing that our metaphors for God are metaphors, which means that they have great power to convey meaning, but also great potential to become idols. God is our father; God is our mother; God is our maker, governor, source, end, hope, and ground of being. God is love. But even more than God is love, God is God. And some mystics have gone so far as to remind us that what we name as "God" is also *not* God. In other words, even the word *god*, and even with a capital G, is still a figurative expression for the ineffable.

One of the formative influences on Christianity was Stoicism. The Stoics formed a school of Greco-Roman philosophy that taught patience, self-control, and submission to fate. It is not difficult to see why the first Christians found Stoicism appealing and why Stoicism would have influenced Christianity. One of the best-known of the Stoics was Seneca, who has some interesting things to say about anger. For Seneca anger is an emotion that arises when our will finds itself in opposition to the world as it is. We want the hammer to strike the nail, for example, and it smashes our thumb instead. So we're angry. In his view anger is the sign of a man not fully resigned to "reality." And Seneca is absolutely right. If he and his followers made any mistake, to my mind, it was to assume that reality was absolutely right.

Stoicism strikes me as a philosophy nurtured by an imperial world. Change yourself, it seems to say, because you're never going to change Rome. Seneca had the dubious honor of being tutor to the emperor Nero, a position that would eventually cost him his life. Put yourself in his position, and you're in a good place to appreciate his point of view. Seneca was not trying to conquer the world. He was trying to conquer despair.

Many Christians of the same time shared Seneca's predicament and shared his fate—Peter and Paul also perished under Nero—so it is not surprising that they would come to share his point of view. And as points of view go, his is an attractive one. It calls out the best in us, and it calls us not to require much of others. There are many things I'd rather not be than a Stoic.

Nevertheless, Jesus is not a Stoic, no more than he is an ascetic, a socialist, a feminist, or a Christian. I would like to think that each of these terms might be applied approximately to him, and as approximations perhaps they can. But only as approximations. The one who "was made man that man might be made divine" (as Athanasius puts it), who turns over tables, who weeps at the grave of his friend, who cries out on the cross, who blesses a woman who anoints his feet with tears and curses a tree that fails to give him fruit out of season, is not a Stoic. He is most certainly a human being, and "dignified" is too small a word to describe the kind of human being he is. In him my own humanity is fully realized because fully felt. Without his anguish, without his anger, without his passion—tell me, who would it be who died on the cross, and how could I ever imagine myself redeemed by his death? Perhaps it was only by cursing a tree that he could hang on one and be cursed for my sake.

In the end there is no good explanation for Christ's cursing of the fig tree, at least none that I can find, but there is a good application. It flies smack in the face of any Stoic acceptance of reality—and of any institution that defends its privilege in the name of reality. What could be more real or more natural than the seasonal cycles of vegetation? If Jesus did not refrain from cursing a tree for following its natural course, then of what use is it to defend the injustices of the market economy or the patriarchal family or even the "one, holy, catholic, and apostolic church" in the name of nature, necessity, or divine patronage? Remember the words of John the Baptist: "Do not presume to say to yourselves, 'We have Abraham as our ancestor'; for I tell you, God is able from these stones to raise up children to Abraham." In other words, do not presume to enter the argument of the "natural" with the Creator of the natural. Do not invoke the sanctity of the house of God as an excuse before God. The Stoic sees the market in the temple courtyard as an annoyance to be endured, the Sadducee as an interest to be preserved, and both as one of the givens in this give-and-take world. Christ sees it as a den of thieves and puts them to rout. And rightly or wrongly he greets the fig tree with this same idealistic expectation, and then with an indignation, that he refuses to suppress. I do not understand his cursing of that tree. I do not like what he does. But on some level, in the same deep place that I believe in the resurrection of the dead and believe, also, that I shall one day see John Brown in heaven, I love him for it.

⌒

I read a story once about the great Shawnee chief Tecumseh, how he received reports that some of his braves, with the connivance of their British allies, had begun scalping American prisoners of war. Tecumseh immediately took horse and galloped to the camp where the atrocities were taking place. Kicking one scalper to the ground and brandishing his tomahawk over another, he is said to have cried out in a loud voice, "Are there no men here?" The answer reverberates throughout history: There is at least one. If the Son of man was anywhere in the American wilderness at that moment, where was he but in the heart of Tecumseh?

I also read (in a book by Andrea Dworkin called *Letters from a War Zone*) of three women in the 1970s who entered a store that sold pornography, whips, and metal-studded dildos and splashed the merchandise with blood. They were splashing nothing less than the Constitution, say the scribes and Pharisees. They were splashing the law. Their actions were completely "over the top." Yet I have found myself thinking of these women every Palm Sunday when we read the account of Christ cleansing the temple. Wasn't their point that a woman's body is also a temple and that we use the phrase "consenting adults" as disingenuously as the money changers spoke of worship and the Romans spoke of peace? Show me the spot where those women stood to throw the blood, and I will kneel and pray there.

And this too—my wife heard the story on the radio years ago and told it to me, how a family of three had picked up a hitchhiker who forced them at knifepoint to a motel room where he tied up the father and raped the mother. Then he turned his attentions to the five-year-old girl. Outraged beyond fear or hope, the mother seized a table lamp and proceeded to beat the man so fiercely that when the police finally arrived he was crawling in his own blood. I see the lamp wire flailing in the air like a scourge of small cords. When people speak with disparagement of anger, or with embarrassment of Christ's anger, I think of that woman. And when my own anger arises at some petty offense, I sometimes shame myself into sobriety by calling their holier rage to mind.

Anger and wrath are abominations,
and the sinful man will possess them.

Ecclesiasticus

THE DEADLY SIN

The writer Georges Bernanos said, "For men it is certainly more grave, or at least much more dangerous, to deny original sin than to deny God." I'm not sure I believe that. Bernanos seems to give too much honor to a doctrine. And yet on the most basic level, the statement makes perfect sense. I can imagine two scenarios, one in which I'm adrift on the ocean in an open boat with a party of atheists who, notwithstanding their unbelief, have a vivid personal and historical sense of evil; and another in which I am also adrift on the ocean, this time with a party of amiable believers who deny that any such thing as evil exists. "People make mistakes, that's all." Which boat would be the safer one to drift in? Even if no disaster arose to distinguish the moral scruples of one party from those of the other, I can barely bring myself to imagine the vacuous conversations I'd have to endure in the second boat. Before it even occurred to its blithe passengers to contrive a theological rationalization for throwing my cannibalized carcass into the drink—and I have no doubt that given enough time it most certainly would occur to them—I would probably jump out of my own accord.

A reader aware of the malevolence at work in her own rage might be close to doing the same thing right now. After reading several chapters on the righteousness of God's wrath and the humanity of Christ's anger and the transforming potential of our own anger, she might feel that we have all but sidestepped the elemental, biblical understanding of anger as a sin. But we are in no such danger. And I would go so far as to say, not only that anger in many of its forms is sinful, but that anger comes close to exemplifying the very nature of sin itself.

Christians frequently define *sin* as separation, from God and from the good intentions of God's creation. The original symbol of original sin is that of Adam and Eve hiding from the voice of God and from each other's nakedness. Given such an understanding, we could say that anger includes forms of separation capable of defining sin even for those who believe in no God. Anger separates us from our own minds and from our own best intentions, regardless of any divinity's intentions. Where else do you find the nerve to cut off your nose to spite your face, except in the heat of rage? "I could have kicked myself" frequently means "I *did* kick myself." I separated myself into two parts, a self that went amok and a self that bore the consequences. And that cleaving apart was the result of anger, which split me away from my better self like lightning cleaving a tree.

So I have no argument with the author of Ecclesiasticus—who describes anger as an abomination—but I do have another argument that starts from a somewhat different place. Yes, I can see anger as an emotion that "the sinful man will possess." I can readily see myself as that sinful man. But I also see anger as part of my nature as a creature made in the image of God. And this is where I part company with what Bernanos said about original sin, in that I insist on taking God, not sin, as my starting point. In other words, I refuse to take sin as my major premise, however major its role in my life. To do so is to reason something like this:

> I am sinful by nature. I am angry by nature.
> Therefore anger is by its very nature sinful.

In contrast, the arguments of the preceding chapters are based on a pair of different syllogisms. One might be stated as follows:

> God is not sinful. God is sometimes angry.
> Therefore anger cannot always be sinful.

The other:

> God's creation is essentially good. Human beings are part of that creation, and anger is a natural part of human beings. Therefore anger is good—at least so far as the divine intention that brought it into being.

Mine is a conservative argument, in the sense that it seeks to conserve as much as possible of an existing order, in this case the order of human emotions.

Nevertheless, it would be foolish to believe that a good thing is incorruptible simply because it is good. Isn't the goodness of a thing often revealed by the magnitude of its potential for corruption? Only a fallen angel is capable of becoming a devil; a lout can seldom manage to be worse than a lout. To explore the excesses of human emotion, therefore, is always to make an exploration of glory confounded. Step back from the circles of Dante's hell, and what do you hear but the music of the spheres gone terribly out of tune.

According to Christian tradition, anger is numbered as one of the seven deadly sins, a conceit that derives in part from the medieval significance given to the number seven. The other six are pride, envy, gluttony, lust, sloth, and avarice (or covetousness). I shall never forget one of my professors ticking off the list and ending by saying, "in other words, all the things that all of us do every day" as if the medieval theologians were being perverse and impossible. But in any practical discussion of sin, as in the practical discussion of any other poison, "deadly" and "daily" mean close to the same thing. A regimen of small doses is usually what kills us.

Leaving aside the dubious numerology of the tradition, the seven deadly sins give us a useful way of looking at anger. First of all, there are features found in at least several of the sins that are also common to anger. What is more, all of the other six can lead to anger; or we could say that anger is often symptomatic of the other six.

Finally, if we pair the sins according to which seem most compatible with which, anger winds up as the odd man out, the sin without a date. Pride goes with envy (as two sins based on false comparisons with one's neighbor), gluttony goes with lust (as two cerebral sins falsely attributed to the flesh), and sloth goes with avarice (as two false opposites in the area of human ambition). And the cheese stands alone. Of course, our concern in this book is with the cheese. But a person attempting to deal with anger does well to look at anything standing in its vicinity. Moral detective work begins by rounding up all the suspects, the usual and the unusual too.

⌒

Pride and envy are companions, strongly with each other and more tenuously with the remaining deadly sins, in that both have to do with disproportion. Both have to do with a lack of proper balance within oneself and between oneself and the world. That is to say, both are grotesque. In some ways the seven deadly sins might be called the seven ugly sins. More than one person has noted that ethics and aesthetics—the true, the beautiful, and the good—have overlapping margins.

Pride is sometimes said to be the deadliest sin, perhaps because the thing distorted is the human soul itself. The proud fancy themselves as something greater than they are. And since the universe appears to be finite in nearly all of its particulars, a person can be more than she is only by attempting to make somebody or something else less. Pride is like one of those ancient Mesopotamian steles declaring this or that potentate "the brother of the sun," the "ruler of the earth," and so on. His larger-than-life image is presented against a decorative background of impaled bodies, severed heads, wailing women, and burning towers. $W - Y = M^2$, where W equals the world, Y equals you, and nothing on earth equals the power of me. If you want to know how you get from

$E = mc^2$ to an atom bomb, from the poetry of the Bhagavad Gita to Robert Oppenheimer quoting it as he rapturously beholds the first mushroom cloud, you need to study that older formula.

"Pride goeth before a fall," says the biblical book of Proverbs; it also goeth before a fit—and for at least two reasons. First, the proud are angry at anyone who challenges their revision of proper human proportions. How dare you not see me for the colossus that I am? With perverse irony, the proud are *also* angry at anyone who *does* see them in these exaggerated terms. Thus, the proud start out by making themselves gods, and end up by protesting, "Who do these ingrates think I am, God?" The petulance of tyrants with their people, or of celebrities with their fans—not to forget that of certain clergy with their flocks—is usually the direct result, and perhaps the well-deserved punishment, of pride.

Wherever pride appears, we also find irony. What can be more ironic, after all, than a proud mortal? For that reason, pride is often a conspicuous trait in both tragic and comic literary characters. The disproportion is portrayed in one genre as a fatal liability; in the other as a joke. Not surprisingly whether we look at Oedipus the king or Mr. Bumble, we see pride giving vent to anger. Hold the mirror of reality up to the midget who imagines himself a giant, and invariably he smashes the mirror, or puts out his eyes.

Envy is superficially the opposite of pride, but it has the same features of disproportion, and often the same symptoms of rage. (Were the two sins completely opposite, we would not so often find them in the same person.) In the throes of envy, the absurd disproportion that characterizes pride is projected onto someone else. The envious person imagines others faring better than himself and almost always in spite of their true deserts. To envy is to see the world as fundamentally unjust and particularly unjust toward you. Of course, sometimes the world is, in which case the imputation of envy seems almost more wicked than the sin itself. I never saw much point, for example, in calling the starving masses of the third world "envious" of American prosperity. The distended bellies of starving children do not amount to a distorted vision of the truth. We might as well accuse them of gluttony for wanting to eat.

Samuel Johnson said that envy is one of the worst of vices because, alone among them all, it is indulged without pleasure. Perhaps for that reason it is seldom indulged without anger. An envious person is polymorphously pissed: at others for possessing what she would have, at herself for not possessing it, at God or fortune or fate for allowing this state of affairs to go on. As with the other deadly sins an element of insatiability characterizes envy. Indeed, if Johnson's observation is correct, then satiation is not even a question: In the absence of all pleasure there is nothing to satisfy.

Actually that lack of pleasure, so extreme in envy, may not be exclusive to envy. To one degree or another all of the deadly sins may be described by an inability and in some cases by a stubborn refusal to be satisfied. In other words, they can be symbolized by an anger that refuses to cool. Conventional wisdom sees it otherwise of course: Sin and pleasure supposedly go hand in hand. Conventional wisdom is mistaken. The delusion by which a gross sinner imagines himself an earthy man of pleasure is not unlike the delusion by which the puerile atheist imagines herself a shocking freethinker. On close examination we often find that the first is about as capable of having a good time as the latter is of having an original thought.

All of this is to say nothing more, and certainly nothing more original, than that sin is at bottom ungodly. The God of Genesis is characterized in part by the pleasure he takes in what he has made. "And God saw that it was good." The worldview of the envious—and to a certain extent, of the lustful and avaricious too—runs counter to God's vision. Nothing they see is good, or good enough, or else nothing they see is enough of the good. In other words, you can never please them, which is as good a definition as you may get of what it means to be damned.

~~

Lust and gluttony are often described as the "gross" sins, the fleshy sins, but they are in fact deceptively cerebral, the cleverness of the mind showing itself in the stratagem of blaming the body. Both sins are essentially denials of the body, which comprehends limitation much better than a mind divorced from the body. Lust is to erotic desire as gluttony is to physical hunger: Both defy limits; both deny satiation. The hungry eater, once sated, leans back at the table and sighs, "What a great meal." The glutton betakes himself to the vomitorium and sticks his finger down his throat so that he might eat some more. In the same way, erotic communion with a beloved human being is never adequate to lust. In its most extreme forms, its vomitorium forms, lust attempts to increase its pleasure through the sensation or infliction of pain. Lust never arrives at the throne of grace. Lust never comes.

The equation of lust and gluttony with "sensuality," whether construed by the prude or the libertine, is a libel against our bodies, our lovers, and our creation. What frequently gives the lie to this false sensuality is the disdain with which the lustful and gluttonous regard the commonplace delights of others. "He actually *eats* in that diner. And probably enjoys it too." "It takes more than a little bare skin to turn me on." This is a credential? I am a typical Westerner in seeing the veil worn by women in some Islamic countries as oppressive, but I find it sad and ludicrous to hear someone express great amazement that "any guy could be turned on *by a face.*" At least the Muslim women are able to see through or over their veils. The veils over our eyes are more opaque.

Neither lust nor gluttony is a stranger to rage. Lust will make a person angry because he imagines his mostly mental illness to be a mostly physical drive. He thinks of his lust as a basic human need, with a correlative basic human right, even though in reality it exists as nothing more than a bizarre distortion of a basic human desire. As he fails to take pleasure, he tends to give offense—to the body, to women, to the world. The language of smut is, of course, the language of lust. It is almost disingenuous to point out that smut is also a language of violence. It is perhaps a bit less disingenuous to point out that our culture uses different forms of the same four-letter obscenity to mean "have sexual intercourse," "confuse," "confound," "cheat," "manipulate," "disrespect," "dismiss," "malfunction," "beat up," "damage," "doom," "destroy"; as the most intensive modifier of the most negative adjectives; and in the imperative, as something *more* offensive (think about this) than "Go to hell." Were some future archaeologist to reconstruct our culture based on nothing but the linguistic record, she could only conclude that we coupled and reproduced in a state of raging fury.

It might appear that gluttony, in contrast with lust, has little to do with anger. Gluttony merely sighs and salivates; anger foams at the mouth. Yet if we were to give the natural world a voice to speak besides our own, I imagine it would describe human beings as furious creatures, and our fury as a distinctly devouring kind. From the ancient Romans who wrung the necks of hundreds of peacocks in order to feast on their tongues, to the gourmets of modern industrial nations who allow whole coral reefs to be dredged up and destroyed in order to provide a few shrimp, our quietest dinners bespeak the most virulent rage. When St. Paul speaks of those "whose god is their belly," he refers to a bloodthirsty god.

The connections here may seem remote and invisible, but you can sometimes see the relationship between gluttony and wrath by observing the behavior of a certain kind of eater—often a man, in my experience—who grows visibly irritated when his food fails to arrive at the table as quickly, delectably, or hot as he desires. I suspect that waiters and waitresses see more anger on a given day than prison guards and taxi drivers see in a typical week. Or observe your own behavior during a fast. Many is the person who fasted thinking to acquire the serenity of a saint, only to find she had the disposition of a bear.

This is where the no-nonsense secularist steps in and says, "Well, of course, one is going to be irritable during a fast, and so-called gluttony has nothing to do with it. If fasting makes you so irritable, you should just eat!" This is to miss both the point of fasting and the nature of gluttony. The most futile of all actions for the glutton is to "just eat." Whether he eats or fasts, in the end he is still fasting. Gluttony is the myth of Tantalus with a twist: In this version Tantalus actually manages to seize a piece of the overhanging fruit that so tantalizes him in the underworld—only to find that it doesn't satisfy him in the least. For one thing, it's a nectarine, and he hates those.

⌐⌐

Avarice and sloth are false opposites because although they seem to represent opposite poles of human activity—for example, the go-getter versus the couch potato—they express the same basic wish, which is a wish for death.

This is probably easier to see in sloth. The attempt to remain as inert and passive as possible is a morbid preoccupation, so much so that one wonders if the typical funeral parlor was originally designed to resemble a suburban living room or the other way around. Dorothy Parker's famous canard in response to the news that President Calvin Coolidge had died—"How could they tell?"—could serve as the perfect motto for sloth. I wonder how many people sit dead in front of their television sets, and for how long, before someone living in the same house finally realizes they're gone.

But avarice too has a funereal smell about it. The love of money is the root of all evil because the ultimate aim of all evil is death. The avaricious person wishes to obtain that morbidly prosperous state that is beyond desire, beyond fear, beyond need, beyond worry, beyond threat, beyond hope. Avarice is nirvana as imagined by someone who is not yet a Buddha. Avarice is the unenlightened wish for sublime extinction.

If the identification of sloth and avarice seems too abstract, try analyzing the seemingly opposite predicaments of someone who complains about an indolent spouse and someone else who complains that a spouse is "married to the job." On the one hand, the spouses in question seem to be completely opposite types in temperament, ambition, perhaps even in the way they groom themselves. Depending on the frustrations of one's own marriage, each might seem like a desirable alternative to the other. But the complaints of their mates boil down to the same thing: The slothful spouse and the avaricious spouse are both absentees. They're no fun. They inspire a sense of bereavement in those who love them. They're as good as dead.

Dead men throw no fits, or it seems they wouldn't. And at first glance sloth and avarice do seem a long way from wrath. But death hates resurrection. No one likes to be woken from a sound sleep. Where those afflicted by sloth and avarice can become most angry is when someone or something—like a dissatisfied spouse—disturbs the tranquility of their chosen sarcophagus. Perhaps this is the psychological truth behind those legends of angry ghosts and vengeful mummies, as well as the adage about letting a sleeping dog lie: Anger comes from an abrupt awakening. Even if we are not especially slothful or avaricious, we can still become terribly angry on being wakened from a reverie, a preoccupation, or an illusion. On the most literal level, this is probably a physiological defense mechanism: the vestige of a saving grace that prevented some of our ancestors from becoming food to the first predator that chanced upon them sleeping. But on another more spiritual level, we are gripped by the same emotion that stoned the prophets. Before I surrender to that kind of anger, I will always want to ask which is of greater moment, the rudeness of the disturbance, or the danger of the sleep.

⸺

I have purposely left anger with no companion among the deadly sins, though I've hoped to show it capable of keeping company with them all—with the false proportions of envy and pride, the false sensuality of gluttony and lust, the false opposition of avarice and sloth. To explain why the devil is sometimes called "the father of lies," we would need to look no further than these seven sins. Each one of them is a lie, anger included.

Perhaps the best way to glimpse the essential falsity of anger is to call it by its older name, "wrath." Nowadays, we tend to reserve that usage for God, especially in his preexilic mode—and therein lies the key. Wrath is the anger of someone who has begun to play at God. Wrath is the anger of one who has distorted his sense of self and the world—a disproportion that he shares with his proud, envious, lustful, gluttonous, and avaricious counterparts. He feels that his prerogatives, his grievances, his right to redress are all absolute. Holy, holy, holy. A person consumed by wrath has eaten and digested the forbidden fruit she thinks will make her a god. She storms out of the garden of Eden cursing and swearing, which is as much as to say acting as though she created the place and that it is her God-damned business and hers alone what happened there.

And yet—even in those curses, and even in that lie, is a vestige of something created and good. Just as all desire is not necessarily lust, or all gourmets gluttons, all anger is not sin.

At least some of it comes out as an expression of faith. A former student of mine tells me that one of her professors remarked how anger is so often accompanied by a spontaneous invocation of God, as in "God damn it." On one level this may be nothing more than the spiritual equivalent of breaking one's dishes or tearing up the flowerbeds. Frustrated by one thing, I defy the consolation of other things. I smash, I shatter, I blaspheme. But even that destructive impulse strikes me as having a vaguely religious meaning. Take back your world, O God, if this is how it works!

But with those angry words we move to another level of religious meaning. The angry person who invokes the name of God is acknowledging that the source of his frustration runs contrary to an expectation of divine benevolence. In other words, the world ought to work better. There ought to be figs on this tree. There ought to be some force, some angel, that prevents hammers from accidentally crushing thumbs. The theology may be crude, but it is theology nonetheless. At the very least, it insists that the source of our frustration is within the control of a greater power—and a good one. Like the child who cries, "You don't love me!" trusting that his parents do indeed love him and thus will be hurt by the remark, the person who cries out, "God damn it" is in some way acknowledging that God has already blessed "it," by making it and by sustaining its cussed existence. If an atheist falls in a forest, do his curses make a sound? They do, but they make no sense.

Abbot Ammonas said that he had spent fourteen years in Scete praying to God day and night to be delivered from anger.

Thomas Merton, *The Wisdom of the Desert*

EVEN IN THE
DESERT

For the Buddha, it was sexual desire; he is supposed to have said that with one more obstacle as strong as that, he never would have reached enlightenment. Apparently for Abbot Ammonas, one of the fourth-century Christian ascetics we have come to know as "the Desert Fathers" (and ought to know as the Desert Fathers and Mothers, for their numbers included women too), it was anger. I have thought of both sayings many times, although I tend to see the Buddha's more as a reflection of his humanity and honesty—and of the tremendous power of eros—than of my own religious struggles. My aspirations are a good deal less lofty than the Buddha's. They are also of a different order. I have not left my wife and child to seek the meaning of life, nor do I wish to. And in place of the Four Noble Truths, I have chosen the one ignoble truth of the cross. So much for nonattachment. Whatever else we may say about the man on that cross, he is most definitely—and painfully—attached.

Certainly my struggles also differ from those of Abbot Ammonas, our common religion notwithstanding; yet his words strike home in a way that the Buddha's do not. For fourteen years he prayed *day and night* to be delivered from anger. He definitely has me on frequency, but I may have him beat for duration. I have sometimes wondered, though, if he made his pronouncement after achieving mastery over his anger or if he continued to pray beyond those fourteen years, perhaps way beyond, for his deliverance.

My differences from the desert ascetic cause me to wonder about other things also. I use the word *wonder* here in the sense of "marvel." I marvel that Ammonas should have found anger so formidable. I can imagine a man afflicted by lust in the desert, that is, even though he is far away from the objects of his desire, but how could he have occasions for anger—and anger to such a tenacious degree—in his solitude? What would he find to be angry about?

An easy answer is found in the phrase "in Scete," which refers to a place where the desert hermits eventually organized themselves into an early monastic community. It may be that Ammonas was not truly solitary, and that would certainly account for his struggle with anger. Any kind of shared life can have its irritating moments—think of all the stand-up comedy made from that material—but imagine living in what amounts to a barracks full of aspiring Buddhas, all somewhat frazzled by fasting and watching and doing without what the Buddha himself found so hard to do without. Perhaps it was this kind of situation that prompted another Desert Father, Abbot Moses, to say: "A man who lives apart from other men is like a ripe grape. And a man who lives in the company of others is a sour grape." You can almost imagine some monastic Henny Youngman opening his routine at Scete with the line, "Now, take my brothers . . . every last one of them."

Still, others whom we know to have been true solitaries also speak of their struggles with anger. St. Anthony wrestled with it during his temptations. We find references to anger scattered throughout the lives and sayings of the Fathers. Abbot Agatho: "Even if an angry man were to revive the dead, he would not be pleasing to God because of his anger." Abbot Agatho's words are good counsel, though we should not forget the case of an angry man who did on several occasions revive the dead, and in whom God is supposed to have been "well pleased."

But why did these hermits wrestle with anger? It is a source of the most ambiguous comfort to hear that they did. On the one hand, it gives further proof that the saints were human and fallible, "just like us"—and that's of some reassurance. On the other hand, we hate to hear of fallibility in such heroic circumstances. After all, the Desert Fathers and Mothers adopted a program such as we sometimes imagine ourselves adopting, if only in the most hypothetical way, and that we're sure would relieve us of much of our anger. They simplified their lives. They set their priorities straight. They were "intentional" and "spiritual." They cut down on stress. They associated only with people who shared their values and objectives. They didn't have—at least some of them didn't have —neighbors. They didn't have families and jobs. And yet they prayed day and night for as long as fourteen years to be delivered from anger. It sounds hopeless, though of course it wasn't.

Our perplexity at the struggles of the desert hermits with their anger arises from several misconceptions. The first is our tendency to see the Desert Fathers and Mothers as embarked on a program of escapism, albeit escapism of the highest, healthiest, and most "spiritual" kind. (Million-dollar footnote: Never be so suspicious of yourself or of others as in the use of the word *spiritual*.) Anger, we assume, is one of those things that the hermits were leaving behind, along with noisy spectacles, streets full of temptation, and platters heaped with peacock tongues. They went into the deserts to embrace a simpler, less stressful life. They went into the deserts to find peace. So it appears.

But on further investigation, we learn that at least some of these hermits went into the desert not to escape the devil but to find him. With the conversion of the Roman Empire to Christianity, and the reading aloud of the gospel in virtually every major city and town, the Christian hermits of the fourth century believed that the forces of evil had fled to the wilderness in fear of the good news. The demons were "on retreat," not the hermits. The hermits went into the desert to take the war to the enemy.

Few details in the history of religion have ever struck home for me with such force. On the one hand, here is a vivid awareness of evil; on the other an even more vivid awareness that evil can be put to rout. How dangerous it is for us when we have one awareness without the other, in which case we shall have either witch trials or tribunals made up of witches; either Calvinism in its most stultifying forms or New Ageism in its most vacuous.

This balance of an awareness of evil and an awareness of our strength against evil will prove invaluable should we choose, like Abbot Ammonas, to do battle with the darker forms of our anger. But it will be every bit as important to remember that the decision to do so can lead us not away from the fire but straight into it. So many people seem to assume that the decision to "become more spiritual," to find inner peace, to get certain emotions under control, must inevitably and immediately and by itself lead to a more peaceful state of existence. In our resolutions, and even in our fantasies, we are continually making that assumption. If I could just get away from here, if I could just be more disciplined, if I could just renew my prayer life, then things would be better, more manageable, quieter. Ultimately this may be true. But the history of the Desert Fathers and Mothers and of other reputed seekers of peace suggests the very opposite. It suggests that conviction and conflict go hand in hand. If you go to slay dragons, you should be prepared to find them angry. You will have passed beyond the provisional peace of "live and let live," where the dragon alternately scorches the countryside and rests in its cave. At the point of deliberate engagement, either you kill the beast or it kills you. And the odds are not necessarily in your favor. This may be why Jesus in one of his parables compares the kingdom of God to a king preparing for war, who first ascertains if he has the resources to engage a superior force. If he doesn't, he asks for terms.

These are not antique insights, lost to us over time. They are as perennial as the human yearning for peace. In May Sarton's book *Journal of a Solitude,* a writer of the last century records her experiences living by herself in a New Hampshire farmhouse. Just that basic idea conjures up all the alluring images of the uncluttered life, the focused existence, the hermit's retreat, the book and the candle—the "desert" with a few less devils and a few more pieces of furniture. Yet here is what Sarton writes at the beginning of her journal:

> Now I hope to break through into the rough rocky depths, to the matrix itself. There is violence there and anger never resolved.

To this all the hermits of the desert nod their heads in recognition.

~~

Another misconception that stands in the way of our understanding how and why someone like Abbot Ammonas might have struggled with anger for fourteen years is our belief that anger is always tied to an objective cause. Something out there makes us mad, and if we can but eliminate whatever that something is, then we shall be at peace again. In a world where every experience of anger was holy, this would undoubtedly be true. Anger would be aimed exclusively at real and deserving targets.

Of course, we know that this is not always the case. It is not even often the case. And lest we forget, we have the testimony of people like Ammonas to remind us. He had reduced his objective world to sand and sky (and as we have noted, perhaps to some like-minded companions). Nevertheless, he not only found anger; he also experienced it as a powerful and tenacious obstacle to his progress.

At this point I can imagine a devil's advocate, or perhaps the devil himself, raising a few objections. "Aren't you ignoring the possibility that Ammonas's ascetic practices could themselves constitute 'objective' causes of anger? Ammonas is in many ways typical of the paradox that lies at the root of so many religious projects: The method he uses to solve 'the problem' only exacerbates the problem. Take somebody like Ammonas, give him a nice house and three square meals a day, a pretty wife, and a couple of good trout streams close by, and he wouldn't be praying to get rid of his anger. That's because anger wouldn't be an issue. Neither would three-quarters of the other things against which he is so 'valiantly' doing battle. Here you have asceticism in a nutshell: Invent the problem, then invent the regimen that will only make the problem worse. Then after you've knocked yourself down so many times that there's not enough of you left even to complain about the problem, declare victory and receive homage from the next generation of dimwits. What nonsense."

Perhaps. But speaking as one who has the nice house, the three squares, the pretty wife, and even the several trout streams—in which I consistently catch trout—I have to say that the devil's argument is a bit disingenuous. History, even history roughly contemporary with Ammonas, bears that out. In his writings on anger, the Roman philosopher Seneca takes his examples from the peevish behavior of the aristocratic landowning class, people who ostensibly ought not to have had a single murmur of complaint, let alone a temper tantrum, but who frequently had both. He tells of one aristocrat, for example, so incensed by the racket made by a slave who had accidentally dropped a tray of crystal glasses that he had the poor man thrown into a pond of lampreys.

Obviously a change of situation or scene or even of religious regimen is not likely to solve our problem with anger, if we do indeed have a problem. For further evidence you might observe your own and others' behavior in the course of a vacation, when some of us attempt for a time to enjoy the luxury of a Roman patrician or the tranquility of an Egyptian monk. For blissful intervals we may have healthy doses of both, and if all goes well, that's all we may have. In that case, great vacation. But if something does go wrong, we may find ourselves as easily aroused to anger as we are back home—perhaps more so, because the mishap outrages the expectation created by the mix of luxury and tranquility that we have contrived.

~~

A third misconception in our list has to do with our failure to see the relationship not only between anger and our unregenerate selves, but between anger and our integrity. We cannot believe that Ammonas or one of his fellows would have had such a problem with anger because we think of them as earnest, sincere folks, and we expect better of them. We also wish better *for* them; after all, don't they deserve it?

We fail to recognize that the anger they experienced may to some degree have been a mark of their caliber as human beings committed to a noble cause. They may have become angry because they cared about what they were doing. Their shortcomings and those of their fellow ascetics were matters of the utmost importance. A more easygoing attitude would not necessarily have proved that they were living in accordance with their vocation.

If I were an abbot, or even a psychotherapist, and someone came to me full of despair over his anger, this is how I might proceed:

Abbot Keizer: For the next week, I want you to make a concentrated study of the people you know who never get angry. I want you to watch everything they do and mark it well.

Troubled Monk: Is that so I'll learn how to master my anger?

Abbot Keizer: No, that's so you'll learn how to master your guilt.

Try it sometime. Spend time in a school, for instance. Locate those teachers who are always jovial, never frazzled, never upset—those who reportedly "never get mad." Sometimes these are individuals of such transcendent competence and compassion that, as my troubled monk above suggests, the best thing you can do is watch them and learn everything you can. But in other cases these are individuals who have succeeded in reducing everything to the least common denominator. Some time ago they stumbled upon a great secret, which is that many people wish for nothing more than to have a little fun while making an even littler effort. And another great secret, which is that they, the teachers, share this very same goal. And a third great secret, which is that *our* goal is best achieved by guaranteeing the fulfillment of *their* goal. That's three noble truths, and the best thing about three noble truths is that they're 25 percent less work than four.

So get to work on time, and—more important—leave on time. Learn to see the mercy in all the little glitches that tend to infuriate the less enlightened. Fire drill at the critical point of a lesson? Try to grab a coffee on the way back. And remember, this one could actually be the real thing . . . better grab a coffee on the way out. Students cut class? If only more of them would do the same. Didn't try their homework? Less to correct. Misbehaving? Today's interrupted lesson is now tomorrow's. And tomorrow is Friday, thanks be to God. See what I mean? Life is good. Anger is bad. Life minus anger equals longevity. And longevity is what it's all about. If Jesus Christ had just strolled into the temple courtyard with a little money to be exchanged and a few jokes to exchange with it, he might have lived to enjoy his retirement.

Sometimes there is no great distinction between laid-back and lying down. Sometimes the worker who is capable of getting angry *about the work* in the most disturbingly "unprofessional" way is the worker who cares about more than looking professional when she works. That Abbot Ammonas became angry was a sign that he had to keep watch on his emotions; it was also a sign that he was capable of watching something besides a clock.

The danger, of course, is that the integrity sometimes revealed by anger can itself become a temptation. Lust and gluttony are not the only kinds of obsession, nor are money and power the only kinds of false gods. We can also make an idol of our own conscientiousness. We grow angry when it fails to stand up against every obstacle, and we may also grow angry when others fail to bow down before it. The devil has often been portrayed as an impish angel who takes perverse delight in confounding the creation. Might he also be portrayed as an overly earnest spirit, convinced to the point of damning rage that the creation would be so much better off in his capable hands? After all, God rested on the Sabbath, but the devil never sleeps.

∽

Finally, we may be troubled at Abbot Ammonas's fourteen-year struggle with anger because we believe, as children of our culture, that all problems exist to be solved. Ammonas ought to have been able to solve his. But Christ did not solve the cross. He suffered it.

Listen again to May Sarton. Here she quotes two of her mentors, Carl Jung and George Herbert:

> Jung says, "The serious problems in life are never fully solved. If ever they should appear to be so it is a sure sign that something has been lost. The meaning and purpose of a problem seem to lie not in its solution but in our working at it incessantly. This alone preserves us from stultification and petrefaction." And so, no doubt, with the problems of a solitary life.
>
> . . . I asked myself the question, "What do you want of your life?" and I realized with a start of recognition and terror, "Exactly what I have—but to be commensurate, to handle it all better."
>
> Yet it is not those fits of weeping that are destructive. They clear the air, as Herbert says so beautifully:
>
> Poets have wronged poor storms: such days are best;
> They purge the air without, within the breast.
>
> What is destructive is impatience, haste, expecting too much too fast.

I am not so sure as Jung about "the serious problems of life" never being solved. I believe that sometimes they might be, but seldom without struggle, never without grace, and never with the guarantee that they will not reemerge in some new form. In Luke's account of the temptation of Christ, the devil eventually departs "until a more opportune time." The battle is won, for the present, but there is no "closure." If there is a word that raises my suspicions as much as the word *spirituality*, it is the word *closure*. Have you noticed how those with an exaggerated fondness for the one word almost always develop an exaggerated fondness for the other? That is because of the life-denying quality implicit in both. The only spirituality I believe in is incarnate. And the only closure I believe in is what will happen when the undertaker screws down the lid on my coffin. Given the resurrection of the body, I cannot even say that I believe in that.

With May Sarton, I do believe that my life can be managed better than I frequently manage it. Like her, I do not desire a different life than the one I have, nor a different range of emotions, but a better way of dealing with both. Like Herbert, I believe that the storms of my life—including the storms of anger—are sometimes no less a blessing than the storms in the sky. Apparently, the poet who asked God to "Throw away Thy wrath" would not have asked him to throw away the thunder.

ANGER
IN THE
HEAD

I refute Berkeley thus.

Samuel Johnson, kicking a large rock

ANGER AS
MENTALITY

I believe that people in the twenty-first century will come to
see Arthur Miller's play *Death of a Salesman* as an even more
groundbreaking work than it seemed when first performed in
1949. And though the themes that moved audiences then
may still ring true in the future, I do not believe that the
play's tragic portrayal of the American dream will be the
main cause of its celebration in decades to come. Instead
playgoers will judge the play important for being one of the
first treatments in modern literature of a man living almost
entirely in his own head. Unless, of course, playgoers are by
that time so much in *their* heads that they cannot appreciate
the play.

In an interview Miller revealed that he had actually first
conceived of the stage set as a gigantic head—Willy Loman's—

in which all of the actors would perform. He wisely abandoned the device. The play itself suffices to show a man who inhabits his own memories to the exclusion of the living stuff out of which further memories might be made. In this he is both a harbinger of days to come, and a holdover from a philosophy at least two hundred years old.

The eighteenth-century philosopher Bishop Berkeley proposed that what we call reality exists only as a subjective phenomenon, something "in our heads." Samuel Johnson dismissed Berkeley—and made Berkeley immortal in the process—by kicking a large rock and saying, "I refute Berkeley thus." Of course, he refuted no one, and proved nothing, but he did memorably profess his faith in a concrete world outside his own mind. The tragedy of Willy Loman may actually go farther by way of refutation. That is because Willy doesn't kick the rock; he trips over it. We cannot say that his mind put it there as part of his wish to kick a rock. God put it there as part of God's wish that rocks, along with salesmen, galaxies, and pineapples, exist as unique and distinct creations.

But Miller has not only given us a tragedy about a man living in his head, and thereby an uncanny prophecy of where more and more of Willy's successors are going to live, he may also have given us an equally prophetic glimpse into how that transformation is going to come about. If you know the play, you cannot forget the scene in which Willy goes to see his boss in the hopes of obtaining an easier sales route. The boss is the son of the man who first hired Willy, and it's clear in the scene that he scarcely knows who Willy is and even more scarcely pities him. What makes the scene so brilliantly horrible is the new toy with which the boss is fascinated to the point of obsession. As Willy fights for his life, the boss fiddles with his tape recorder, subjecting Willy to various inane recordings of his children. In some ways the boss is also a man living in his head. The voices on the machine are more real to him than the man standing before him in the flesh.

What Miller is showing us—years before the widespread use of television, computers, and VCRs—is the technological creation of an alternative reality, a "virtual reality" if you will, that is ruthlessly isolating, endlessly repeatable, seductively controllable, and utterly dead. The play does not suggest that this alternative reality is in any way responsible for Willy's retreat into his own mind. But it does foreshadow the way in which Willy Loman will become more, not less, of an Every-man even while *Death of a Salesman* recedes more and more into the past. We all have those recorders now, and the other devices they have spawned, and it seems that they have led us willy-nilly to a Willy Loman place where each of us acts in his own movie, scored by his own music, but influenced by some master script.

Many forms of anger partake of this same false reality; they amount to storms brewing in our heads over grievances that are also, to a large degree, brewed in our heads. And to some extent, our electronic media have become the brewery. It may be too that this condition does not so much owe to the content of what we watch and listen to, as is sometimes alleged, as to the actual process of watching and listening—of repeatedly entering a situation in which the flesh and blood people around us are less real to us and we to them than the phantoms occupying our attention. It was once assumed, for example, that young lovers would go to movies in order to make out. It would now seem that many of our contempo-raries are making out even as the movie plays in their heads, more real to them than the person in their arms. The word *fantasy* buzzes around our use of the word *sex* like bees around a flower, but no flower was ever pollinated by a fantasy. Something similar might be said about our anger. It might seem real and visceral and ecstatically primitive, though when we look at it closely, we discover that it is, in many cases, unreal, totally cerebral, and fashionably up-to-date.

As a simple example, try to gauge your sense of violent crime, that is, to assess in as realistic a way as possible your own degree of danger from violent crime. First, make a quick mental estimation, like a tire gauge pressed onto a valve: What's the pressure? Next, ask yourself how many violent crimes have actually been committed in your neighborhood. How many times have you come even remotely near to being a victim of violent crime? Which for you is more real, your imaginary sense of crime or your lived experience?

Of course, if you have actually been a victim, or if you live in an abusive relationship or in what amounts to a war zone of violent activity, you can hardly be accused of exaggerating your danger. In fact, you may discover that in order to maintain some kind of sanity you have consciously de-emphasized the danger. In other words, you have created a sense of safety that is to some extent unreal—though it may be helping you to deal with your environment in a more rational and humane way.

For many of us, however, I suspect that the opposite is true. We have an exaggerated view of the dangers of our neighborhood, because our neighborhood is perceived as a composite "world," which, strictly speaking, does not exist except on paper, on a screen, and in our heads. Inhabiting such a virtual neighborhood is not necessarily a humanizing experience. It can engender a kind of fantasy life in which the dangers of people everywhere add up to the sum total of our dangers, not by way of sympathy, but by way of paranoia, which expresses itself in daydreams of revenge and self-defense. These daydreams can often be formulated as a series of "if" clauses: "if someone ever did something like that to my family," "if what happened six thousand miles away ever happened right here," "if this stranger I'm seeing before me turned out to be another version of the person whose face and name are now on the news," and so on. The "then" clauses that follow the "if" clauses can amount to actual anger in response to imaginary provocation. With the right stimulus, they can lead to actual violence.

I used to wonder what Jesus could have meant in the Sermon on the Mount when he said, "Whoever is angry at his brother without a cause is in danger of hell fire." How, I asked myself, could one be angry "without a cause"? Quite easily. I have been angry in that way many times—as the result of just such a fantastic process as I've described. And in those cases one doesn't have to take the fire of hell on faith; one can actually feel it. One could be in heaven itself, as Satan supposedly once was, and still be in hell by virtue of the seething and fantastic raging of one's own mind. "If that angel over there were ever to insult me, I would grab him by his wings and . . ." Sooner or later the hypothetical "if" becomes the hallucinated "because," and Lucifer falls from the sky.

⌒⌒

The recent phenomenon of road rage is a good example of the anger that results from exaggerated subjectivity. It is also an example of how the gadgetry of the modern world helps to foster that subjectivity. Driving, after all, is an experience not unlike that of watching television, with a windshield for a screen. But whereas a TV show is an illusion we take to be real, the world outside our windshields is a reality that we sometimes treat as an illusion. We act as if we were doing something other than piloting one- and two-ton masses of steel with the power to kill and maim in an instant. Until a cop, a collision, or a close call tells us otherwise, we are to a great extent in our own heads. Have you ever noticed how putting your feet on the ground of a highway rest stop can feel like a more powerful sensation than it somehow ought to be? It's like going to the kitchen for a snack during a television commercial— the world seems so overwhelmingly solid in three dimensions and in real time. The teakettle sounds like an alarm clock.

Sometimes, though, the image coming through the windshield doesn't even register; the "show" we're watching is entirely fantastic. The music from our radio or tape player is the score—not for the fleeting images we see on the screen of our windshields, but for the imaginary dramas in our heads. A rude or careless driver's sudden interruption of our on-the-road daydreams can have the same stress-inducing effect as being awakened abruptly from a sound sleep. We wake as if to hungry jaws open above our face; the reaction is automatic and extreme.

I love the road as much as any American, perhaps more than most. If I couldn't be a writer, I would be a truck driver. Still, I find it unfortunate that so many of our American metaphors and myths come from auto travel: life in the fast lane, in the driver's seat, put the brakes to, take a backseat, head-on collision. I say "unfortunate" because auto travel is often an isolating experience, asocial and hypersubjective. Safe driving, as I'm rediscovering in the process of teaching my teenaged daughter to drive, is an act of contrived paranoia. You improve your chances of survival by distrusting the other drivers' signals, by resolutely expecting them to do the worst. It might be said that this is nothing other than how we survive at life in general, but I wonder if the prudent guardedness we bring to everyday life isn't exaggerated by the isolation and illusion of "the cockpit"—by the speed of the vehicle and the corresponding fleetingness of every encounter with another driver. There are things I would not dare do as a pedestrian among other pedestrians that I might be tempted to do in a car among other cars, where the fear of retaliation and the human claims of a face-to-face encounter are radically reduced.

It's hard not to wonder, also, if the daily experience of being in the car, along with the metaphorical constructions of being "on the road," don't eventually lead people to behave as though they're driving even when they're not. Watch shoppers in a supermarket. Watch friends "navigate" their love lives. In essence what they're doing is driving. You almost expect them to honk a horn. There's that sense of an accident waiting to happen.

Road rage is typically a loss of reality. Both the perceived offense and the response to it are completely out of proportion. Someone cuts you off, and suddenly you want to cut her throat. Someone seizes an advantage, and you're ready to hunt him down like prey. Surely there's a primitive physiology at work in all of this, as in any case where stress triggers our flight-or-fight response. But that response can also be triggered, and indeed is intentionally triggered, by loud music in a gym or in a high action movie. Because the response functions naturally does not mean that its occasions are all natural. It's perfectly natural to scream, for instance, but something's wrong if we're screaming all the time.

Perhaps the best way to grasp the unreality of road rage, its extreme subjectivity, is to notice how selective and relative our sense of justice becomes during the experience. The person poking along in front of me is an idiot; the person on my tail is an idiot too. The person who takes advantage of an opening in traffic is a pushy bastard; the person who checks my doing the same thing is an uptight jerk. If I'm lost, the other driver has no patience; if the other driver's lost, I have no time. The only thing real in this picture is *me*. There are plenty of out-of-car examples of this kind of meanness and madness, to be sure, but rage on the road offers one of the best illustrations I know of the connection between egoism, anger, and too little else in the concrete world of creation.

Another danger of living too much in our own heads is the inevitable assumption that others live in our heads too. Not in their heads, but in our heads. In other words, we begin to assume that others are aware of our doubts, fears, and sensitivities, and that they therefore hurt us with the perfect knowledge of what they're doing. It's not simply that they have acted with a malicious intent, which they may indeed have done, it's that they have acted with inside information. Of course, they could only have such inside information if they were indeed inside, which is where they would have to be if no such thing as outside exists. When we live too much in our own heads, every careless injury is seen as a calculated insult, every tactless boor as a clever sadist, every enemy as the devil himself.

A minor and relatively harmless form of this delusion occurs when we assume we've told someone something that we never have. "Didn't I tell you that Martha and I were going hiking this Saturday?" "You most certainly did not," says your husband. Either you only daydreamed that you told him, or else you really did tell him, but he was too lost in a daydream of his own to hear you. If taken in the right spirit, misunderstandings like this can be one of the comic endearments of a long-standing relationship. They suggest that the partners are "talking to each other" even when they're not talking. But they also serve as a gentle warning that the imaginary conversation is beginning to supersede the actual, or that even when the partners are actually talking, they're not actually listening.

We know we have stepped onto more dangerous, if even less substantial ground when we hear ourselves saying, with a frequency that amounts to a refrain: "She *knows* what she's doing." In other words, she knows where my most tender places are, and she's doing what she's doing on the basis of that knowledge. Perhaps she is. There are certainly ways to wound one another without having to know the intimate particulars of one another's previous wounds. Human beings are not so unalike—we all bleed blood. I grow increasingly impatient with that glib "interpersonal" strategy that attempts to render all conflicts moot by rendering all grievances subjective. We're terribly sorry that *you had such a problem* with our dropping a bomb on your village; if we *made you feel* like a victim of genocide, we regret it. This kind of qualified apology is nothing more than a different form of living in our heads; we could call it hiding in our heads. The bombs don't exist, just our differing feelings about them.

Nevertheless, we need to be on guard against confusing the motives of our adversaries with the vulnerabilities of our own minds. Remember the prayer of Jesus on the cross: "Father, forgive them, for they know not what they do." Of course on the most basic level, they *do* know what they do; it's hard to be oblivious to the act of driving nails into a man's flesh. But the soldiers cannot know the identity of the man they crucify—even the insightful centurion who calls him a son of God cannot know—any more than they could know the minds of the two thieves. The soldiers are too caught up in their own assignments, in their own game of lots, even in the habitual gestures of their own brutality, to know on the deepest levels everything subsumed in the cry of "My God, my God, why have you forsaken me?" Recognizing that they knew not what they did must have increased Jesus' sense of alienation, surely, but perhaps it also mitigated his sense of outrage. The assumption of their ignorance, like vinegar on a sponge, must have provided him with a few drops of sour comfort.

So too will the hunch that my absorption in my own head corresponds to a similar absorption in the heads of my adversaries. Most people are too self-preoccupied to *mean* much of anything. Replacing a worldview in which everyone is calculating to get me with a worldview in which most people don't give a damn about me one way or the other is not necessarily a move toward consolation, but it is, in many cases, a move toward reality, and therefore toward sanity too.

‎⸗⸝

At one point in *Death of a Salesman*, Willy's wife, Linda, speaks a line that could serve as her husband's epitaph: "Attention must be paid," she says. She means (and Miller means to say through her) that we must acknowledge Willy's struggles and suffering and goodness. So we must, if we are to avoid dismissing Willy. But attention must also be paid if we are to avoid becoming Willy. Attention must be paid if we are to avoid becoming trapped in our own heads, our own anger, our own hell. "The virtue of humility," said Simone Weil, "is nothing more or less than the power of attention." Attention to what? To everything that reminds us of our humble place in this world: to the other drivers on the road, even to the rock at the side of the road, which has much to tell us if we will but get out of our comfortable cars once in a while and give it a good kick.

Love casts out fear.

St. John

ANGER
AS FEAR

Once during a discussion at my church, a man remarked that "Anger is nothing but fear." He claimed to speak from experience. I was immediately skeptical, in part because I'm always skeptical of any statement phrased in the reductive terms of "nothing but," in part because I could not believe that a man of his formidable size and commanding personality had found much to fear in his life (an assumption that was far more reductive than his statement), and in large part because I resisted the humbling connection between my own robust capacities for anger and anything as paltry as fear. Was my friend suggesting that anger was "nothing but" an indication of cowardice?

Of course, if we locate the source of anger in our primordial flight-or-fight response, there's nothing especially shocking or profound in what this man had to say. It is a simple thing to prove, and on any number of occasions, I have discovered that I was indeed angry because I was also afraid. I have noticed my rage rushing to encase and contain my fear like the antibody of some emotional immune system. And this is basically a good thing, because while fear paralyzes you, anger prepares you to act.

In some cases, though, acting on anger can be more dangerous than not acting because of fear. Anger is constructive only to the extent that fear is reasonable. But knowing as much is not very helpful once you're angry. Trying to eliminate anger can be every bit as futile as trying to eliminate any other emotion—as trying to be happy when you're deeply depressed, for instance, or to "get over it" when you've been shamefully humiliated. You feel what you feel. So often the attempt to rise above anger can amount to a vain exercise in fakery—like sitting on a bed of nails and pretending that it doesn't hurt—which gives way in a howling cry of pain once the ruse becomes unbearable.

This is where the recognition of a link between anger and fear becomes useful, something much better than one of those bar-stool equations to which we respond, "Ah, I see what you mean"—though what we *don't* see is how the equation has any practical relevance whatsoever. Sometimes I have found that the best way to overcome my anger is to deal with it indirectly by overcoming my fear. It may sound as though I'm doing nothing more than giving my anger a different name. But fear can be opposed by a simple act of will in a way that anger often cannot.

Once I was prevented from pulling into a supermarket parking lot by a pickup truck idling just inside the entrance.

The driver and his two passengers were chatting with someone who'd just come out of the market, and though I suspected that the driver was aware of my presence in his rearview mirror, he was in no hurry to be on his way. So there I sat, pulled in as close behind him as I could get, with my own behind sticking out on the busy main street.

I did not honk my horn, which probably would have been the most reasonable thing to do. I have certain scruples about car horns: I use them liberally as a warning, but I generally refuse to use them as a prod (as at a red light that has just turned green) or a threat. In this case I might not have used the horn because I preferred being ignored with at least a pretense that it was not deliberate to being ignored outright. I also preferred to avoid an escalation: Would I get out of my car if the horn didn't do the trick? And would I get out of my car if these three scruffy rednecks decided to get out of theirs first?

In a situation like this, my mind tends to overload with considerations. One of the foremost for me is always time: These guys were wasting mine, but a confrontation was likely to waste still more. I also remembered that I was supposed to be "living the gospel." Shouldn't one be prepared to bear these innocuous injuries with patience? On the other hand, are you truly loving your neighbor as yourself if, through a cowardly tolerance of someone's boorish behavior, you set a precedent for your neighbor to be similarly abused? How often don't patience, mercy, tolerance—all the so-called liberal virtues—come down to drinking a toast to your own benevolence and leaving it to someone else to pay for the drink?

Well, of course, by the time you've listened to even a few of these voices, the truck has moved, and you're ready to go grocery shopping—except by that time you're so angry you could spit and, what is more, deeply ashamed to recognize that in the end you were not rational or charitable so much as you were simply afraid. Anger may arise from fear; it may also arise from recognizing the fear, and loathing it.

Somewhere in the supermarket, in the midst of deciding which size box of crackers to buy and which kind of apple, I decided that I hated the way I felt and that I wanted to feel different, no matter the cost. And so when I came out to my car with my groceries, instead of driving directly home, I began to search for the truck, which was identifiable by a faded sign painted on one of its doors. I wasn't sure what I was going to do if I found it, but I was going to try to find it.

Although this was a Saturday morning, and although searching for a particular pickup truck in my region is a little like searching for a particular alligator in the Everglades, I did happen to sight the truck parked outside a down-at-the-heels mechanic shop. The garage door was down and the windows covered, so I wasn't sure at first that the shop was even open. But when I went inside, I found three men under the hood of a car.

I asked them if they were connected to the truck parked in front of the garage. When they said that they were, I recounted what had happened at the supermarket and the fact that I didn't appreciate being treated as they had treated me. What happened next is barely remarkable, though what might have happened next—if, for instance, one of the men had decided to deck me with a lug wrench—might have been terribly remarkable, but what interests me here is what I felt at that moment: a total absence of anger and, if not a total absence of fear, then a mastery of it so complete that I might almost have been disappointed were the fear to have vanished. I felt calm. More important, I felt alive.

All of the men were looking at me now; none of them seemed sure what to make of me. Later I would recognize their response as a main advantage to calming anger by facing fear: One's adversaries are momentarily thrown off guard. It is much easier to classify and therefore respond to an angry person than to one who is . . . well, acting with all the chutzpah of an angry person but with none of the anger. After a moment one of the men said, "That wasn't us."

Of course it was, but I saw no reason to argue the point. The man's lie may have been his attempt to save face, but it was no less a concession than if he'd been forced to cry, "I'm sorry!" on his knees—indeed, it was more so, because no one was forcing him to do anything. Our business was finished. I had told a simple truth, without bluster or accusation, and he had defended himself with a flimsy lie. I left the shop feeling better than many a cathartic explosion of rage has made me feel. What is more, I didn't have to spend any extra emotional capital on feeling sorry for my adversary or retroactively foolish on my own behalf, as I might have felt had I gotten mad at him.

Of course, an episode like this doesn't amount to the epiphany I might like to make of it. The same problem handled in the same way might end in disaster. The same problem handled in the same way might lead me back to the very same dilemma that created the problem in the first place—except that I would lack the advantage of sorting the problem out within the protective enclosure of my car. Still, the episode was not without some value for me. For one thing, I feel that I can better understand the phenomenal equanimity of certain persons who have carried on campaigns of nonviolent resistance: Perhaps they did not so much overcome their own anger through nonviolence as they used nonviolence to face and overcome their fears. Given that victory, their anger was almost moot.

I feel too as if I can better appreciate, in spite of some reservations, the conspicuous adventurism one sees in our culture of late—all of this artificial risk-taking and compulsive gear-mongering, people shooting down rapids and clambering up cliffs, like old-time flagpole sitters and goldfish swallowers reincarnated minus all sense of proportion and any sense of humor. The thought of a grown man or woman with a family, a full refrigerator, a well-stocked bookcase, and enough dirt to grow a garden going off to scale the higher Himalayas strikes me as little short of obscene, like a man who forsakes his beautiful wife to seek out the company of needle-scarred teenaged prostitutes. I want to know how he became so jaded and twisted as to need that kind of prurient thrill. And when a crew of these explorers finds itself in jeopardy, my distaste and incredulity turn to out-and-out disgust at the prospect of other men and women risking their lives to rescue those who were so perversely incapable of enjoying their own. More than once I've said to myself, Let them perish. What is the point of their "risk" otherwise? Do we parachute philanthropists onto the roofs of Las Vegas casinos whenever a gambler loses his shirt?

But in a more charitable frame of mind, I have wondered if some of these seeming fools haven't tapped into a wisdom that is only beginning to dawn on me: that in the overload of stimuli and responses that comes of living in our frenetic civilization, life can sometimes come down to a simple choice between daring and rage, between the risk of freezing one's nose in an Arctic snowstorm or breaking someone's nose (or having one's own broken) in a parking lot brawl. They opted for the first, and though there may be a more constructive way to frame the choice, who dares reproach them for choosing as they did?

⌒

If anger is sometimes "nothing but fear," then what do we fear that has such power over our emotions? One of the things we fear most is losing a battle. It is as if the primal emotion of anger arises in us because every conflict in some way recalls some primal conflict, when our very lives were at stake, though the conflict at present may in fact be no more primal than an argument over the minutiae of office procedure or the up-or-down position of a toilet seat. Remember that we have been talking about "anger in the head." Anger that arises from a dread of losing, when the consequences of losing are a good deal less than dreadful, is obviously the result of a mental distortion. We've all had the experience of playing a recreational game with someone, or even *as* someone who could not stand the idea of losing, whose keenness for winning spoiled the fun, who was a jerk, in other words. But in the day-to-day business of our lives, many of us play in the same way, so that a keenness to win becomes an irresistible rage to win.

Admittedly we sometimes fear losing because we see some higher principle at stake in the conflict. It is that principle, we insist, and not our own pride that motivates our passion. This may be true. And I have little sympathy and recommend giving no quarter to those who try to ignore principles or belittle conflicts because, as they're fond of saying, "This is not a matter of life or death." Not a matter of death, perhaps, but always a matter of life. If principles have nothing to do with the quotidian details of office equipment and toilet seats, if they have only to do with the Vast and the Vague and the Grand Scale, then they're worthless. The same goes for that hackneyed evasion, much beloved by traveling bigamists, serial killers, and the winners of contested presidential elections, "It's time to move forward now." As soon as you hear someone use those words, you know that of all things possible at that moment, moving forward is not on the list. Any housekeeper can tell you that. People who "move forward" from their messes rather than cleaning them up only go on to make other messes—usually bigger ones.

So it is not a delusion to insist on "the principle of the thing" in a given conflict. The delusion comes of fearfully assuming that the principle is defeated just because we are—that truth loses out because a liar wins, or that justice no longer exists because we fail in our attempt to challenge some injustice. The partisans who fought in the Resistance during the last world war seem to have possessed a confidence that went beyond the fear of any such outcome. Certainly they were afraid, and should have been afraid, of the kind of world that would result if Hitler prevailed. But could they have believed that all decency would die if they lost? I don't think so. If decency were so terminal, they had lost already.

It is also a delusion to believe that in losing some conflict we ourselves are diminished, even in our very being. We believe so when we have thoroughly identified ourselves with the issue at stake. "If I lose, I *am* a loser." But defeat in itself is no diminishment, which may be one reason why conquerors have routinely followed their victories with torture, rape, and other brutalities: to accomplish, if possible, the subjugation that victory alone can never accomplish. The vanquished are not less for being defeated; indeed, they sometimes grow stronger in defeat, just as a cause sometimes gains permanence through being lost.

I try to remind myself of that now and again. I am suspicious of self-hypnotic formulas, self-help mantras, and all the rest, but I'm also suspicious of letting my suspicions deprive me of good comfort when it's available—so I've composed a simple motto that has sometimes proved useful for me:

> You do not have to win;
> you only have to fight.
> And you have to remember
> that any cause worth fighting for
> is larger than you.

Another way of saying that is "You do not have to be afraid"; and another way still: "You do not have to be angry."

On the most basic level of all, deeper than our fear of losing, we are afraid to suffer. As a mere statement of fact, this hardly deserves mention, but it always comes to the forefront of my consciousness like a sudden flash of light. I am afraid to suffer. I am a Christian. I worship a man nailed to a cross. But I am angry; I am angry because I am afraid; and I am afraid because I do not wish to end up like the person I believe to be the end of all human love, hope, and striving. The absurdists of the last century boldly proclaimed that life has no meaning; they were amateur absurdists. In so many of my words and actions, I proclaim that life *has* a meaning but that I want no part of it. That is an absurdity beside which any other form amounts to a mere posture. I think of Peter on the night of Christ's trial: Asked if he knows Jesus, he begins to curse and swear. That is the archetype for a good deal of my anger. I curse and swear by way of denying one of the few things I know for sure.

⌒

Examples of that denial are as common as the occasions of pain, even those mundane varieties that we locate figuratively in the buttocks or the neck. And how great a variety! Young students are often amused to learn the types of neurotic phobia, to memorize the various "silly" things that people fear. In time we come to see the catalog as nothing more or less than a partial listing of all the ways that human beings can suffer and be traumatized. My daughter came home from school not long ago amazed and amused at having learned of optophobia, the fear of opening one's eyes. I am glad that, at the age of seventeen, she can find such a fear ridiculous. Nearly thrice as old as she, I can only think of it as rare, and strangely so.

I can recall a time in her childhood when I could easily have imagined a fear of opening one's ears—a very formidable fear, in that it is most potent at the very times when a person is most desirous of hearing. I remember, to be more specific, her Christmas concerts, and one in particular. Student bands and choirs from several neighboring towns were to join in the all-purpose room of her elementary school for a precious hour of public performance. For months she had practiced her parts on her clarinet, after school on Wednesdays with the whole band and most evenings at home between cleaning out the rabbit's cage and starting her math. From the time when her instrument was almost as tall as she, I had watched her struggle with it, her eyes those of an overloaded pony as she strained with all her might to make the notes. That night she would be the only first clarinet on a difficult song. She dressed early in her holiday clothes, new evergreen dress, candy cane–colored sweater, snowman earrings—she was almost as nervous as she was beautiful. Her mother and I told her she'd do fine.

I was going to the concert for her, of course, but it was not as if my only pleasure came from her. How many things on earth are as lovely as a children's chorus, to name but one of the night's attractions, especially when the choristers not only desire to sing but *dare* to sing, especially when their young teacher is even more nervous and almost as endearing as they are, especially when they perform in a place where life can be so hard and the winters so bleak that any single thing of beauty is a grace so amazing it hurts.

All I wanted to do was sit for an hour and enjoy these kids and this music in peace. I wanted to hear the words that they had struggled to memorize. I wanted to follow the notes that they had struggled to produce. An artistic performance is like a Thanksgiving meal—be it Grandma's or the Holy Eucharist: Someone has gone to a lot of trouble on your behalf, and all you're required to do is sit down and eat, watch, or listen. And in the right frame of mind, that is all you want to do: be nourished and be grateful. As an aside, I would note this frame of mind as worth the attention of any careful student of anger. Learn to recognize the mood and moment when "All I want is such a little thing," that is, when you have reduced your negotiation with the world to one modest requirement that ought to be yours by virtue of its being so modest. This is often a prelude to anger, first of all because you're already drawing a line in the sand by demanding that one small thing, and second because even that one small thing can turn out to be more than you're going to get.

It would be more than I got that night. Behind me, as there must always be behind me, two women were chattering away. One leaned forward now and then to talk to her husband or boyfriend, who for some reason was sitting beside me instead of her, and who in his antsy distraction made a Saint Vitus' dancer look like a tree sloth on a particularly logy day. The other woman, when she wasn't blabbing to her friend, was telling her little boy to keep quiet. To sit still. To "be-have." Except for the patter of his feet when he ran away from her, I could hardly hear him. Mainly, I heard her. This was her performance too, you see. I have been audience to a hundred others just like it: the performance of ostentatious parental control by a person with absolutely no parental control and not a clue how to achieve it. Within the space of two songs, a sixteenth-century carol and an Appalachian folk ballad, the last stanza of which was drowned by her nagging, she had exhausted her entire repertoire, threatening to make the child sit out the concert in the cold parked car or else on her lap "like a baby." Finally, she seemed to wear him down. At last she had the opportunity of setting him a good example of how you behave at a concert—by carrying on with her friend like a couple of Klondike barmaids.

During the intermission a good-natured neighbor of mine shook her head and whispered, "Well, it takes all kinds, I guess"—which was the last straw for me: rudeness under the auspices of diversity. I supposed that "all kinds" might eventually include the Ku Klux Klan.

Of course, my neighbor was only trying to commiserate, to be reasonable—except that reason and reasonable solutions were all meaningless here. Someone might say to me, "Why didn't you turn around and simply ask the woman to be quiet?" This is reason? To suppose that a person who would not attend to *her own child* making music would nevertheless attend to a perfect stranger making a fuss? "Well, you should have moved, then," says another reasonable voice. "Change your seat. For that matter, maybe you should change your address!" Yes, maybe I should have annoyed a dozen other people by crawling over them on the rare chance of finding a seat where I wouldn't be annoyed. And yes, maybe I should move away to some genteel place where instead of showing off their poor parental skills the backseat blabbermouths show off their superior knowledge of Renaissance vocal music. Only a hick believes that urbanity exists in a more urban place.

Nothing reasonable could have worked here. And to reason with my anger was as pointless as reasoning with the two women. So what could I do? Suffer. I said the word to myself as an imperative sentence: *Suffer.* That is what I could do, maybe all I could do. I could suffer. And that is surely what the mother who sat behind me does, whatever else she does or doesn't do—and I bet, and I could hear it in her voice, that she does it a lot more than I do: She suffers.

Finally, I could remember that above all, in all, and in spite of all that we suffer, at least at that moment, our children were singing. A man's daughter was going to play her clarinet. And I could applaud.

⌒

The resolution to suffer will not last long apart from a willingness to love. In fact, we could go so far as to define love in terms of suffering: *love,* the only thing for which a sane person willingly suffers. Love is the missing link in a Stoic's scheme of personal evolution. It is the critical link in a Christian's. My friend at church said that anger is often based on fear. I have said that fear is often of suffering. And St. John closes the circle when he writes, "Love casts out fear." In other words, love enables us to suffer, to embrace the cross of Christ and, as part of that same embrace, the other people at the Christmas concert, including the woman who annoyed me so.

Love does not cast out all conflict, however. If that were so, then Jesus would never have said, "Love your enemies," because love would make us incapable of having enemies. Perhaps love makes us *more* capable of engaging with our enemies. That is because love makes us willing to suffer, on behalf of those we love, and in conflict with others whom we may, in the course of our struggle, come to love even as they come to suffer with us. This may sound like a tangle of abstractions, and as a string of sentences, so it is. But in concrete, day-to-day situations, I find that these abstractions go a long way toward clarifying what I want to do and what I don't want to do. Why am I angry? Is it because I am afraid? Then what do I fear? Is it suffering? If so, what must I suffer in order to maintain some semblance of humanity? And is it as unbearable as I fear?

All these questions ultimately lead me to the same place: Whom do I love, and what does that love require? Sometimes it requires me to wield my anger like a sharp sword. But more often it requires me to suffer, and to do so fearlessly and without complaint.

Anger hath a privilege.

Shakespeare, *King Lear*

ANGER AS
PRIVILEGE

The scene opens at the torch-lit entrance to the duke of Cornwall's castle. Two messengers named Kent and Oswald surprise each other in their haste to reach the duke. Kent comes from King Lear, hoping to prepare the way for his master's arrival; Oswald comes from one of the king's heartless daughters, hoping to sabotage any asylum the king might find here. Offended by the very sight of Oswald, Kent draws his sword, and when the cowardly sycophant refuses to accept his challenge, Kent begins to beat him. The duke enters with his retinue and demands an explanation for the assault. Kent is scarcely more deferential to the duke than he was to Oswald. When Cornwall warns him to mind his manners, Kent speaks his memorable line: "Anger hath a privilege."

We love Kent, or at least I do; he's everything that many of us would like to be: brave, forthright, and angry in a good cause. In a tragedy filled with vice and folly, he stands as a paragon of selfless devotion. Nevertheless, though his line is spoken in a good cause and among reprehensible characters, its ring of truth reverberates with an echo of hollowness.

Anger does indeed have a privilege. In many cases it amounts to a privilege. The angry person is often confident that he will be able to get away with his anger, either because he is strong or because those around him are compassionate or weak. Anyone who would look consciously at his own anger would do well to ask, first of all, To what extent am I allowed this storm of mine? To what extent does it represent a privilege—of my size, my sex, my reputation, or my status?

The second question that needs asking is like the first: To what extent does my anger *create* a privilege? Many people will defer to anger, and not necessarily because they fear it. Sometimes people defer to anger in the same way that they defer to tears. Something in a healthy human being responds to signs of distress in another. What's wrong with him—and how might I make it right? A person given too easily to anger can be too much aware of the deference his outbursts bring. Like the person who has learned how to shed tears at the most opportune time, he gets angry as an act of manipulation. In the scene where Kent speaks his line, the duke of Cornwall, insufferable monster though he is, shows himself quite perceptive in the following remark:

> This is some fellow
> Who, having been praised for bluntness, doth affect
> A saucy roughness, and constrains the garb
> Quite from his nature. He cannot flatter, he—
> An honest mind and plain—he must speak truth!
> An they will take it, so. If not, he's plain.

These kind of knaves I know, which in this plainness
Harbor more craft and more corrupter ends
Than twenty silly ducking observants
That stretch their duties nicely.

The knaves of which Cornwall speaks are common enough. The sad thing about them is that to some extent they have lost touch with their anger. People appalled or frightened by their outbursts will exclaim, "I wish that guy could get rid of his temper!" The irony is that he has already gotten rid of it. By giving vent to it at every opportunity, by coining his passion and spending it, he has cheapened its value. Not for nothing do we say "get mad" for "get angry," because true anger is like madness in its ability to lift someone out of his everyday mind, either for better or for worse. But anger that hath a privilege or that seeks a privilege is not a matter of getting mad. It's a matter of getting what you want. It's a lion in a circus cage, snarling and clawing the air in exchange for its preset reward of slaughterhouse meat.

～

Privileged anger comes in several forms. It might, for example, appear as an identity. In that case it amounts to saying that you get mad because that's who you are, or at least a big part of who you are. Anger is what you're known for, your trademark, and it ought to be respected as such.

In our society people seem to have a great need to define themselves in this way. And it may be too simplistic to restrict the need to our society. I think of Homer's warriors in the *Iliad*, announcing their names, ranks, and pedigrees before flinging a challenge to their opponents, who must then reciprocate in kind. War as an exchange of résumés—sometimes the introductions take longer than the actual combat. I knew the routine long before I knew Homer. When I was growing up in New Jersey, it was not unusual to go to a kid's house and have his mother ask "your nationality." I knew who in my class was Italian or Dutch, Catholic or Protestant, even though that information had no relevance whatsoever to our studies and games or even to our fistfights. The forms change, but the phenomenon doesn't. Nowadays I'm no longer surprised when a new acquaintance tells me where he fits on the Myers-Briggs inventory before he's even told me to take off my coat. And I have caught myself doing the same thing by confessing, with a subtle hint of disdain, that I have absolutely no idea whatsoever where I fit on the Myers-Briggs inventory. It is a part of my identity not to be concerned with such things.

Emotions can also serve as identifiers, that is, as cut-rate substitutes for what used to be called character. If I am known for displaying a certain emotion, it saves me the trouble of knowing what I actually feel. An identity is like a precooked dinner: No mess, and the instructions are right on the package. The problem with an identity, though, and with the politics of identity, is that one must be forever certifying his credentials. The more people who claim the same identity, the less it actually identifies, and so the ease of "knowing who you are" is sooner or later contradicted by the suspicion that you are not what you seem. Perhaps you are not really a lesbian—just a confused bisexual. Or perhaps you are not really a bisexual, just a lesbian afraid to come out all the way. Perhaps too your anger was just a passing phase, and now you're mellowing out. Perhaps you're losing your edge.

In Hemingway's novel *For Whom the Bell Tolls,* one of the Spanish partisans recounts how during the running of the bulls that traditionally precedes a bullfight, he had jumped onto the back of one and bitten off a piece of its ear. The bravado of the act had so impressed the people in his town that it had virtually become his identity. He was the man with *cajones* enough to jump onto the back of a running bull and bite off its ear. And so every year he was expected to repeat the stunt. What had been an act of spontaneous abandon in the heat of the moment had become a duty, a performance, and—in the sense that it belonged to one man alone—a kind of privilege. In the same way, a reputation for always giving people a piece of your mind can amount to little more than the predicament of continually having a piece of bull's ear in your mouth.

The conundrum of the Spanish bull-biter calls to mind what Jesus said about losing one's life in order to save it. In some sense, one's "life" may be taken to mean one's identity. If your life is defined by jumping onto the back of a charging bull and biting its ear, then losing that false life is, perhaps literally, to save your true life. Or rediscover that life. At the very least, it's a saner way to enjoy a bullfight.

⌐

Another way that "anger hath a privilege" is in the guise of inspiration. By this I mean the belief that anger takes possession of us like a religious ecstasy, as when Samson, inspired by the spirit of God, smites a thousand Philistines with the jawbone of an ass. He couldn't help it, in other words. Anger certainly can come as such an inspiration; I have already given several examples where I believe it came in just such a way and for a similarly liberating purpose.

But not every fit is an inspiration. As God says in the book of Jeremiah, noting those prophets who pass off their dreams for oracles, "Let the prophet who has a dream tell the dream, but let the one who has my word speak my word faithfully." In other words, there are visions, and then there is vision. I tend to be skeptical of any claim for anger as an uncontrollable impulse in the same way as I tend to be skeptical of the "call" of clergy from one church to another. I would frame my skepticism as follows: Why is it that a professional minister is so seldom called to serve a poorer church, or a temporarily insane person moved to attack a more powerful opponent? I'm not saying either can't happen, or that God never works in harmony with our best interests; I'm just saying I have my doubts.

We sometimes hear an abusive spouse or parent talking about how he "lost it," that is, how he lost all control, all sense of the harm he might do, in an overwhelming fit of rage. We might even hear his victims come to his defense with the same argument: He just wasn't himself. He was out of his head. He couldn't do otherwise.

Really? Why then is there nothing in his long violent history that has him walking into the poolroom of a biker bar on Saturday night and, beside himself with rage, kicking one of the burliest patrons in the behind? Why do people "go postal" in post offices but never in precincts? Does inspiration, much less insanity, make such fine and self-serving discriminations between relative degrees of personal danger? In contrast, the hallmark of Samson's inspiration is the fact that he willingly took on a thousand men with nothing but the jawbone of an ass. Would he have seemed as inspired if he had knocked Delilah around with it?

If a person is alive, and out of jail, and gainfully employed, it means, among other things, that his inspirations usually tend to be mixed with a healthy dose of self-interest. He should remember that fact whenever he's tempted to assume the privilege of losing his temper in situations that pose no danger of losing anything else.

One last example of anger as a privilege has to do with the assignment of blame. Anger and blame are often found together, sometimes as fire and fuel, other times as fire and extinguisher. We can feed our anger through dwelling on blame; or we can use blame to dampen our anger—as when we blame the victim of an injustice in order to stay calm in the face of the status quo. In either case, the blamer presumes a certain superiority. The blamer is the one without sin, who dares cast the first stone. It is he who exists to be pleased, he whose business is of the greatest importance, he whose prerogative it is to interpret the merits and demerits of a given issue. The blamer may not be in control, either of the situation or his own emotions, but he acts as though he was somehow in charge.

The book of Genesis treats blame as the second great sin of humankind, older than envy or murder. Only Adam and Eve's eating of the forbidden fruit takes precedence. As soon as God calls them to account for that transgression, they fall to blame, or at least Adam does; it is almost as if we do not realize that humanity has fallen until that point when Adam says to God: "The woman whom you gave to be with me, she gave me fruit from the tree, and I did eat." What words could more succinctly express the idea of a paradise lost than such a paltry and prosaic reversal of the man's exclamation on seeing his wife for the first time:

> This at last is bone of my bones
>   and flesh of my flesh

—now turned to the thorn in his flesh, the supposed cause of all his problems.

That blame should be the second great sin of the Eden story makes perfect sense. To see that, we need to remember what Adam and Eve hoped to gain by eating of the tree of the knowledge of good and evil: They hoped to gain the knowledge of good and evil. "You shall be as gods," said the serpent, "knowing good from evil." In other words, you shall not need a directive from God in order to determine wrong from right, but rather you shall possess that discrimination as a category of mind. (Adam and Eve already had some sense of right and wrong—they knew it was wrong to eat from the tree—but only in relationship to God and his guidance.) I have never ceased to be amazed that the Bible, the *Bible*, should present the prototype of all sin as the willful acquisition of an independent moral consciousness. Not power or pleasure, a quiver of invincible arrows or a cache of giant chocolate bars, but the knowledge of good and evil. Not the stuff of brothels but of Sunday schools.

Of course, the more one thinks about it, the more plausible it seems: the moral discrimination of a god apart from God is hell, like a "relationship" apart from love or a "community" apart from any meaningful communion of human beings. A morality apart from God is a morality apart from mystery and mercy, where the adventure of being alive is reduced to a guided tour of "must see" and "must not see" attractions, where the poetry of the Bible is reduced to the wooden prose of an owner's manual.

Blame inevitably follows that kind of reduction as surely as anger follows blame. The next step after knowing wrong from right is knowing *who* is wrong or right—in other words, knowing whom to blame. And that secondary knowledge can prove as irresistible as the fruit that gave the first knowledge. It comes over us so powerfully because it speaks to our mind's yearning to be free of all constraint. The relationship between anger and blame is not unlike the relationship between anger and hurry. In the latter case, time is what seems to constrain us. You will notice how often your day-to-day anger arises when you're in a rush. Hurrying lowers the threshold of your frustration, even as anger urges you to hurry more. On some visceral level, it makes sense that the engines we employ to give us more speed so often sound angry.

Blame, on the other hand, is not so much a rage for speed as for clarity. In the instant when we make that cause-and-effect connection, the world lights up—things finally make sense. Much of our mortal time we spend like dazed slot machine addicts in front of the absurd combinations and configurations of our lives: two lemons and a banana; an apple, a banana, and a pear; two trips to the hardware store on the same day plus one bolt that still doesn't fit; an unhappy marriage, an ill-fated affair, a bitter divorce. We pay out, we pull the handle once again, we keep our eyes on the wheel. Blame is the deceiving mirage of three lemons. All of a sudden, everything makes perfect sense. It's instructive to remember what the Nazis called the Holocaust: the Final Solution, that is, the promise of everything coming clear and clean at last, like some grand geometric proof.

The wisdom of the Genesis story consists to no small degree of locating the origins of this phenomenon in a man's blaming of his wife and his God. To locate the primary origins of the ovens of Dachau, one must stand by the oven in his own kitchen. When a man is capable of blaming both his loving Maker and the one to whom he makes love, then scapegoating anybody else—even everybody else—is no great stretch. The same can be said for Cain's killing of his own brother and all the mayhem that followed.

⌐⌐

I hesitate to observe that in the Genesis story Adam comes off as more of a blamer than Eve. There is a trend these days toward biological determinism in the discussion of gender that I would prefer to avoid. I question how great a distance lies between talking about "masculine consciousness" and "feminine consciousness" and talking about, say, "Aryan art" and "Semitic art," or the "Negroid brain" and the "Caucasian brain." Men are from Mars and women are from Venus—so we've been told, and so it can seem—but the men and women I love and revere are all from planet Earth. I'd like to remain there with them if I can.

Still, I have to admit that men often seem more ready to blame than women. That should come as no surprise if blaming amounts to the assumption of a privilege. In any situation where men have first position, men will be more likely to accuse and blame. If we would cast a kinder eye on men, we would also point out that their predilection toward blame may arise from a perceived disproportion of responsibility placed on their shoulders. In a creation story where man is made before woman, where he names all the animals and woman as well, where it is apparently his job to tell his wife about the forbidden fruit after she is born from his side, where it is apparently also his job, or rather his sons' job, to "leave father and mother and cleave to a wife," who presumably need do nothing more than wait to be wooed, it is understandable that in a crisis he will anticipate all the blame coming home to him by attempting to shift that blame onto someone else. Blame is the proverbial hot potato, and in a world where men are expected to take charge and be responsible and snatch their potatoes hot from the fire with their bare hands, men are also more likely to blame.

I have more than once observed a pattern in domestic quarrels that goes something like this: The woman expresses her concern, worry, or chagrin over a certain situation. The man, assuming he must somehow be responsible for preventing or rectifying that situation, interprets the mention of it as an insinuation of blame. Resenting that supposed insinuation, the man explicitly blames the woman, who in reality never intended to blame him at all. The woman therefore concludes, as conclude she must, that in the man's eyes she is to blame for all her own problems. Of course, somewhere in this process someone is going to get mad.

The anger will be unhealthy if the partners direct it at each other. It has the potential to become healthy if the partners direct it instead at the fact that they're fighting with each other instead of fighting the source of their frustration. I think of those lines from Homer about marriage:

> the best thing in the world
> [is] a strong house held in serenity

> where man and wife agree. Woe to their enemies,
> joy to their friends! But all this they know best.

Aside from changing "wife" to "woman" or "man" to "husband," all that remains to do by way of bringing the passage up-to-date is to note that the "enemies" are, more often than not, the mechanisms for misunderstanding conditioned in our heads along with every Martian or Venusian notion of what constitutes a real woman or a real man.

⌒

The Russian Orthodox priest Alexander Elchaninov wrote in his extraordinary *Diary:* "In all life, including the Christian life, wisdom consists of this: not to be exacting towards people." This is an excellent piece of advice, and one easily reduced to absurdity. Should the Nuremberg tribunal have been less "exacting" toward Eichmann? Of course not. But such a question betrays the very propensity toward excess that characterizes much of our anger, many of our privileges, and a good deal of our blame. Most of our adversaries are not Hitler. Few if any of our indignities are those of Treblinka. The well-worn habit of invoking the Holocaust in every moral argument says less about the Holocaust than it does about the hubris and disproportion that lie at the root of so much of our rage.

Anger frequently arises from excess and can itself be excessive. A world in which 6 percent of the population consumes 40 percent of the nonrenewable resources and a world in which a motorist can shoot down a stranger for cutting him off on the highway are instantly recognizable to me as the same world. And if anger is often excess, then excess is always the assumption of privilege. When my share of the rights and goods exceeds your share, my share of the rage will do the same. Big palaces and hideous punishments—the Hanging Gardens of Nebuchadnezzar and the grisly "forests" of Vlad the Impaler—are but the yin and the yang of the same gross misappropriation of the world.

That is to put the matter in its negative form. In a positive form, a person might come to see the struggle to check her anger as an act of conservation, as of a piece with her efforts to recycle and to dispose of toxic chemicals safely. She might come to see civility as another endangered species, and rage as another form of consuming fire: something to be kindled with one eye on its safe containment and the other on its polluting effect to the atmosphere.

That is not to suggest that there is no good time to strike a match. "I have come to set fire to the world," says the Prince of Peace. Perhaps the most legitimate expression of anger is not an act of excess but a protest against it. The best kind of anger always "hath a privilege"—by the throat.

Malcolm: Dispute it like a man.
Macduff: I shall do so.
But I must also feel it as a man.

Shakespeare, *Macbeth*

ANGER
AS GRIEF

Sometimes people will respond to a show of anger or irritation by saying, "Don't give me any grief," meaning, I suppose, "Don't make my life any harder than it is." But there is a variant to this expression that goes, "Don't give me *your* grief" or "I'm not going to take any of *his* grief"—and in that case the meaning is more subtle. What it might suggest is that anger is an expression of unresolved loss. In other words, we grow infuriated at one thing because we are not done—or perhaps haven't started—mourning another.

The relationship between anger and grief is treated in Ernest Hebert's novel *The Dogs of March,* which tells the story of Howard Elman, a laid-off mill foreman in rural New Hampshire. Elman is a man trapped in his own unarticulated thoughts and emotions no less than in his poverty and in the press of unforeseen events. The genius of the novel is in giving a voice to Elman's inner life and in showing how his actions say what his words often cannot; the power of the story comes in large part from recognizing how much Elman's inner disquiet reflects our own, no matter how verbal we might be. In the following passage, Elman attends the funeral of his coworker Filbin.

> The minister had entered the pulpit and was speaking. Howard could hear the voice, but the words were mumbled, like a radio blaring in the next house. Something about Filbin's family, something about his work, his devotion to . . . what was it? God? Something or other. And then there was an organ playing in the balcony, and then singing, soft and beautiful. Filbin's cousin, Merwin, Howard guessed. And then the minister read from the Scriptures. More music. And, goddamn, he could feel Carsons quivering beside him, could feel him begin to weep before he heard the strained hiccupping sounds. He was both sympathetic to Carsons and enraged at him. Carsons, he wanted to say, what the hell are you doing breaking down at a goddamn memorial service? There ain't even a body here. You don't even know if there is a body. Smarten up. That Filbin, who the hell does he think he is? What kind of a goddamn joke does he think he's pulling? . . . And Howard found that he too was sobbing.

In his mind Elman is ready to "give people some grief," *his* grief, which finally bursts forth as what it is. But had he not broken down sobbing, he would have left the church with a burden of suppressed rage, or rather with a burden of rage greater than the one he already has.

I suspect that many of our angry outbursts are the result of grief that never comes to sobbing. Our most grievous losses represent obstacles that we cannot overcome, sources of frustration that we cannot staunch, and that certain lesser obstacles have the power to recapitulate. If accurate, this is a valuable insight that can, nevertheless, lead to a good deal of silliness. For example, we can assume that a more effusive style of mourning will make us more genial people outside the funeral parlor (it won't), or we can assume that every experience of anger ought to be cured by a search for hidden grief (it shouldn't, and it can't). What is more sensible, I think, is to assume that anger can in some cases be controlled and eventually channeled into meaningful action by first determining what is truly bothering us. It's not that the anger is somehow illegitimate, but rather that the assumed cause is inadequate. The real cause lies buried, sometimes literally in a casket, sometimes figuratively in the heart.

Some years ago I found myself furious at a delivery truck driver, not a usual object of my hostility. When you live as I do, well off the main drag, where the main drag is one of the last exits off the interstate, delivery drivers of all kinds are familiar and welcome connections to the world at large. The wood truck, postal, UPS, and FedEx drivers who come to my door know my name, even my dog's name, and I know many of theirs. (The editor of my first book went from wonder to incredulity when I told him, first of all, that his letter of acceptance had come to me under a rainbow and, second, that the UPS driver on our route was named Judy Garland.) In fact, I also know the name of the driver in this story, and I know him to be a likable man. On one afternoon, though, I found myself ready to take a tire iron to his truck. Of course, there was a background to my rage, though I did not perceive all of it at the time.

Bus service had recently been eliminated at my daughter's elementary school, the local cheapocracy having seized power yet again. My wife and I had always driven our child to and from school anyway, but of course now everyone else was forced to do the same thing, so the situation had a great potential for stress.

Instead, with a resourcefulness that should have come as no surprise from an institution that has learned to address all manner of difficulties with a bake sale, the school devised a practical arrangement for dropping and picking up children, one car at a time. It was orderly, safe, and—because teachers and the principal served as valets and doorman—remarkably gracious as well. So what had promised to be a small disaster at the hub of a divided community became instead an oasis of day-to-day patience and civility. Of course, an oasis can be a dangerous place.

Enter the driver. For some reason he had decided to make his delivery at the very same time when the children were being picked up from school. His was a local business, so it was not as if he had come a long way. Fifteen minutes out of what I assume is an eight-hour day—this is when he had to show up. He mounted the driveway parallel to a line of waiting cars, something he wouldn't have dared to do with a school bus. A teacher halted him in a most apologetic manner and told him, no, you cannot pull up and risk running over some first-grader's sneakers. As a gesture of conciliation, the teacher meekly took the delivered boxes into the building and brought what I assumed was a check out to the waiting driver—smiling all the while. The driver was not satisfied, however. He began complaining about having to back his truck down the drive, giving the teacher—perhaps the gentlest man in the school—a hard time.

At this point I was out of my car, body tense, lungs full and ready to shout. But the driver was already backing sullenly down the drive. I picked up my child, took her home, and called the business that had sent the truck. I doubt the manager there will ever forget my call.

Now some readers might be saying, "Good for you." But the rage I felt was so intense, so white hot. Why? No one got hurt here. The driver did not defy the teacher's directive. Who knows but that he had some very good reasons to be angry himself that afternoon. I had never known him to be irritable before, nor have I seen him so since.

I can attempt to explain my anger by saying that I hate to see any self-styled special characters defy good rules of courtesy and propriety. It annoyed me when I worked as a teacher, it can annoy me in my work in the church, and it annoys me whenever I see it. Fair enough. I can say that where the safety of children is concerned, I have a right to be as angry as I choose, and I certainly do, though no child was endangered here. I can say that one of my "buttons" is wired to a mechanism of instantaneous outrage whenever I see a kind and considerate human being abused, though in this case both human beings were fundamentally considerate, and the "abusive" one had willingly yielded his ground.

Something deeper was at work in my anger, and I think that it amounted to grief—grief because the bus situation was just a small detail in a whole sad school scene, where my daughter had spent year after year in an overcrowded class with a sizable number of miserably unhappy kids from intricately screwed-up households, where so much promise had been lost and wasted, so many hopes had failed to be fulfilled —where every single afternoon I dreaded to go because of the shell-shocked expression on my kid's face when I went to pick her up, the "nothing much" response to my question, "What did you do at school today?" Six years ago she was teaching a song about an inchworm to her teacher; three years ago she was saying that she wanted to be a scientist; two days ago she was saying that she wasn't "good at anything."

"Dispute it like a man," says Malcolm, attempting to stir Macduff against the tyrant who has slaughtered his wife and children—"all my pretty chickens in one fell swoop." "I shall do so," Macduff replies from the depths. "But I must also feel it as a man." I must grieve this before I can even begin to avenge it.

Even those of us with lesser grievances than Macduff's must learn to recognize how to winnow and refine our anger by first admitting and expressing our grief. I had to do the same. Eventually my wife and I would make some critical decisions about our daughter's education that would give us some peace. We also resolved not to lose sight of all the good things that happened at her school and all the good people in our community, including those whose opposition to school budgets would soften and even reverse itself over time. These days, with our daughter happily ensconced in high school, I try to remember the lessons I learned from her younger years, when I was younger too. I keep an eye out for anger that is actually unexpressed grief. And I try to fight the issues before they become grievous, which is to say, a long time before I get mad.

⌐

Of course, we do not grieve only for our loved ones; we also grieve for ourselves. On some level, I think anger is a protest against mortality. Its highest form is the resurrection, so beautifully depicted in that painting by José Clemente Orozco, where a defiant Christ with clenched fist has just chopped down his own cross, thus adding it to the heap of trashed idols and armaments that lie piled in the background. If we never lost our lives, perhaps we would never lose our tempers —but only if we had never lost our innocence. St. Paul says, "The wages of sin are death," but sin without that wage would be hell. It would be a world where torture could literally be endless. As it is, death cheats every torturer in the end.

In other words, death is God's mercy on our fallen condition. So if at least some of our anger arises from grief at our own mortality, we are in effect angry at mercy itself. We are angry at the reprieve that eventually lets us off the barbed hook of human misery. Our anger amounts to absurd ingratitude.

Recognizing this ingratitude is not without practical application. In moments of extreme frustration or stress, we tend to personify the world as malignant. We see it as consciously out to get us. The gods—or Murphy's Laws—have conspired once again to take us down a peg. But if we must personify the world, we might better choose to see it as a gentle teacher, preparing us by progressive stages for the fact that we are destined to die and the equally compelling fact that, given all we are and are not, we are fortunate to die. Dylan Thomas urges us to "Rage against the dying of the light," and so we are entitled to do, but we do not have to rage against every flicker that prepares us for the light's inevitable extinction.

Rage belongs more properly to tragedy, where the light of life burns with heroic luminosity before being extinguished, often abruptly and prematurely. But even in tragic works of literature we often see mortality embraced with something more sublime than rage. "I am ready," says Tess of the d'Urbervilles when the gendarmes come to arrest her for murder. And when a soldier urges Breaker Morant in the film of that name to devise an escape from his impending execution, Morant responds in a manner worthy of the great tragic heroes. His companion urges him to "See the world," to which Morant says, "I've seen it."

So have you and I, our lesser statures and our lighter burdens notwithstanding. We see the world, and it helps to remember that what we often see is a gentle—not a mocking—reminder of who we are and where we are going at the end.

There is a cottage on an island off the Maine coast that I love as much as any place on earth. My wife and I went there on our honeymoon more than twenty-five years ago—two kids who had lived at home all through college and never under the same roof. The cottage faces the mainland, separated from it by a channel of water in which loons, cormorants, and lobstermen do their fishing throughout the day. From the back porch, you can watch the sun set over the coastland; a long stairway descends through the woods to the shore, a rock-fancier's dream at low tide.

We stayed in the cottage several times after our marriage, losing track of it in the years after our baby was born. During that time the owners' name disappeared from the phone directory; we assumed they were dead. When our daughter was older, we wrote to inquire about another cottage on the same island, only to discover when the photo came in the mail that it was the same cottage with new owners. The fortuitous rediscovery made it seem all the more romantic and magical. So we began going back. During the summer of my ordination as a deacon, I walked that shore for the first time in years, with my little daughter shell-gathering in front of me, and thought to myself, "The One you have been called to serve made all of this." The slight repulsion I had felt at having my ministry "regularized" by an institution broke at that point, like a wave on the rocks.

Part of the place's beauty comes from its seclusion. There are other houses not far away, but invisible. The cottage is itself an island in a sea of ferns and pungent evergreens, giant ash trees, and glacial boulders. At least it was.

Several summers ago we trod the familiar path from the car to the screen door, luggage in hand—and noticed through the thinned-out forest the foundation hole of a new house. It was closer to the cottage than our nearest neighbor at home in Vermont. Very soon we would be able to wave back and forth from our respective decks.

It would take many more pages to describe the sinking feeling, almost of despair, that took possession of my bowels with that sight. I was dismayed, then angry. Why so many trees cut? Why not cut down every last one instead of leaving this ridiculous impersonation of a screen, like a see-through garment worn for no other purpose than to add titillation to nakedness? Why this obscene need to be "in somebody's face," even when money and the lay of the land allow for some privacy? You may have found a quiet spot to eat your picnic, a seat far off the aisle to watch the show, but I choose to present myself as an unavoidable blot on your landscape, an inescapable ringing in your ears. "Hi. We're the Dingdongs. We're up from Massachusetts, where we made a big pile of money, and now we travel all over the world giving people a big pain in the ass. See you in a bit." I could envision it all.

Then I looked toward the west, the direction from which I had come and would return soon enough, and remembered the old lesson. This is not your permanent home. Nothing is. The reason is that you yourself are not permanent, at least not in this world. As it turned out, no one showed up to work on the house during the entire week we were there. So we were able to enjoy a brief stay of execution. We never went back. Perhaps in the not-too-distant future we shall find a place that we like even more. It's doubtful we could ever love it more. For someone my age, that's not necessarily a bad thing.

~~

So we are angry because we die, and by accepting death we might become less angry, is that it? Yes, but only in part. I think it can work the other way around too. Anger is not only a protest against death, and it is not the only protest against death. Sometimes I think that anger can be a wish for death, a rash impulse to throw life away and have done with it. In that case, patience, calmness, and forbearance amount to the most effective protest against mortality. In my experience, this happens most often in the case of people poignantly aware of death, and especially thankful to be alive. Anger, like diving into cold water or smoking a cigarette, is simply more extravagance than they can afford.

When Jesus enters Jerusalem in triumph and finds the money changers in the temple, he angrily throws their money onto the floor. But when he enters the garden of Gethsemane "sorrowful unto death," only to have his disciples fall asleep during their watch, he cannot be angry with them. He is not even angry with the guards who come to arrest him—nor angry with Judas, Pilate, or the soldiers who nail him to the cross. Well, you say, he is dying for their sins. So I believe. But perhaps we can achieve something like the same equanimity by living with their sins, by bearing with them, because we recognize that life is so dear and irreplaceable that Christ himself does not lay it down without some reluctance.

My father-in-law lives in a three-story house on a small yard in the middle of a blue-collar town in northeastern New Jersey. He's one of those men who like to keep their places neat, their porches painted, their walks swept, the grass mowed and trimmed. It is not easy for him to do so because he's in poor health, with heart disease and emphysema, and because his yard is full of leaves and twigs from his neighbors' overarching trees and litter from God knows where, seemingly from every human being who walks or drives by.

Still, the litter does no more than annoy him. It doesn't seem to make him mad. Every day he goes out and picks up the wrappers, the plastic straws, and coffee cup caps that have blown or been thrown onto the lawn. He sweeps the sidewalk, stopping periodically for a toke from his pocket inhaler. Some weeks it may take him a couple of days to finish the round. But he never loses his mortal perspective. As he likes to tell door-to-door salesmen and Jehovah's Witnesses who come to call: "The owner isn't home. I'm just the gardener." I think of him as Adam, a little worse for wear, but doing the best he can in the territory east of Eden. For me, he represents the possibility of making a conscious choice to bear with whatever garbage blows over the fence into your life, if not happily at least not angrily, though often happily, because you're so grateful to retain the wherewithal to pick it up.

His secret was revealed to me one day when we were inspecting the estate, so to speak, and the subject came up of a relative's attempted suicide. "One of the goombahs" had unsuccessfully tried to end his life in desperation over his mounting debt. And my father-in-law had sent him this message of goodwill, something I repeat to myself when a dark mood takes me or a bad temper is about to.

"I told Mike to tell Joey, if he's planning to make another attempt, I can use a heart and two new lungs. And if his prostate's any good, tell him I'll take that too."

Then he added, not unlike Christ in his own littered garden, though laughing instead of praying, but maybe praying: "Hey, I want to live."

'Tis a weapon of novel use, for we move all other arms, this moves us.

Montaigne, "On Anger"

ANGER
AS GRACE

If anger were the only trouble in our heads, we might be done now. If the only mental forms that anger took were those of blame, fear, grief, and things of that ilk, then all our prayers in respect to anger would be either petitions or confessions. Cleanse me. Forgive me. But there is also an anger that comes as grace, and a prayer about anger that rises in thanksgiving. I can even imagine a prayer of intercession that implored God to give someone the gift of anger: "Feed my sister with the grace to know what it means to be fed up."

That is because there are other sins and delusions in our heads that have nothing to do with anger, that in some cases are the very opposite of anger, of anything that might be called an outburst. There is crippling guilt, for example, which presumes to deserve every misfortune that befalls us. There is a desire to please others, a desire for their favor that puts us in their servitude. There is a wish to be invisible, to be a germ so small that no other creature on earth can think of us as prey, and by means of that invisibility to be immune from every pain. All of these are ways in which the Samson of the human spirit can be bound and which anger can dissolve "like flax in a fire."

And there are other ways as well. We can also be bound by burdensome labor, impossible demands, ridiculous expectations, imposed from without or within. In these cases anger can amount to the overtaxed mind or body's cry for mercy. Adults are usually quick to recognize that cry in their young children: "He's up past his bedtime, and that's why he's throwing a fit." They are less ready to see the same cause-and-effect relationship at work in themselves. Failure to do so may lead to regrettable consequences, even to violence, and thus to the conclusion that the phrase "anger as grace" is an oxymoron.

But grace does not absolve us of responsibility. I am not sure that grace automatically saves, nor was I ever comfortable with John Donne's depiction of grace as holy ravishment. I prefer Julian of Norwich's vision of the "courteous" savior. Grace comes, and we decide whether to act on it or not —and sometimes how to act on it too. For all we know, there was as much grace at work in the garden of Eden as in the garden of Gethsemane—there was certainly temptation at work in both places—it's just that Christ said yes, and Adam and Eve said no. Likewise, there may have been as much grace at work in the cleansing of the temple as in the cleansing of the lepers, and Christ said yes in both cases.

~~

Perhaps the strongest forms of bondage in our particular place and time are the chains of comfort and security. These can amount to an implicit sadomasochistic pact to endure every form of intellectual, political, and environmental degradation, all for the luxury of new sensations. Beat me and debase me, so long as you feed me and fondle me too. Entertain me most of all. Give me bread and circuses, and if I can eat the bread while watching the circuses, so much the better. Show me documentaries on the turbulent 1960s; I promise that I will pay the homage of a few nostalgic tears, even if I wasn't alive at the time and am only half alive now, so long as I can enjoy a premium beer and a big-screen picture of the March on Washington as I sniffle.

I am talking about no one so much as myself. In an earlier chapter, I spoke incredulously of the "conspicuous adventurism" of my peers. Here is the less attractive side of my touted ability to enjoy an "ordinary" (that is, extraordinarily fortunate) life. Whenever I see televised footage of a mass demonstration in some foreign country, and sometimes even in our own country, I seldom marvel at the zeal of the demonstrators or ponder the justice of their cause. I do not ask myself why these people hate Americans so much or what they hope to accomplish by creating such a stir. More often than not, what impresses me most powerfully is the extreme *bother* of it all. I imagine myself in their shoes—except that I am still myself and still shod in the shoes of a comfortable middle-class American—and I can scarcely think of leaving my house, driving to the center of some sweltering dusty city, parking my car (of course I wouldn't have a car in most of these countries), milling about with a bunch of smelly, jostling people, and then marching myself lame and shouting myself hoarse when I might have been home planting hyacinth bulbs or reading *The New Yorker.* What grievance could possibly be so galling as to make me leave my little homestead to shake a Qur'an, a homemade placard, or for that matter a palm branch cut on the outskirts of Jerusalem, at the wicked world? I sometimes realize with a shudder that had I lived when Jesus lived, I probably would never have gone to hear him preach. I might have thought about going, but then, considering the bother involved, I probably would have settled for reading the book whenever it came out. He would have had to come to me.

I am probably not all that unusual. I am one of the sheep who lie down in dollar-green pastures beside domestic still waters, who will accept almost any rod or staff so long as it holds the promise of additional comfort. In such a pastoral arrangement, the ability to feel anger is seen as an undesirable trait, evidence of a bad gene, to be bred out of the line even as the defective individual is culled out of the herd. Do you want people to think of you as an ingrate, say the shepherds, a Luddite, a nut? Do you want to wind up like the Unabomber? Are any of you willing to lose this succulent green grass, this lion's share of a lamb's consolation? Not I, say the sheep.

But not all of us are sheep. I watched those young people riot at the World Trade Organization's meeting in Seattle in the late 1990s and found myself inspired, convicted, and hopeful beyond anything I ever expected to feel from something so familiar as a fracas in the streets. The Chicago Seven were a cliché even before I graduated from college. But without the reassurance of belonging to a mass movement, without the benefit of an anthem "blowin' in the wind," without the certification of a cover story in *Life* magazine or the kudos of a William Kunstler, without so much as an identifiable charismatic leader, these kids made their unsung way to the barricades. Never mind my sympathy with their cause—and I felt plenty of that—what moved me most of all was an overwhelming sense of relief at knowing that human beings are not dead, that the potential for righteous and inconvenient rage is not dead either. For unlike many of those arrested in Seattle, I never believed that it was carcinogenic growth hormones or omnivorous global corporations that would do us in at the end, but rather the sweet taste of the goodies produced thereby—even the miraculous restoration of a natural environment so safe and pristine that justice would not dare light a fire.

⌒

Moses the lawgiver comes down from Mount Sinai with the tablets of the law in his hand. Seeing the Israelites worshipping the golden calf—that holdover from the land of slavery, with its cloying abundance of "garlics and leeks" in the slop buckets and visible divinities on their thrones—he breaks the tablets into pieces.

The action amounts to an eleventh commandment: Thou shalt break the law itself for the sake of righteousness. Of course, it can also amount to a rationale for every form of self-righteousness. For better or for worse, it serves as a justification for anger. Enraged at the sight of that golden idol, Moses rejects even the potential idolatry of the tablets themselves. Like a wife finally angry enough to pull off her wedding ring in the face of abuse, like a priest finally angry enough to tear off his collar in the face of ecclesiastical hypocrisy, or a cop finally angry enough to rip off his badge in the face of legally sanctioned hooliganism, Moses in his moment of wrath is full of the grace that St. Paul says "abolishes the law." Granted, he eventually heads back up the mountain for another copy. He knows, as Jesus surely did too, that we cannot do without laws any more than we can probably do without temples or money changers. Moses never sets himself up as a law unto himself or unto his followers. But his anger insists that life is more than regulations, and deserves more than they can give.

Jesus knew this as well. "It would be better for you if a great millstone were fastened around your neck and you were drowned in the depth of the sea," he says of those who offend one of his "little ones." Whether "little ones" refers to literal children or to all innocent souls, "millstone" refers to a millstone, and "sea" refers to the sea. The anger born of grace, so strikingly revealed in the violence of Christ's language, often comes in response to some little one's helplessness and the cruelty of power. In James Agee's novel, *A Death in the Family,* a young boy's uncle and father convince him that they are able to make a piece of cheese jump off the table by magic. In a spontaneous explosion that shocks her husband, the boy's normally meek mother chastises the men for exploiting her child's innocence. They protest that they were only having a bit of fun. The people worshipping the golden calf were, by all reports, doing the same. On another level, so were the Congolese soldiers who brutally raped and tormented Belgian women before sending them into exile. Of this Susan Brownmiller writes in her book *Against Our Will:* "Rape in the Congo was shrouded in the cloak of vengeance and made plausible by an historic view of woman as the property of man, but we should not forget that beyond the shiny patina of ideological excuse, it was also rape amid the levity and frivolity of men having a good time."

Agee's angry mother gives the lie to all such fun and games. In so doing, she seems almost divine, a reflection of her namesake, Mary the Mother of God, "full of grace." Apparently, anger is a part of that fullness. "Blessed is the fruit of thy womb"—and anger is also a part of that fruit.

⌐⌐

When I was a boy, probably not much older than the character who believed his uncle could levitate a piece of cheese, my father took me with him one night to "check on a trouble." He was a high-ranking supervisor in the maintenance division of the New Jersey telephone company, and it seemed as though much of his job consisted of going out at all hours of the night to check on a trouble. He accepted the inconvenience as part of the bargain. "I have a college man's job without a college degree," he once told me. The implication was that you had better be willing to work hard for such a distinction, and he certainly did work hard. He had started climbing poles at the age of nineteen, once falling straight down the length of one, so that my mother wound up spending a good part of that evening tweezing the splinters from his chest and stomach. By the time I was old enough to know what he did for a living, he was no longer climbing poles. He was a boss over the guys who did.

The trouble we went to see that night was not up a pole, however; it was underground. After telling me to wait by the car, my father walked in his fedora and overcoat (a kid in the inner city had once referred to him warily as "that big detective fella") to the edge of a hole ringed by the silhouettes of men. A light issued from the opening, so that I saw other men's faces flashing in between the shadows. I kept my eye on my father as he joined the circle.

Then I lost sight of him. For a while, he seemed to have disappeared. Perhaps I had simply looked away; as my father often reminded me, I was easily distracted. Then, just as suddenly as he had disappeared, he was near me again. "Let's go," he said.

As soon as we were in the car, I was aware of a change in my father's mood. He seemed angry—he was angry, though when he spoke he seemed to be standing above his anger somehow. With more maturity and a bigger vocabulary, I would have described his tone as one of exultation.

"They've got this one poor guy working down in the hole and all these supervisors up on top telling him what to do." My father shook his head as we backed decisively out of our parking space. "And the more they got on his back, the more mixed up he got. He didn't need somebody to tell him what to do; he needed somebody to *show* him. So that's what I did. I got down in that hole, and I showed him. The two of us had the problem taken care of in a couple of minutes." He glanced down at his dirty knuckles, where he gripped the steering wheel. "I used to work with these hands, you know."

Sometimes in my sermons I have used this story as a parable of the incarnation, of the Word made flesh and dwelling among us. Prophets and lawgivers told us what to do, I will say, but Christ shows us. There came a point in the history of salvation where God could no longer be our boss alone, but needed to become our companion in the depths of human existence.

The story might also serve as a parable of anger as a form of grace. Anger pushes us out of our confining roles and identities, out of the ring of censorious heavenly beings—which also includes the adversary we know as Satan—and ultimately out of our heads, into the down and dirty place where people suffer. Had my father not acted on his anger, he would have carried it home as an undigested lump in his stomach. (God only knows when the man in the hole would have gotten home or what undigested thing he would have taken home with him.) On the other hand, had my father chosen to lash out at his peers on the rim of the hole, he might have experienced a certain kind of catharsis, but nothing so liberating as his rediscovery of himself as a working man who could still work with his hands and in solidarity with other men. In some ways, his descent into that hole and his emergence from it amounted to a kind of baptism.

With that analogy in mind, we may be able to go one step further. Perhaps these two ways of dealing with the story, as parable of the incarnation and as example of anger as grace, are not so distinct as I imply. Perhaps every grace-filled expression of anger is in some ways incarnational and sacramental, an embodiment of God's loving and maternal desire to be with her children and to advocate on their behalf. Remember that the name for the Holy Spirit given in the New Testament, *parakletos,* is sometimes translated as "Advocate." And that "Advocate" is the antonym of "adversary," which is what the name *Satan* means.

Likewise, the incarnation itself may be understood as a highly refined expression of the wrath of God, the force that cleaves the rocks, parts the waters, and ultimately breaches the barrier between the human and the divine. It is the thunder of Sinai subsumed in a baby's cry; the bread of life furiously hungry at our breasts; the Lord made visible in his holy temple and rearranging the furniture.

ANGER
IN THE
HOUSE

When the rooms were warm, he'd call
and slowly I would rise and dress,
fearing the chronic angers of that house . . .

Robert Hayden, "Those Winter Sundays"

THE CHRONIC
ANGERS OF
THE HOUSE

All tragedy is domestic. Although Aristotle famously pointed out that tragic figures like Agamemnon, Medea, and Oedipus tend to be kings and queens, most of us will see them as mothers and fathers, husbands and wives—sometimes in some pretty weird combinations, true, but all people distinguished by having their hardest knocks at home. There is nothing extraordinary about that connection. After all, only among those we love are we capable of the most stubborn blindness, the most fatal vulnerability, the deepest regret—in short, of the basic ingredients that make life tragic.

How strange, though, that a social institution intended to be our chief refuge from danger should so often prove so dangerous. In that regard, we can take the image of our prehistoric ancestors living in caves as an appropriately ambiguous symbol of their decision to live in families: We can picture a band of hominids retreating from some wild beast to the dark recesses of a cave, only to come upon another beast waiting there to devour them. Frequently the name of the beast is Anger.

It is probably not all that mysterious to find such a dangerous emotion lurking in what we trust to be our safest place. Perhaps the greatest danger of domestic life resides *in* the safety, that is, in the sense of license that comes with safety. Home is where you hang your hat, where you let go of the conventions that govern your behavior in the world. In societies of excessive formality, there must be enormous relief in having a place where you can dispense with the curtsey, the veil, the formulaic reply—the hat. But in societies like ours, where formality has been replaced on the one hand with a have-a-nice-day friendliness (probably a more demanding act than rote formality), and on the other hand with an in-your-face attitude (which can irritate us more than we dare show), the release of coming home at the end of the day can be like the release of a shaken jarful of wasps. Something besides Jack Nicholson's over-the-top performance makes us remember that scene in the film *The Shining* where, having hacked through the front door with an ax, the insane husband thrusts his face through the splintered boards and announces, "Honey, I'm home!"

The human household is a strange mix of the sacred and the profane. We speak of its various privileges and pleasures in the language of sanctity: the sanctity of marriage, the sanctuary of hearth and home. The person who exclaims, "Is nothing sacred?" is in all likelihood bemoaning the loss or the perceived loss of something close to family life. Yet homes can be dismally profane places, the very opposite of churches (though churches too can be dismally profane). I hesitate to say the opposite of synagogues, for the home in Jewish tradition seems to be an extension of the house of prayer in a way that Christians have seldom managed. Assuming the contrast exists, we can speculate on any number of reasons: the sacerdotal self-absorption of the institutional church, the domestic aspects of kosher law, the longer history of persecution and therefore of household worship in Judaism, the deeper suspicion of the flesh in Christianity.

In Liz Harris's fascinating book about the Lubavitcher Hasidim, entitled *Holy Days,* she tells of a Hasidic husband singing softly to his wife on Sabbath eve. By custom, he is not even permitted to kiss her in public, but there at the candlelit table, with a number of guests in attendance, he sings what amounts to a kosher serenade. Harris says the words were from the Song of Solomon, an appropriate choice, I think, not only for its tone of intimacy, but because the man who sang it seems very wise.

The point here is not to imagine oneself as a Hasid. The point is to imagine this particular Hasid screaming at his wife. It takes some effort to do that. It would probably take some effort for him to do that.

The Hasidic family points us in a good direction. The sanctification of our households through prayer, custom, and ceremonies of tenderness works to curb anger. Of course, for those who live ritually prescribed lives, sanctification is meant to come with the territory. That does not mean, however, that the rest of us cannot keep some version of a kosher home, or what Christians might call a sacramental home. I know of households where the brewing of the first pot of coffee, where the waking of the children, where the warming up of the boots or the starting up of the cold car amount to intentional acts of service performed quietly, habitually, and—when people are paying attention—lovingly. The speaker in Robert Hayden's poem "Those Winter Sundays" describes how, in spite of "the chronic angers of that house," his father would rise early on Sunday to build a fire and shine his son's good shoes. "What did I know," the son exclaims years afterward,

> what did I know
> of love's austere and lonely offices?

Apparently, the father knew enough to perform them, whatever his other shortcomings, which might have been far worse without those offices of love.

We need not dwell long on the office of grace at table, but few indicators better describe the spirit of a household than the manner in which its members sit down together to eat, or if they eat together at all. It's interesting that the prayer said at meals is the only one we call "grace," as if to acknowledge that reverence, graciousness, and elegance exist there or nowhere. Likewise, I have always been fascinated by the crucifix I've seen in Catholic households hanging above the marriage bed. I suppose one could take it for a censorious witness, the "blessed passion" asserting its claims above every other kind, but that's not the sense I've often gathered from the casual affections of the couples themselves. It says in the *Zohar*, a Jewish mystical treatise, that "this pleasure [of sexual intercourse] is a religious one, giving joy also to the Divine Presence." Who knows but that the couple making love under the crucifix doesn't have that same sense of giving delight to the

Sacred Heart. If so, then a cross word in a bedroom must seem as out of place as an obscenity scrawled upon the cross.

I suspect that some might find all of this a bit precious. How can a few homely gestures and table graces have any mitigating effect whatsoever against the full-blown force of wrath? Perhaps they have no effect at all. But perhaps too a rare explosion of full-blown wrath in a sanctified house—provided that the wrath is not expressed in violence or insult—is a necessary thing. Even a temple must be cleansed from time to time. A house where no one ever gets mad might not be any more healthy to live in than a house where no one ever opens a window. Aside from the obvious pathological exceptions, I do not think it is the big blows that cause the greatest harm anyway, but rather the constant and petty outbreaks of simmering ill temper—what the poet Hayden so aptly calls "the chronic angers of that house." These are mainly what we try to keep at bay by the sanctification of our domestic lives.

That sanctifying aim is surely what Yeats had in mind when he wrote these lines in "A Prayer for My Daughter":

> And may her bridegroom bring her to a house
> Where all's accustomed, ceremonious;
> For arrogance and hatred are the wares
> Peddled in the thoroughfares.
> How but in custom and in ceremony
> Are innocence and beauty born?
> Ceremony's a name for the rich horn,
> And custom for the spreading laurel tree.

No doubt we could dismiss these sentiments as a prescription for the most anemic kind of gentility—as the vain wish of

the father of the bride to see his daughter married to a surrogate father of the bride, more master of ceremonies than
love of her life. Ceremony and custom are nice, but what
about spontaneity and passion?

Experience tells us that they go hand in hand. Experience
tells us that we never really know the one without the other.
There is no nakedness without clothing, no consummation
without courtship, no Feast of Fools without a calendar of
the saints. The shade of "the spreading laurel tree" is the fairest
place on earth for an honest quarrel, and the most delicious
for a good roll in the grass.

⌐⌐

The effort to sanctify our households leads us to the recognition that our worst enemies are often within us, just as our
worst behaviors can appear within the safe precincts of our
homes. The beam that Jesus tells us to take from our own eye
before attempting to remove a splinter from our brother's
can amount to a beam in our domestic architecture. Clarity,
like charity, begins at home.

We may also come to recognize that the act of sanctifying
a household or a life is only secondarily an act of exorcism;
primarily, it is an invitation to the exorcist. We are more on
track when we think of welcoming the holy one *in* than when
we imagine ourselves casting the evil one *out*. That emphasis
on positive action, on the virtues of praise as opposed to the
power of curses, on invocation as opposed to repression, will
also carry over into the various ways that we attempt to raise
our children and make accommodation with our neighbors
and our mates.

One of the sacraments of this holy invitation is hospitality. The guest mirrors the Guest. This is an insight older than the Bible; we find it in the most ancient of myths, where people entertain strangers who turn out to be gods in disguise. Given the right conditions—considerate guests, a minimum of fuss, a total absence of any agenda besides mutual enjoyment —hospitality can work as a potent charm against anger. The Greeks believed that the Furies, those snake-haired divinities who gave us another name for rage, punished crimes between host and guest. Turn that idea around, and it also holds true: Graciousness between host and guest tends to pacify fury. There are at least several reasons why.

The most obvious has to do with the courteous demeanor we put on for the benefit of our guests. In its best form, the act of hospitality combines the public face we wear for the world—sometimes a kinder face than we wear for our loved ones—with the private ease we feel at home. The effects of hospitality can be similar to those of a restful vacation: We come away from the experience with that sense of "That was so nice" followed by the questions "What made it so nice?" and "Why can't life be that nice all the time?"

Hospitality also reminds us of the purposeful nature of the household itself. A home is not merely the lounge where we crash when we finish with the "real work." At least it cannot reduce to that for anyone who calls herself religious. A household is a workshop for the preeminent business of justice and mercy. We could gain much by cultivating that awareness. Have you ever noticed how some people are far more fastidious in the keeping of their work spaces than they are in the keeping of their homes? The farmer whose barn looks neater than his house is a standard joke in many rural communities, but the joke often applies to the rest of us as well. If we saw the household as the place in which we do some of our most important work, we might be more conscientious in maintaining it as a place of loveliness. Hospitality can bring us closer to that insight.

It can also provide us with a foil for our day-to-day domestic behavior. If I am a reflective host as well as a gracious one, then I shall sooner or later ask myself if and why I am any less gracious after the guests go home. If I made myself seem like a considerate partner in their presence, why am I less so in the solitary presence of my mate? Hospitality compels me to recognize the differences that exist between my behavior as an attentive host and a careless occupant, an ardent suitor and a complacent spouse, a persona masquerading for the approval of others and a genuine person acting in the best interests of those I love.

Finally, hospitality transfigures those I love. In the presence of company, I hear my child's conversation from a different vantage point; I see my partner's face in a different light. More than once I have looked at my wife across a table surrounded with guests, unable to touch her or engage her attention as fully as I might were we alone, and felt I was the witness to an inscrutable physical change. It was as if the molecules of her skin and the tissues of her eyes had reconfigured ever so slightly. It was like seeing her in the resurrection—"Touch me not," yet know me as you have never known me before. Walk beside me every day for years, but recognize me for the first time in the breaking of the bread. "Fear not," yet do not presume either. This is not only the bone of your bones and the flesh of your flesh, but bone and flesh of an entirely separate human being, at once familiar and utterly mysterious. Avoiding the irritable word is not even a question at that point, but rather finding the voice to speak any word at all.

⌒

The chronic angers of the house may have more than a little to do with our chronic passivity in the world. They may represent a sad disproportion in the expenditure of our aggression, whereby goodwill in the world is purchased at the cost of ill temper at home. In that regard, we might consider the questionable domestic conduct of our great nonviolent saints —Tolstoy and Gandhi, for example—in comparison to the at-home benevolence of some of their more militant counterparts. Perhaps being a bit more fiery abroad would make us act with greater kindness and fidelity at home.

It is not unknown to discover a greater freedom for women and a more pronounced tenderness toward children among notoriously warlike societies. This flies in the face of one of our most cherished myths, namely that matriarchy and nonviolence would go hand in hand. Perhaps that was indeed the case in prehistory; yet when we look at the record of warrior societies as diverse and far-flung as the Scythians, the Celts, the Spartans, the Vikings, and the Iroquois, what we tend to find is an uncanny combination of aggressive males and comparatively emancipated females. In the case of the Scythians and the Celts, we also find evidence of warrior females.

Of course, we must be wary of jumping to conclusions. Societies in which men are frequently away at war must confer greater autonomy and authority on women simply to function; this does not necessarily mean that the actual status of women increases in direct proportion to the aggressiveness of men. (In both world wars, we saw "emancipated" women put back in their places as soon as their men were discharged from active duty.) But neither can one conclude that beating swords into plowshares is a foolproof first step away from beating women and children into submission. Outward ferocity and domestic tenderness, like loyalty and aggressiveness, sometimes exist side by side. More than one explorer has noted the conspicuous affection and forbearance shown by headhunting tribes to their children.

This is not to suggest that the best way to keep our heads at home is to bag a few some distance from camp. It is only to suggest, in the most tentative way, that domestic anger may amount to little more than the vestige of unexpressed outrage in the world at large.

Emerson wrote that "Society everywhere is in conspiracy against the manhood of every one of its members. Society is a joint-stock company, in which the members agree, for the better securing of his bread to each shareholder, to surrender the liberty and culture of the eater." The language here is masculine, but the observation is by no means exclusive to men. Perhaps a better metaphor lies in the history of the ancient Babylonians, among whom every woman, at least once in her life, was expected to serve as a prostitute in the temple of Ishtar. According to the Greek historian Herodotus, a woman took her place in the temple gallery, waiting for a male worshipper to toss the required coins into her lap. (Herodotus notes that a few of the less attractive ladies sat there for a humiliatingly long time.) The man would then lead her to an adjoining room by the scarlet cord attached to her body. After servicing him and donating the proceeds to the temple, the woman had fulfilled her obligation. Presumably, she did not then go home to write any cuneiform dissertations on the liberating glories of goddess-worship.

Most of us, male or female, have sat in that temple gallery. Most of us have sat waiting for the coin to be thrown into our laps, hoping we could make a good enough appearance to finish our business and be home in time to eat supper. We have sat down to table in the company of our loved ones with the souvenirs of Ishtar like bite marks on our flesh. On some level, don't we feel ashamed in their presence of the work we have done? Aren't we secretly resentful of their implied complicity in that demeaning arrangement? Is it any great wonder that sometimes we lash out in anger?

I can imagine a hybrid myth, applicable to both women and men, that combines the image of Christ cleansing the temple in Jerusalem and Herodotus's description of the temple in Babylon. I can imagine a woman ripping the scarlet cord from her wrist and using it as a whip to drive the money changers from the temple of Ishtar. I can imagine her walking home purged and at peace. No doubt tomorrow she will learn the price of her revolt, but for now and for once her children will not have to pay the price for her compliance. The Great Mother can turn her own tricks; this mother has just turned the front door key. Honey, I'm home.

Our stories, Wade's and mine, describe the lives of boys and men for thousands of years.

Russell Banks, *Affliction*

ANGRY MEN

AGAMEMNON AND SAUL, MICHAEL HENCHARD AND WADE WARD

Sometimes we meet someone for the first time who reminds us so much of another person that science itself seems like just another branch of the occult. Reincarnation, astrological influence, doppelgängers—we can understand why each of these ideas has adherents. We also meet doubles in books; were it not for our experience outside of books, we might be ready to believe that they had all been plagiarized. But after a while, through the books we read and the people we meet, we come to recognize that the patterns of human life are not infinitely various, just profoundly strange. No man is an island, and more men than suspect it are twins. Two such twins are the ancient commanders Agamemnon and Saul, who, taken together, constitute a distinct type of angry man. Perhaps *the* type.

The story of Agamemnon, which we first hear in Homer's *Iliad*, is set around 1190 BCE, though the epic itself is several centuries younger. The story of King Saul, which we find in the first book of Samuel, dates from about 1020 BCE. In the larger context of history, these men are practically dorm-mates, though neither is likely to have known of the other's existence (that is, if they both existed). Both men are presented as mighty and courageous leaders, with brooding and irascible spirits that eventually undo them.

Agamemnon is the commander of the Greek military force that besieges the city of Troy in order to retrieve the supernaturally beautiful Helen, who has run off with a Trojan prince. (The situation can seem absurd even to characters in the story; in a memorable scene from the *Iliad*, some of the old men of Troy sit grumbling over the waste of a war fought over one woman—until Helen herself comes gliding past them, at which point they more or less say, "On the other hand . . .") Agamemnon's brother, Menelaos, is Helen's aggrieved husband. The cloud that seems to hang over Agamemnon's head turns especially dark on three occasions.

The first of these occurs when the Greek fleet is unable to set sail for Troy because the wind is against them. A prophet advises Agamemnon to placate the gods by sacrificing his own daughter. A nobler man than Agamemnon would have refused to do it; a less noble man would have required a more self-serving temptation. Agamemnon lives too much in the regard of others; he exemplifies that all-too-typical masculine reflex of saving face even at the cost of losing one's head. We see the same thing in Saul: Before ascertaining who has violated one of his strictures, he rashly vows that even his own son, if found guilty, shall not be exempt from death. It turns out that his son Jonathan has indeed transgressed his command, though out of ignorance. Only the intervention of Saul's men prevents him from executing Jonathan on the spot. Agamemnon's officers, on the other hand, do not intervene; they're eager for war, and the sacrificial victim is only a girl. So Iphigenia is put to the knife.

Agamemnon's second big mistake involves a conflict with his greatest warrior, the all-but-invincible Achilles. One of Agamemnon's prizes in the war is a slave girl who happens to be the daughter of a powerful Trojan priest. When the priest's entreaties fail to set the girl free, he calls on the god Apollo to plague the Greeks until Agamemnon is pressured into relinquishing his prize. In a tantrum of resentment, Agamemnon confiscates the prize of Achilles, that is, *his* captive woman. Achilles responds by sulking in his tent, refusing to fight, and the war is thus prolonged. (Not surprisingly, the *Iliad* has sometimes been titled *The Wrath of Achilles,* though it is Agamemnon's wrath that concerns us here.) If we can see beyond the spectacle of women being used as the pawns of men, we can see the related spectacle of men as the pawns of their own codes of honor. The conflicts that result are, of course, utterly devoid of honor; they resemble nothing so much as "puppy-dog fights" on the rug of a preschool classroom. He took my toy, so I took his.

The best retelling of Agamemnon's final mishap is found in a play by Aeschylus named after the doomed conqueror. Returning in pomp and pride from his sack of Troy, Agamemnon is cleverly murdered by his wife in revenge for his sacrifice of their daughter. Before striking the fatal blow, she coaxes Agamemnon to walk from his chariot to his house on an expensive purple carpet. By acquiescing to her demands, he reveals his vanity, his wife's strength, and not least of all his willingness to trample on precious things, even those of his own house. He claims he doesn't want to perform the gesture, but finally gives in under the pretext of satisfying his wife. It is impossible to describe the power of this scene in the play: It is like watching every one of your own grossest sins reenacted in a single, slow motion.

The biblical King Saul is a far less grandiose figure than Agamemnon; at the same time, he serves a grander god. For these reasons, we may find it easier to sympathize with his plight. His stature is closer to ours, as is the venality of most of his mistakes. It is debatable whether he is even tragic in the strictest sense of the word. He is certainly pathetic.

A physically imposing man, Saul is anointed as the first king of Israel in response to the threat of marauding Philistines. Prior to his coronation, the people of Israel have lived in a loose confederation of tribes, each with its own "judge," a charismatic leader combining the roles of adjudicator and military chief. The last of these judges is a man named Samuel, who accepts his divinely appointed role as kingmaker with considerable reluctance.

In all of his subsequent dealings with the new king, Samuel shows himself to be every inch a judge. At first, having Samuel's blessing, Saul enjoys military success, but he soon runs afoul of God and his spokesman. As familiar as I am with the Bible, I always have to go back to its pages to remember what it is, exactly, that Saul does wrong. A few things as it turns out, though none of them seems to merit his fate. Briefly, he fails to wait for Samuel to give an invocation; he spares a king he was supposed to have killed; and he makes booty of what he was supposed to have sacrificed. If we cast Samuel in the role of father figure to Saul, we are presented with the familiar image of the son who can never do anything right in his father's eyes—a recognizable archetype for many angry men, including several we meet in the fiction of Russell Banks.

After a while, God's favor shifts from Saul to David, the charismatic killer of Goliath. Apparently, everyone else's favor goes the same way. "Saul has slain his thousands, and David his ten thousands," the women sing in the street. Even Saul's own son Jonathan becomes David's dearest friend. Saul tries to kill David in several bursts of bad temper, but fails. These are rash acts, which the author attributes to an "evil spirit," but it is hard not to feel some pity for Saul; at least it is hard for me. Interestingly enough, Samuel himself seems to have shared the sentiment: At one point, God asks him, "How long will you grieve over Saul?" Not that Saul is dead, only doomed. Samuel dies before Saul does.

In what may be Saul's most pathetic moment, he visits a witch and asks her to conjure up the ghost of his dead mentor—this in defiance of his own law against sorcery. Samuel is just as full of disapproval in death as in life. So much for any hope of "closure" after the death or estrangement of a stern father figure. Eventually Saul commits suicide rather than be captured after a disastrous engagement with the Philistines. His armor bearer refuses to give the coup de grace, and so Saul falls on his own sword. Thus dies the great king, heavy with suspicion and perceived threat, having no one in his life treacherous enough to relieve him of it.

⌣

Saul and Agamemnon are both brave men whose strong sense of outrage is matched by formidable temper. One gets angry enough to sack a city; the other, angry enough to break the siege on a city. When Saul hears that the Ammonites have surrounded Jabesh demanding terms of surrender that include the privilege of gouging out the right eye of every survivor, "the spirit of God came upon Saul in power . . . and his anger was greatly kindled. He took a yoke of oxen, and cut them in pieces and sent them throughout all the territory of Israel by messengers, saying, 'Whoever does not come out after Saul and Samuel, so shall it be done to his oxen!'" Ox-lovers from near and far rally to their king, and Jabesh is liberated.

Of course, these two mighty avengers are less than gallant toward their own families. Both were willing to sacrifice their own children. It is a mistake to see too much irony in this. "Men of vision" are notorious for their willingness to pay that sort of price. On one level, that's what the story of Abraham and Isaac is about. Very soon after your father meets a new god, he's going to start building a new altar, and he may not be overly sentimental about what he puts on it. God's seemingly perverse testing of Abraham may in fact be a preemptive strike on the sacrificial leanings of masculine idealism. Command the patriarch to do what he's only going to dream up on his own anyway, and then nip it in the bud. Sometimes I wonder if the single most compassionate decision Jesus ever made was to remain childless. In any case, boys who wish their fathers were more messianic are just that: boys. A full-grown man learns to give thanks for every contented bourgeois bone in his father's body. You take the father with the altar on the mountaintop; I'll take the one with the workbench in the cellar.

Agamemnon and Saul also engage in tragic confrontations with men more gifted and attractive than themselves—though not necessarily more virtuous. Agamemnon's rival, Achilles, performs outrages on the corpse of Hector in full view of the slain man's family, and David's shenanigans with Bath-sheba and his murder of her honorable husband are far more reprehensible than any of the errors of rash Saul. Nevertheless, neither of these warlords is quite so dangerous as his overlord suspects. Achilles and David are perhaps the natural rivals of their captains, but not their inevitable enemies. The stories suggest that the outcomes might have been better. Both Achilles and David refuse to kill their commanders; Achilles suppresses the urge "within his shaggy breast," and David scorns the opportunity when he comes upon Saul asleep in a cave. Though David and Achilles can be ruthless, both are possessed of profound capacities for loyalty and friendship. In fact, their most striking similarity, aside from the rivalries under discussion here, is an intense and possibly homoerotic alliance that each man forms with another comrade, Achilles with Patrocles (who sleeps in his arms) and David with Jonathan (at whose death David says, "Your love to me was wonderful, passing the love of women"). Rapprochement, reconciliation —what the popular psychology books call male bonding— would not have been impossible with such men. Rage and insecurity are what make it impossible.

And here I cannot resist one of those nickel and dime generalizations that, for the low price of a nickel or a dime, hold a lot of truth. One of the best ways to discriminate between a healthy older man and a damaged one is in their contrasting attitudes toward younger men. A healthy man may attempt to restrain some of the foolishness of his juniors, but overall he cannot resist a certain affection for "the young dogs." It escapes him as naturally as his own sweat. Those suffering from the spirit of Saul are more likely to want to pin a few to the wall with their javelins. Some of the sanest older men I've known always had younger ones under their wings; the losers and the lunatics only wanted them under their thumbs. Granted, a few sly ones may have affected the first course as a way of effecting the second.

Finally, and perhaps most significantly, both Agamemnon and Saul are at odds with priests and prophets, while at the same time both are also undone through their reliance on augury. Agamemnon offends a suppliant priest by enslaving his daughter; he obliges another priest by sacrificing his own. Likewise, though Saul offends Samuel repeatedly, he goes so far as to employ the services of a witch to bring Samuel's spirit before him. What this paradox amounts to, once we trim off the mythological fat, is a kind of degenerate fatalism that often seems to characterize angry men. They are firm believers, not only in their own iron hands, but in the iron hands of genetics, race, culture, bad luck, "the will of the gods." I am reminded of the volatile Joe Christmas in Faulkner's *Light in August,* who begins his journey toward murder with the words, "Something is going to happen to me." Agamemnon and Saul prefigure such men in their slowness to embrace repentance, which implies free will, and in their speed to embrace destiny, which does not. The prophetic warning, the priestly supplication falls on their deaf ears. But fatalistic oracles and rigid predictions hold them in superstitious awe. Change Agamemnon's chariot to a pickup truck, and we know immediately what the bumper sticker on its tailgate says: "Shit Happens." And there's nothing you can do about what happens. Likewise, there's nothing you can do to change what I am.

The stories of Agamemnon and Saul are themselves prophetic warnings to rash, brooding, and irascible men. Behold the *real* shit that can happen. You will fall on your own sword in the end. You will either destroy someone you love or be destroyed by her, or both. These are the wages of unchecked wrath. Of course, the warning is effective only to the extent that one is able to see himself in the character, so that when God is quoted in the Bible as calling David "a man after my own heart," we can admit that to some degree Saul is a man after ours. Who knows but that to transcend these characters, we must first learn to love them. It remains for an artist like Thomas Hardy—or in our generation, Russell Banks—to show us how.

Thomas Hardy was not a man you would have wanted to ask, "What's the worst that can happen?" He would have told you more than you wanted to hear. He is known as the great pessimist in English literature, but his pessimism is more than balanced by his compassion. That is one reason that I think people continue to read him: Behind all of the disasters and fatal errors of his characters is the author's worrying love.

Hardy's *The Mayor of Casterbridge* may contain the most fully developed literary expression of the Saul-Agamemnon archetype. Hardy may even have had these figures in mind when he created Michael Henchard, an itinerant laborer who, in a drunken fit, auctions off his wife and child to a sailor at a country fair. There's some suggestion that the "auction" is nothing more than a display of intoxicated bombast, but then the sailor makes his bid, and Henchard says yes to the awful momentum he has set in motion. Like the sacrifice of Iphigenia and the near-sacrifice of Jonathan, the auction has something to do with face-saving. Aeschylus would have said the same thing about Henchard's sale as he said about Agamemnon's sacrifice:

> Then he put on
> the harness of Necessity.

Add to this masculine vanity the abuse of patriarchal power, the dark connotations of the phrases "my wife" and "my child." If you own them, you see, you ought to be able to sell them.

Henchard also mirrors Saul and Agamemnon in his rivalry with a young man of promise, the Scot Donald Farfrae, who comes to work for Henchard after the latter has had the improbable good fortune of building a new life as the mayor of Casterbridge. Like David and Achilles, Farfrae is charismatic and gallant where Henchard is brooding and irascible. And as with its Homeric and biblical precedents, Henchard's rivalry with Farfrae does not have to be so bitter or disastrous as he makes it. Farfrae is a decent enough fellow. That said, he cannot know all that Henchard has suffered, and in some ways his attractiveness as a character suffers by comparison. In Hardy's novel, the ambivalence one feels in the Saul-David story is completely fleshed out: We like Farfrae more than Henchard, perhaps even more than David himself, but it is Henchard whom we love, or at least I love him, to an extent that we are not permitted to love Saul. What the nineteenth-century novel gives us that the biblical narrative doesn't is the wounded heart of the hero.

The Mayor of Casterbridge is as grim a novel as one can find. All of Henchard's attempts to make up for his past meet with failure and heartbreak. His last wish is for the utter annihilation of any trace that he ever walked the earth. Few passages in literature move me so powerfully as "Michael Henchard's Will":

> That Elizabeth-Jane Farfrae [his stepdaughter] be not
> told of my death, or made to grieve on account
> of me.
> & that I be not bury'd in consecrated ground.
> & that no sexton be asked to toll the bell.
> & that nobody is wished to see my dead body.
> & that no murners walk behind me at my funeral.
> & that no flours be planted on my grave.
> & that no man remember me.
> To this I put my name.

At this point we might be inclined to ask what Hardy's novel has to offer us besides a highly literate version of that other fatalistic bumper sticker, "Life's a Bitch and Then You Die" with "Good riddance" added as an afterthought. Granted that Hardy didn't write his novel to serve as an exhibit in a book about anger, what purpose does it serve to mention it here? At least three purposes, I think.

First of all, Hardy's novel comes with another stern warning to angry men, so stern it cannot even be called didactic, because it tells us that we can quickly reach a point where life lessons don't amount to much. There may be no way left to apply them. Rage always seems so ephemeral once it has passed, no more than a brief storm, but it can leave irreparable damage in its wake. This is what an angry man forgets even more than his manners; at some level, he is convinced that "we can always fix it later." Not always. In some cases, there is simply no room to say "I'm sorry" to anyone but God. I think of that scene in *Raging Bull* where the boxer Jake La Motta, having terrorized his wife and trashed their kitchen, calls to her where she is hiding with the words, "Let's be friends." It's a funny line—and a terrible one in its implications. Hardy's story says that a man of Henchard's cast of mind has good reason to be afraid. "The fear of the Lord," says the book of Proverbs, "is the beginning of wisdom." The fear of one's own wrath can be a beginning of wisdom too.

Second, the novel is telling us the corresponding truth that we have no worthy choice but to *attempt* to repair any damage we have done with our wrath. It may do no good, it probably will do no good, but de Motta needs to pick up the mess in the kitchen. This is where Henchard differs from Agamemnon and Saul: in his effort to make amends. That his eventual fate is little better than theirs compels a reader to cry out, "What else could the poor man have done?" And the answer of the novel, at once dreadful and sublime, is "Nothing." What makes Henchard a good man and Hardy a great novelist, what gives each his stature in the end, is that the mayor of Casterbridge tries to be good and to make good in the face of inevitable failure. Our prospects are not always so dismal as his. But in making his so dismal, Hardy forces us to ask what other course there is but to struggle, to hope, and to endure —even if redemption is beyond us. Would we have wished Henchard to go on drinking? Would we have wished him to take his own life? He is happy for annihilation when it comes at last, but the words that move us so powerfully in his will could only have left us cold in a suicide note. Henchard's last will and testament amounts to his bill of inalienable rights. He has earned every one.

Finally, *The Mayor of Casterbridge*, like the best of literature, gives us a glimpse of what Albert Camus called "the solidarity of all man in error and aberration." The viewpoint of the archetypal man of wrath, be he Agamemnon in his chariot, Saul with his javelin, or Henchard or King Lear in the pouring rain, is the viewpoint of a man who believes himself to stand alone. Whether the belief is based on egotism, desperation, or grief, the great ragers all see themselves as armies of one. But literature reminds us, through the repetition of their type, that they are merely members of an army.

> [O]ur stories, Wade's and mine, describe the lives of boys and men for thousands of years, boys who were beaten by their fathers, whose capacity for love and trust was crippled almost at birth and whose best hope for a connection to other human beings lay in elaborating for themselves an elegiac mode of relatedness, as if everyone's life were already over. It is how we keep from destroying in our turn our own children and terrorizing the women who have the misfortune to love us; it is how we absent ourselves from the tradition of male violence; it is how we decline the seductive role of avenging angel; we grimly accept the restraints of nothingness—of disconnection, isolation and exile—and cast them in a cruel and elegiac evening light, a Teutonic village in the mountains surrounded by deep dark forests where hairy beasts wait for stragglers and deer thrash wild-eyed through the deep snow and hunters build small fires to warm their hands so as to handle their weapons gracefully in the cold.

So writes the narrator in Russell Banks's novel *Affliction*, which contains a recent incarnation of the angry figure we have met in three earlier guises. Banks's Wade Ward is neither king nor mayor, but a part-time cop and plow truck driver in northern New York state. His sacrifice of his daughter is done for no higher cause, nor even for a base one. He is scarcely aware of any cause at all. He has simply lost her, officially to divorce, and actually to his own clueless ineptitude as a father. But many familiar features make up his story, the simmering rage, the oppressive sense of doom, the disapproving father, not least of all the young rival, who is not even a rival in any rational sense, but whom Wade kills anyway. In a brilliant twist on a familiar theme, he shoots his young friend in the way that Saul, Agamemnon, and Henchard sacrifice their children, as if the deed somehow needed to be done.

The narrator who frames the words in the long quotation above is Wade's younger brother, and in his view, the annihilation that Henchard wished for in death amounts to a sad covenant that angry men like Wade make with life. He explains their acceptance of nothingness as a pitiful attempt to resist the temptations of rage and violence. In some ways, the narrator presents us with a choice that differs markedly from the one presented by Hardy. The mayor of Casterbridge had to choose between annihilation and a futile hope for redemption, between despair and some kind of tragic resignation in the face of despair. Apparently, Wade has made a different choice, one between rage and nothingness, between a direct and emotional engagement with life, which could prove dangerous to everyone that he loves, and an "elegiac" detachment that amounts to acting "as if everyone's life were already over."

I find myself wanting to close with some kind of answer to Wade's brother. I want to pose a better choice than he does. But I am not sure that I have one—except to say that the choice he implies goes to the very heart of what this book of mine is about. If anger cannot be redeemed, then the choice for those men scarred by its uglier manifestations is very likely what the brother proposes: either to embrace "the tradition of male violence," or to effect some kind of nihilistic disconnection from life—through ironic detachment, through hedonistic indulgence, through rituals of male bonding that are certainly not homosexual, but that are even more certainly not heterosexual. That is precisely the choice that I see many of my male contemporaries making; their numbers do indeed comprise an army. And for those who love them, it amounts to an army in a foreign war on ever-more-distant soil.

The glib ideology that would purport to solve this predicament "by getting rid of all the macho stuff," by turning the word *testosterone* into an epithet of contempt, is a bit like resolving the abortion debate by sterilizing every potential mother. Anger is a part of our created nature as human beings, both male and female, in the image of God. The choice, then, is to redeem our anger or to become something less than human, either by making the tragic mistakes of Saul and Agamemnon, or by making an equally tragic covenant with nothingness. Perhaps the best alternative lies in using one's rage to annul the covenant. As the poet William Carlos Williams wrote in his long poem *Paterson:*

> A man is under the crassest necessity
> to break down the pinnacles of his moods
> fearlessly —

to the bases; base! to the screaming dregs,
to have known the clean air
From the base, unabashed, to regain
the sun kissed summits of love!

Compared to Banks's "Teutonic village" surrounded by "deep, dark forests" and "hairy beasts," those "sun kissed summits of love" sound awfully good. They're where I'm headed in any case.

Unless carefree, motherlove was a killer.

Toni Morrison, *Beloved*

ANGRY WOMEN

CLYTEMNESTRA
AND BOUDICA,
MEDEA AND SETHE

A deceptive show of balance pairs the last chapter with this one, matching four angry men with four angry women. It is deceptive in that the women are not and can never be as representative of their sex as the men. Of the four, Clytemnestra and Medea are both the creations of male authors (though the myths in which they first appeared may be more authentically feminine than we shall ever know). Queen Boudica is an indisputably historic person, who nevertheless comes to us exclusively through the eyes of historians who were males as well as citizens of the nation that conquered hers. Only Sethe is a woman made by a woman. Nevertheless, it is a man who interprets her in the pages that follow.

Although the balance of these two chapters may be deceptive, that fact alone says something important about women and their anger. At least some of women's anger derives from an imbalance that is never entirely internal. It lies outside their heads, in the world at large. Aeschylus tells us that Agamemnon "put on the harness of Necessity"; that is, he chose to embrace his fate. In contrast, these four women seem to have had their harnesses put on them at about the same time as they were first swaddled. This is not to say that they lack free will or responsibility for any of their actions. In many ways, their actions are more decisive and consequential than those of the men. Still, taking all these stories together, one cannot escape the impression that the men slept in the beds they made, whereas the women merely woke up in the same beds in which they were born, suddenly unable to sleep.

Medea's male antagonist, her husband, Jason, arrogantly says something like that very thing:

> A man dares things, you know, he makes his adventure
> In the cold eye of death; and if the gods care for him
> They appoint an instrument to save him; if not, he dies.
> You were that instrument.

This is the point in the drama where every woman in the audience with at least one feminist bone in her body groans out loud, but in fact Jason is giving a very accurate, if vain and callous, description of the predicament of all the women in this chapter. Yes, they are able to "dare things" as well as any man, but their daring comes in response to the consequences of their secondary status as the instrument of man. In other words, their daring is never without a certain desperation. Most of them are avengers, but none is an adventurer. In some ways, this makes their anger, and the anger of women like them, a different sort of problem than the anger of their male counterparts. In some ways, their anger is not the problem at all. Whoever first said that "Hell hath no fury like a woman scorned" failed to take into account that the position of being perpetually at the mercy of another's scorn is itself hell.

⌒

Clytemnestra is the wife of Agamemnon and—as even those familiar with classical literature sometimes forget—the sister of Helen of Troy. Both women were born of Zeus's fabled mating with Leda, in which he came upon her in the form of a swan. Long before she performs a single one of the deeds that will make her name a byword for treachery, Clytemnestra finds herself bidding her husband good-bye as he goes off to war on behalf of her famously beautiful sister. Clytemnestra is a second-class person two times over, in subordination to Agamemnon and in comparison to Helen. If anger is frustration poised on the threshold of action, then a woman's anger can come from being forever stalled on that threshold itself, forbidden to act, unwilling to submit. As the narrator in Tillie Olson's short story "I Stand Here Ironing" says on behalf of her daughter: "help her to know . . . that she is more than this dress on the ironing board, helpless before the iron."

Clytemnestra is also the mother of three children. Agamemnon, Saul, Henchard, and Wade are all fathers; and all these women are mothers—but here too the symmetry is misleading. None of the men is defined by his parenthood as the women are. Take the men, make them childless, and you can still salvage their stories. You can certainly locate their anger. This is not so for the women. Take away their motherhood, and they become different women in stories with very different plots. The absolutism of motherhood in their lives does two things: It makes them particularly vulnerable through their children, and it makes their children as instantly susceptible to their mothers' rage as to their fathers' power.

You will recall that Agamemnon sacrificed his daughter Iphigenia to gain a favorable wind for sailing to Troy. The ruse by which he accomplished this is both horrible and emblematic. According to the legend, Agamemnon sent word to his household that he had arranged a marriage between his daughter and the great warrior Achilles. Iphigenia arrived at the Greek camp dressed in her wedding finery, only to be seized and slaughtered. In a sense, she and her mother suffer similar fates: That is, they are each reduced to a very specific role, that of bride and mother respectively, and then that role itself is reduced to a cruel joke. It is not enough to say that the frustration and therefore the anger of women derive from the limitations placed on their freedom, identity, and talent. This is true, but only half true—it amounts to the great half-truth of talk-show feminism. Women are also frustrated and angry because *even that limited role* is demeaned. We could express this by changing a few pronouns in that "riddle of inequality" found in the Gospels: "Whosoever hath, to him shall be given; and whosoever hath not, from *her* shall be taken even that which *she* seemeth to have." A life confined to the kitchen cannot be completely assessed without mention of the muddy footprints left carelessly on the kitchen floor. The scene in *Raging Bull* where Jake La Motta trashes his wife's kitchen calls to mind the scenes in Faulkner's *Light in August* where the misogynistic Joe Christmas throws Joanna Burden's proffered food against the wall. Both are examples of the same reduction that names a woman after her sexual parts and then abuses her sexual parts, that sees a woman as nothing but a bedmate or a baby-maker and then forsakes her bed and kills her babies. If there is any more compelling justification for rage than this, one should like to hear it—or perhaps not to hear it, because it would be unendurable.

⌇

Clytemnestra gets even, for a time. With the connivance of her lover, she murders Agamemnon on his return from Troy. She has woven an ingenious robe that acts as a straitjacket when the conqueror steps into it after his ritual bath; with her husband confined in its coils, she stabs him to death. She also murders his captive concubine, Cassandra. Clytemnestra herself will eventually be murdered by her son, Orestes. The moral conundrum of his vengeance forms the major theme of Aeschylus's masterwork, the *Oresteia*. By its close, Clytemnestra and her grievance are nothing more than shadows on the stage.

And yet the questions raised by her vengeance continue to haunt the audience until the very end of the play and beyond. Does righteous wrath necessarily lead to righteous action? And do righteous actions, by themselves, make a righteous world? The story suggests that even when the claims of justice are irrefutable, the instruments of anger are seldom precise.

Ostensibly, Clytemnestra acts out of outrage over what was done to her daughter. She has another daughter, Electra, in addition to her son, Orestes. Clytemnestra follows her act of maternal retribution by sending Orestes away to live with relatives (she claims to do so for his safety) and by relegating her daughter to the place of a servant in the palace where she and her lover now reign. At least that is how Electra sees her situation. Electra has no sympathy for her mother, and no visible resentment over her sister's death; she's the classic daddy's girl, who gives her name to Freud's Electra complex. But it is Clytemnestra who concerns us here.

Clytemnestra's righteous rage on behalf of her daughter Iphigenia is contradicted by her indifference to her surviving children. Perhaps this can be explained by Aeschylus's need to diminish our sympathy for her in order to gain our support for Orestes' eventual vindication. Perhaps too it can be explained by the fact that neither Orestes nor Electra comes across as a particularly likable child. Then again, given the family, what can we expect?

Nevertheless, even if Aeschylus is manipulating our emotions so that the male avenger gains ascendancy over the female avenger, even if Clytemnestra is given all her due, there remains a very trenchant insight in Aeschylus's characterization of her selective love. How often have we seen someone enshrine the dead or lost child or lover in preference to the living—even to the extent of wronging the living in order to honor the dead? Once again, we see the tyranny of the mind, and the mentality of anger. The dead child, like the beautiful dead woman of romantic poetry, is a secure object of adoration, and an equally secure excuse for anger. Iphigenia offers no challenge. Unlike her brother and sister, she has no life to call her own. This is not to suggest that Clytemnestra has no reason to seek vengeance; she has a reason if anyone has a reason. It is only to say that her anger has the same dimension of unreality as have most other angers, and that this dimension is the chamber in her heart where she has entombed her dead daughter, having first banished the living children who also have a claim there.

As for her murder of Cassandra—

> Brought as a variant to the pleasures of my bed,
> She lends an added relish now to victory.

—here the unreality of Clytemnestra's anger propels her from injustice to further injustice. The neat rhetorical parallelism of her speech obscures a parallel more terrible: Avenging a girl brought bound to the altar, Clytemnestra slaughters another girl brought bound to the bed of her conqueror. Clytemnestra's rage on behalf of a helpless feminine instrument of a man's blood lust finds its object in another helpless feminine instrument of this same man's sexual lust. In the broadest sense, Clytemnestra murders her daughter all over again.

Boudica, the Iceni queen who led a devastating revolt against the occupying Romans in first-century Britain, bears several comparisons with Clytemnestra. First of all, she is given her "harness of Necessity" in the context of a man's world; that is to say, it is thrust upon her without invitation. Second, she is outraged partly through her daughters. And finally, though her vengeance falls on men and women both, it seems that women bear the worst of it.

The story of Boudica's grievance is a dreadful one. It parallels the stories of millions of nameless women throughout history; only Boudica's stature as a noble lady makes her story seem more tragic than theirs, and more unusual than it truly is. The wife of an Iceni king who had reigned peacefully as a client of the Romans, Boudica inherited the throne after her husband's death. Sensing an opportunity for extortion, the local Roman governor contested the dead king's will, in which he had left a portion of his estate to the emperor and a portion to his own two daughters. (Apparently, this kind of division had legal precedents; the first legacy was intended to safeguard the second.) The governor's agents mounted a ruthless campaign of plunder and land confiscation. As a prelude, they decided to make Queen Boudica an example in the hopes of demoralizing her subjects. In the presence of her people and the Roman soldiers, the queen was stripped and flogged. Then, she was forced to watch as her two daughters were raped.

Archaeologists tell us that there is still a noticeable layer of red dust in the soil strata under the present-day city of London, dating from when Boudica's army burned the Roman town of Londinium to the ground. Under the command of their furious queen, the Iceni burned two other cities and destroyed the better part of a Roman legion until they in turn were crushed by superior force. No one is sure what became of Boudica, though she lives as a legend—usually with the name of Boadicea—and in a bronze statue of the queen and her daughters that stands in London today. The statue is obviously intended as a symbol of nationalist pride—the native queen taking up arms against foreign occupation—but it might also stand as a monument to righteous anger everywhere.

The atrocities alleged to have been committed by Boudica's troops are, like many reports of atrocity, subject to conjecture. The enemy recorded them, perhaps embellishing them in the process, and we have no way of knowing for sure if Boudica sanctioned those that actually occurred. Her tribe was hardly a disciplined army, one reason the Romans were able to rout it in the end. In any case, the atrocities seem to have been directed with particular cruelty against women. The Iceni are supposed to have cut off the breasts of the women they captured and sewed them to their mouths to create the macabre impression that they were eating their own flesh. The victims were then impaled on long skewers. It takes no great imagination to guess how the latter operation was performed. The impulse to retaliation probably explains both the brutality and the methods: We saw what you did to our royal women; look what we're doing to yours.

Beyond such an explanation, however, it is hard not to see yet another ironic spectacle of women's vengeance falling disproportionately on women. Setting aside gender politics, we may also be seeing the general tendency to treat the collaborator more mercilessly than the enemy, to hate Judas more than Pilate. I imagine that at least some of the consorts of the occupying Romans were native Britons; certainly none of them were Roman rapists. But then, it was not white South Africans who were "necklaced" with burning tires, nor Ulster Protestants whose heads were shaved in the streets of Northern Ireland. Not infrequently, blind rage attacks its own kind first; like lightning, it takes the shortest path home. This may be where men and women show themselves the most alike. The difference is that, in a world where women have second-class status to begin with, they are more likely to be perceived as collaborators. The role of instrument is the role of a collaborator, after all, so that even when the role of avenging angel falls to a woman, other women are invariably going to pay the price. Earlier, I had said that women's anger may in many cases amount to a different problem than men's anger —I meant that, on the whole, women have greater justification for getting angry. They certainly have no lesser reason to be cautious in the application of their rage.

When we were first married, my wife worked as a clerical assistant in an academic department of a college. Of the various indignities that she bore from professors and graduate students alike, the worst came from two women who could not resist a single opportunity to present themselves as angry "feminists." And against whom did they direct their militancy? Pornographers? Rapists? Pimps? Right-wing clerics? No, but a woman like themselves, who shared nearly all of their convictions, though she lacked their affectations, not to mention their adjusted gross incomes. (One of the two, it should be said, did eventually show a change of heart.) Similarly, when my wife was first looking for a job, her most humiliating interview—in fact, her only humiliating interview—took place at a family planning center where a haughty women's advocate grilled and belittled her without pity for the horrendous crime of failing to type fifty words a minute. I must admit that my ruminations in this chapter derive as much from these vicarious experiences as from any work of literature. Never mind if the latter are the works of men; the proof has come from the acts of women. If, as a slogan once popular among feminists puts it, "the personal is the political," then according to certain personal experiences of certain women, the politics of sisterhood most certainly stink.

~~

We may know Medea better than any of the other heroines of classical Greek drama, in part because of a well-known adaptation of Euripedes' play by American poet Robinson Jeffers.

We may also know Medea because, amid all the acts of human sacrifice and self-mutilation that we associate with Greek tragedy, hers are the most extreme. She murders her own children, because, as she will tell her incredulous husband, "I loathed you more than I loved them."

She has every reason to loathe him. This recurring theme of reasonable loathing makes these four women in some ways more interesting than the four men. The women's anger derives from a just cause more than from an inscrutable condition. For that reason, we can move beyond the question of whether or not their anger is justified and move to the more complex question of whether it does them more harm or more good.

Medea is a foreign princess who falls in love with the Greek adventurer Jason. He has sailed with his famous Argonauts to her country in quest of the Golden Fleece. A sorceress, Medea uses her magic powers to assist Jason, even going so far as to kill her own brother to advance Jason's cause. Hell hath no fury like a woman infatuated with a thug. Jason takes Medea back to Corinth, where he marries her and fathers two sons. (In this, he takes one tentative step beyond that other mythic adventurer, Theseus, who abandons his female deliverer on an island.) Jason and Medea might have lived happily ever after. But always mindful of advancing his own interests, Jason decides to marry the king's young daughter and abandon Medea. To safeguard against Medea's well-known acquaintance with the black arts, the king announces that she is to be exiled. He gives her a day to pack.

Medea responds with cunning and ruthlessness. She sends Jason's bride a gift, a beautiful dress that catches fire as soon as the girl puts it on, and that clings magically to her flesh when she tries to tear it off. Her father dies in a vain attempt to extinguish the conflagration. Then Medea murders both of Jason's sons and departs in a chariot drawn by dragons.

It is no surprise that the modern adapter of this tale espoused a philosophy he called "inhumanism." In Medea, Jeffers saw, not a reason for his misanthropy, but a figure to admire, one who was strong above all else. His heroine shows the clay feet of his idol: To worship strength is inevitably to destroy oneself; it is to join in the project of one's enemies. Medea even admits to breaking her own heart in order to break Jason's. The great irony of her story is that none of the other female characters seeks so deliberately to triumph over her circumstances, and none, it seems to me, is so utterly self-defeated.

Medea has always struck me as a typically Greco-Roman creation, in that she achieves ascendancy only by acting "the part of a man." Her sacrifice, after all, is more typical of Agamemnon than of Clytemnestra, though her immolation of Jason's bride-to-be—another hapless pawn in the power games of men—is reminiscent of Clytemnestra too. The Greeks could only conceive of feminine power as an impersonation (and usurpation) of masculine power. Its operative symbol is the Amazon warrior, who cuts off her right breast (the word *amazon* means "one-breasted") in order to pull a bowstring. Emancipation through self-mutilation. We find the same idea in the Gnostic Gospel of Thomas, a golden oldie among the heterodox since its discovery in the 1940s, where Jesus is recorded as saying that "every woman who will make herself male will enter the kingdom of Heaven."

Impersonation, though, is the ultimate exercise in futility. At the end of the day, nobody "does Elvis" better than Elvis. The crowd may love you, but you'll never sleep in Graceland. Drag queens teach us no less than tragic heroes, and often they teach us the same things. The monumental irony revealed by Medea is that the attempt to rise above second-class citizenship by "making the female male" is an automatic admission of inferiority. To rage against men in conscious imitation of men is only to cut off your own breast, to break your own heart—to put on a phony beard and let the knife fall on your own flesh and blood.

⌒

Then comes Sethe, hushing all pronouncements. Toni Morrison's 1988 novel, *Beloved,* took its inspiration from an actual event in which a slave woman killed her own child rather than have her raised as a slave. The story of her protagonist Sethe is the extreme form of the tale in which woman is born into "the harness of Necessity"—in this case, the harness of American slavery. Sethe's circumstances are relatively benign at first; she comes of age on a plantation known as Sweet Home, where the master speaks of his male slaves as "men" and does not molest slave women. (We are left to wonder if this makes him more enlightened than his peers or more benighted, since he continues to keep slaves anyway.) A change in plantation ownership straitens the harness that Sethe wears. Her baby's milk is sucked from her breasts by two of her new masters. She is beaten mercilessly when she reveals the atrocity to her sympathetic mistress. Her husband, who had watched it in helpless anguish from his hiding place in a barn loft, goes mad. Eventually Sethe escapes to freedom, sending her three children on before her. During her exodus she gives birth to a fourth, the girl Denver, who will become the Electra of this story, the daughter neglected in favor of a ghost.

When slave-catchers come to retrieve Sethe and her family,

she attempts to kill her children, though she only succeeds in killing one girl. This is Beloved, the child who returns years later "from the other side" to haunt Sethe's life as a weird young woman, at once nubile and infantile. The novel is largely about Sethe's struggle to be reconciled with this creature, and eventually to exorcise her from her life. It is also about the struggle of her daughter Denver to be something more than Electra in a head cloth. That both women seem likely to succeed makes Morrison's novel into something more hopeful than a typical tragedy. "Call no man happy till he's dead," says Sophocles. Morrison seems to counter, "Call no woman dead until she has had her last chance to be happy."

Sethe is beyond our judgment. Even her wrath is beyond our judgment, if for no other reason than that it strikes us as an emotion beyond wrath. Her blade is poised, like Abraham's, above the level of normal emotions, common experience, or "universal morality." Who dares say that she was wrong or right, a good mother or a bad? Her lover Paul D. is not so deferential. When he learns of her past, he chides her with the words: "You have two legs, not four." His response is as understandable as it is short on understanding. Morrison told the director Jonathan Demme that of all the characters in her novel, her favorite was Paul D. It must have hurt her, then, almost as much as it hurt Sethe, to have him say this to Sethe's face.

But Paul D. redeems himself at the end, as if to emphasize that redemption is also possible for Sethe and Denver and perhaps for Beloved too. After the undead daughter is at last banished from her life, Sethe comes close to dying herself. Paul finds her delirious and filthy on the floor, mourning her loss. "She was my best thing," she cries. To which Paul D. answers, "You your best thing, Sethe."

This is Toni Morrison speaking, though on first reading I almost mistook her for Whitney Houston. Was she telling us nothing more than that "Loving yourself is the greatest love of all"? Much more, I think. In fact, she may be giving us a key, not only to a better understanding of Sethe, but to our understanding of Clytemnestra and Medea and of the rage that inspires them all.

When Sethe says that Beloved was her "best thing," she is saying what many of the other characters imply, and that many of us feel in our hearts: that our children are absolute in their importance and in their claims upon us. One is inclined to add, "and so it should be." The problem with making children into absolutes, however, is that it eventually makes them into something less than children. It makes them the first thing we seize when fury, despair, or divinity seems to demand the ultimate sacrifice. After all, isn't sacrifice a matter of giving up your "best thing"? To make children less than absolute, on the other hand, is to make them closer to absolutely safe in our arms.

Any healthy attempt to do so is of necessity a religious one. The only absolute capable of interposing itself between our children and our misguided fury is God. Muhammad is supposed to have said that marriage is one half of religion; in the absence of religion, however, marriage (or motherhood or manhood) can become all of life. In the presence of extreme stress, that sense of totality can backfire in tragic ways. This is the meaning of the Abraham and Isaac story, revealed at the moment when the voice from heaven says, "Do not lay your hand on the boy or do anything to him." By teaching Abraham to place an absolute above his only son, God has exempted the child from the sacrificial danger that awaits all absolutes. In

Christian terms, Abraham puts Christ on the cross at the same moment as he takes his own son off the altar.

Perhaps the long white beard on Abraham prevents us from seeing how applicable the story is to mothers as well as fathers. Perhaps what we need is an Abraham and Isaac story for women, and perhaps Toni Morrison has given us the closest thing we have thus far. When Paul D. says, "You your best thing, Sethe," he is urging her to take a step toward that same recognition of motherhood *in relation* to other claims as great as or greater than its own. It is too facile to say that Beloved might have been spared had Sethe known this all along. All we dare say is that many women—and men—might find better objects for their anger and frustration, and more appropriate sacrifices to their gods, than unfortunate children harnessed with the terrible necessity of being their parents' "best things."

Anger which breaks a man into children . . .

César Vallejo, first line of an untitled poem

ANGER AND
CHILDREN

Iknow people who were so traumatized by the anger of
their parents, or by the anger of some other adult in their
childhood, that they never developed an anger of their own.
Even now a confrontation with someone else's anger all but
paralyzes them. To give but one interpretation to Vallejo's enigmatic line: Anger always breaks these adults into children, intimidated and helpless. We could say that they have been
"cured" of wrath in the same way that a sexually abused child
might grow up cured of lust. It is not an enviable cure.

But on the near side of trauma—and in certain psychotic
cases, on the far side of it too—children learn how to be angry
from adults. Anger breaks fathers and mothers into protégés
of their own emotion. Even the child who resolves to be calmer
than her parents is still shaping herself in response to their

influence. A parent or teacher does well, then, to ask, What am I teaching my children about anger? It goes without saying that the most effective lessons will be taught by example. It also goes without saying that the most successful self-improvement plan often has the desire of raising happy children as its driving force.

Perhaps the first thing we need to teach our children about anger is that human beings are allowed to be angry. If emotions are made to count as misdeeds, then it follows that emotions are matters of choice. Believing as much, a child might go on to believe that his choices are as uncontrollable and subjective as his emotions. The result is either an emotional cripple or a moral misfit, not that much difference exists between the two. It is one thing to tell children that no amount of anger gives them the right to say or do whatever they want. In that regard, I used to tell my students that Malcolm X, who called himself "the angriest man in America" and had good enough reasons for being so, did not leave us a single four-letter profanity in print. To tell an angry child that he needs to watch his mouth or to take his anger outdoors or to his room is not to stifle his emotional development. But it is wrong, I think, to tell him that he cannot scream or stamp his foot anywhere on the premises. It is wrong to say to him, "Don't you dare be mad at me," even if his anger strikes you as groundless. It may be even more wrong to say that to *her*. You had better refrain from teaching your daughter that anger is not feminine unless you also intend to teach her that getting smacked around is.

Equally wrong is the practice of aggravating a child's anger unnecessarily. I have been in households where parents seemed to find a certain grim amusement in a child's impotent fury, even going so far as to rile him up further, all under the pretext of demonstrating that "throwing a fit gets you nowhere." This doesn't teach patience so much as sadism. As it says in the Bible, "Fathers, provoke not your children to wrath." I think that means more than try not to get your children upset. I think that it also means try not to create situations that will trigger your children's wrath in later life. Don't behave like an implacable boss, or every boss in the future will wear a father's implacable face. Don't play on your kids' guilt, or every manipulator of conscience will be capable of making your grown-up child feel like a ten-year-old again. If a child's experiences at home are healthy ones, her bad experiences later on will have less power to unsettle her. They'll still be capable of stirring up rage, perhaps, but not the memory of rage, which can sometimes be more volatile.

Something else to teach a child is that anger, like other storms, often follows a warning and always comes with a price. We can't stop a hurricane, and maybe we can't help losing our tempers. What we can do is predict the blow before it arrives and get the breakables out of harm's way. So if the teacher is making you angry, ask to leave the room. If you have enough confidence, tell him *why* you need to leave the room. And if he still withholds his permission, maybe you ought to leave anyway. Maybe it would actually be a good idea to channel some of your rage into dignified defiance instead of abusive language or destructive behavior. Learn your own best way to blow off steam. And learn to recognize the worst ways: for example, driving a car as a form of emotional release, which is often nothing more than a legal variation of driving drunk.

One of the hardest things for a child to learn is how to look beyond his own nose, and perhaps this is one of the ways in which young and old complement each other: The old continually need to learn how to live in the moment, while the young need to learn that the moment only lasts for a moment. The question we all need to ask before rage takes us too far is this: Will my anger lead me out of the frustration that is enraging me, or will it only cause me a bigger frustration on the back end? In the second case, I shall need to be careful—and it's usually the second case. I know a man who became so frustrated by a malfunction in his chain saw that he heaved it down a hillside. Thus, a problem that might have taken him ten minutes or cost him a few dollars to repair became the headache of an entire day. He'd have done better to put the saw back in the truck bed and quit work early. That said, he was wiser to pitch the saw than he would have been to use it as a tool of emotional therapy—with the need for long-term physical therapy as a likely result.

Of course, these kinds of lessons come with living, and rarely without having lived for a while. Some years ago a school bus driver told me that one reason teenagers commit suicide is that they haven't lived long enough to learn that most things get better in a day or two. Adulthood might be described as having that lesson by heart. In the meantime a parent can sometimes point out the disproportion of cause and consequence that goes with every calamity, big or small—how easy it is to break an arm, how long it takes for the bone to mend; how quickly you can be fleeced of your allowance, how long it takes to earn the next installment.

Not least of all, we need to teach our children about moral ambiguity. Not moral vacillation, which often tries to dignify itself under that name, but the possibility of being right and wrong at the same time. It is possible, for example, to have every right to be angry and still to do something wrong as a result. It is also possible for two very different kinds of actions to both be right. I was told once about a village of Jews forced to dig their own graves before being machine-gunned by the Nazis. Two men stood out from the rest: the rabbi, who walked among his people helping them to say the Shema, and the village butcher, who grabbed one of the S.S. officers and bit out his throat. The commentator who told the story posed this question, "Which man was the better Jew?" A kid hears a question like that and automatically assumes there is a right answer. Most adults do too; only they are not so quick as the kid to risk giving the wrong answer. But the commentator who told the story said something like this: "Each man, according to his temperament and station in life, gave an appropriate response to the outrage that was taking place."

In other words, integrity comes in different forms. Parents would do well to remember that when they presume to second-guess every decision of their sons and daughters. Perhaps running from the bully and standing up to him are both acceptable responses. Perhaps it is wrong only to allow oneself to be demeaned—but that too may not be so easy to sort out from a distance.

In the same way, a child needs to be taught that even an appropriate action may lead to an equally appropriate, if decidedly unpleasant, consequence. The consequence doesn't need to be received in the bitter spirit of a condemnation. So, for example, maybe the time had come to lash out at a classmate's taunts, and maybe it was better to vent that rage on him than to turn it inward against yourself. Still, no school can run safely or long if students are allowed to overturn each other's desks at every provocation. What that means, my child, is that I support your having to serve a detention after school even though I also support the action that led to it. It wouldn't surprise me to learn that deep down your teacher feels the same way. But face the consequence with dignity. On another occasion you may be able to bear the taunts in silence. This time you weren't. Events may show that your outburst was beneficial, but we can't always foresee events, and even if we could, the wrong or right of an action is not determined entirely by its results. You did the best you could, that's all. Live with the repercussions; work for the peace. Pray for the strength.

In other words, live by faith. If I could teach my child that, I would not concern myself greatly with what I taught her about anger. But this may be another case where our children are better suited to teach us than we them: "Unless you become as a little child, you shall not enter the kingdom of God." It is characteristic of adults to live by rules, by customs, by the given odds, by the measure of what we can get away with. Very few of us, me included, have that sense of complete freedom and complete reliance on God that defines faith. It might even be said that faith casts out rage, in the same way that St. John says love casts out fear, by giving all frustrations, mistakes, and scruples their proper weight. I can get mad or I cannot get mad, but God is still God, and therefore, why get mad? If that sounds less than clear, it is because I have intuited the truth much more than I have lived it. In a very real sense, I have chosen to write about anger because I did not have enough material to write about faith.

Anger can also break us into children in the sense that it reduces us to callow versions of ourselves. As we "come apart," we begin to regress, recapitulating the tantrums, the sullen withdrawals, the pointless rebellions we knew at the ages of three, ten, and fifteen. This can be disconcerting enough, but if we have three-, ten-, or fifteen-year-old children of our own, then our anger can amount to a nightmare in which the parent virtually disappears into the child he has become. The actual child finds himself suddenly abandoned, at the mercy of someone still more powerful but apparently no more patient than he is. This can be a terrifying experience. And, as I have learned, it can be deeply disturbing even when the parent's anger is a good deal less than fury and even when it is not directed at the child.

This came poignantly to my attention when my teenaged daughter said to me not long ago, "It used to bother me when you got mad at the dog." The remark had no relevant context and seemingly no motive beyond that of stating a simple fact, almost as if she were musing to herself. "I used to believe that a face was looking at me in the tree across the road"—it was that sort of statement. In fact, she did believe she could see such a face; she called it "the Blink," and it sometimes worried her as she sat in her high chair. I could make her squeal with laughter by telling her that if the Blink came anywhere near us I would punch it in the nose. She would ask me again and again to tell her what I would do, and I would always oblige her, glad to see her gradually turning her attentions from the Blink to her noodles. Yes, Daddy would punch that Blink in the nose so hard it couldn't stop blinking. But it had upset her, a few years later, to see me slap her dog on the rump. I wonder now if it was all the more upsetting to see me angry at the dog because I was so seldom angry at her.

Being the parent of a young child is a curious stage of life: Perhaps no experience requires us to be more unselfish and attuned to the needs of another person, and it may be that we approach no other experience more self-importantly or less awake. Only now, when my daughter is a young woman, am I able to grasp how things like my anger may have touched her as a young child. I have a vivid recollection of her out in our backyard, at the age of two or thereabouts, singing with a tape of Roy Orbison. We are painting the house, I with the bucket of yellow and she with a small brush and a coffee can full of water. She is already showing the marked fondness for babies that will eventually determine her plans for college and a vocation, though at the time she is little more than a baby herself. And as she paints the clapboards with tap water, swaying with the music coming from the tape box and clutching a doll maternally to her chest, she sings with old Roy, "Your baby doesn't love you anymore" in a tone that I now recall as especially plaintive. Of course, the song itself is plaintive. But her misinterpretation of the words is so poignant as I think of it now. Does she imagine the loss of love as some terrifying mystery? All at once a baby stops loving its mother. Did she ever worry that the spell might come over her, or over one of her own babies in the future? Was she capable of wondering, a few years later, when she was ready to start school and her puppy was starting its wild adolescence, that the same kind of spell might come over her father and overshadow her dog? Your master doesn't love you anymore.

In fact, I was usually angry at the dog on my daughter's behalf. I was able to laugh when it snatched a Christmas pie off the table, but I found it difficult to keep my humor when it indulged in its favorite prank: snatching the mittens from the little human's hands and running away with them. Of course, in the dog's eyes, my fuming pursuit was all part of a grand game, what made the prank so irresistible, what made it worth the scolding and the slap that followed if ever I caught up with the animal, which was rare enough.

I was foolish to be angry, though the reader ought to know that I had just gotten a child into a snowsuit. Anyone who has ever done the same will require nothing further by way of mitigating circumstances. What is more, on some days her mother and I would have finally managed to hustle her outdoors on the first afternoon in a week or more when the wind chill was above zero. Then the dog took the mittens, like a harpy, like some cruel joke of the gods.

That my daughter would have been bothered by my reaction is, of course, not at all ironic. Perhaps more than any concern for her pet, perhaps more than any alarm at seeing her normally gentle father in an ugly mood, what may have disturbed her was feeling that she was somehow responsible for this trouble. After all, they were her mittens. Had she managed to keep them on her hands, the dog would not be in trouble with Dad. And this leads to an insight that every child knows but that many parents, most fathers, and nearly all fathers of girls forget: In some cases, protection is more frightening than the thing you're being protected from.

I've sometimes wondered if that is a reason for the enduring appeal of dramas about the Mafia. They are double-layered thrillers, because it's frightening to imagine what it would be like to have the Mob after you, and almost as frightening to imagine what it would be like to have the Mob on your side. To spend half your life telling your big brother or your father: "He didn't mean it, I swear. The mittens just came off by themselves. They fell into his mouth." We are reminded of the fairy-tale princess who languishes between a rock and a hard place, between the dragon outside the castle walls and the guardian who keeps her locked within. The hero's job is to rescue the princess from both, though not a few princesses have needed to be rescued from their heroes as well. We endanger even as we protect, even when we have no reasonable choice but to protect.

From time to time my wife has cautioned me, in regard to some injustice my daughter may have borne, "Try not to let her see that you're angry. I'm angry too. But if she sees you get mad, she won't tell you anything that goes wrong." It may already be too late for me to profit from that good advice; I notice that my daughter's grievances almost always go to her mother first, and the worst go to her mother alone. That's fine by me. Perhaps one advantage of having two parents, or of being one of a pair of parents, is that the chores of speaking softly and carrying a big stick can be divvied up according to each partner's inclinations. There may yet be occasions that call for a big stick. Still, I try very hard to be as calm as possible in the face of my child's heartbreaks, which may be the only laudable way under heaven to play God. It is definitely not an easy way.

Finally, I try to be patient with the dog. At least that is not too hard. She is the best of beasts, much slower these days, and hard of hearing in the selective manner of the old, which now that I think of it, is not all that different from the selective hearing of her youth. One of my professors said that the dog is a common dream symbol for the soul; I've not encountered that interpretation elsewhere, but I have noticed that my dog wants pretty much what my soul wants, the companionship of its housemates, a pat of approval from its master, the opportunity to run and sniff at will, with the chance of discovering something delicious and even slightly disgusting to chew on now and again. Anyway, it's good for the dog and me to be at peace. My daughter leaves for college in another year, and we shall want each other's consolation.

The true revolutionaries of the twentieth century will be the fathers of Christian families.

Charles Pierre Péguy

DOMESTIC
REVOLUTION

I was never a big John Lennon fan. It wasn't until recently that I would even admit that I liked the Beatles. Ever since the day in fifth grade when I was ridiculed for not knowing who the Beatles were (having missed an historic episode of the *Ed Sullivan Show* the night before), I nursed something like a secret grudge against them. To an unpopular eleven-year-old, *they* were the establishment. It was a notion that stayed with me, though I did not remain unpopular forever. Years later when one of my friends was all in a gush because John had "taken the courageous step" of staying home to raise his son —this when my working-class neighbors were struggling to do the same thing, minus all the self-dramatization, not to mention the leisure that comes of having a few cool millions in the bank—I could barely contain my disgust. Though I was sorry over his violent death, it did little to change my attitude toward his fans—quite the contrary. I could almost believe that the CIA had engineered the whole thing in the certain knowledge that four Maryknoll sisters raped and murdered several weeks earlier by right-wing paramilitaries in El Salvador would have no chance of competing for our grief and outrage with the unthinkable death of a Beatle. Christ himself could have died at that jungle roadblock and scarcely made the back page of the *Times*.

Grudges are ugly things—very different from anger. If anger is a consuming fire, a grudge is a smoking stinkpot. If you can't honestly say that you're angry with someone, then why would you hold anything against him—except for reasons that can best be described as perverse? In this case, the reasons for my grudge had less to do with John than with the cult of celebrity. Anyway, I no longer hold anything against the man. In fact, I can admire him. Knowing that everything he did would be a public act whether he liked it or not, he chose to perform a decent private act—that of raising his son—as a public statement. To say, as I was once fond of saying, that his money made the whole thing easy, is to lack imagination. In spite of his wealth, in spite of all the insanity that goes with stardom, he took an honorable shot at being a sane man.

Significantly he took that shot by staying at home. Like many people, he was at first inclined to confuse staying at home with staying in bed. But once he had gotten out of bed and down to the business of fatherhood, he was embarked on a program that was arguably more revolutionary than anything else he had done or would do. It was something much more than getting off "the merry-go-round," as he would say in one of his songs; it was an act of personal sabotage against the merry-go-round itself. The Industrial Revolution began by exiling men, women, and children from their homes. When Marx and Engels called for the "abolition of the family," they were merely repeating the marching orders that had created the proletariat in the first place. Better paid and infinitely more pacified, we are nevertheless the natural heirs of Marx's workers—rootless and expendable, frequently bored to tears, and just as frequently fit to be tied. We can only speculate how much of our anger comes from domestic estrangement, of the upheaval involved in leaving home, and of the frantic struggle to return there, day after day. Who knows but that John Lennon's modest (and immodest) gesture will one day be remembered as his major contribution to his times.

He might have balked at such a statement. He might have said, with justice, that it misses the point entirely. His choice was not to be remembered as a figure in an era but to remember himself in the act of being a father to his son. In any case, I find myself thinking of John more often and more fondly. As with others who died too soon after making a radical change in direction, I wonder where he would be today if he had lived, and if we'd even know.

⌒

John came home, and Yoko went to town. Bearing in mind what Wendell Berry once said, that we do not necessarily liberate Blondie by turning her into Dagwood, it is still important to note the contrast in direction. *Home* has not always signified the same thing to women and men. The irritability of men and the irritability of women have often arisen from different spheres of confinement. What John and Yoko tried, and what many of us have in our own way explored, is the attempt to open up those spheres for both partners. You can call it role reversal if you like, though that sounds too superficial to me, as if all our work in the world is about dressing up in different wigs and standing next to various props. I am much more interested in how men and women assist each other in the struggle to break out of the theater than in how they manage to upstage each other in the attempt to broaden their repertoires.

In a number of the healthier households I know, I have observed what might be called a changing of the guard. In the earlier years of the marriage, when the children were young, the husband was the family's chief ambassador and advocate. He went to meetings, offices, agencies. He was the presence of the marriage in the world. He was "the redeemer" in the original biblical sense of the kinsman who gets justice for his family. With the growth of children and the arrival of middle age, the guard seemed to change. The man is now the bigger homebody of the two; the woman is out and about more often, and she bears the standard into the public arena.

It would be foolish to describe this pattern as an ideal, or to prescribe it as a model. It would also be foolish, as well as arrogant, not to admit that I am observing this as a heterosexual phenomenon, that it might not be an exclusively heterosexual phenomenon, and that in any case it probably has to do more with individual character traits than with stereotypical gender traits.

But I am what I am, which is a very ordinary, middle-aged heterosexual man. Speaking as one, I would say that this changing of the guard bears some relation to the different ways in which men and women seem to manage anger. It may also have something to do with the different ways in which men and women age.

Women of middle age seem to grow in wisdom, generosity, and grace. Not always, but often. If God turns out to be female, my fondest hope is that the Ancient of Days will be revealed to us in the autumnal bloom of forty-nine. That's the age I should like Divinity to have if ever I should lose my mind or break my heart. If, on the other hand, God is masculine, then let him be either the age of Christ on the cross, or that of Methuselah at the height of his reputation. Nothing in between, I think. A male god of middle age is too much a God of the Middle Ages. At least men of that age can seem darkly medieval in their battle-ax moods, their fortified paranoia, their dungeons of periodic depression. This is not to say that men of middle age cannot achieve a wisdom equal to that of any woman of their years, only that the wisdom most often consists of being able to acknowledge the strength, competence, and surpassing good sense of their wives.

When our daughter was very young, it was I who went to school board meetings, I who negotiated with contractors and bank officers. I was as fair and firm as I could be. I did nothing without my wife's advice, but I did some things alone. I have not necessarily gained patience with age. My wife, without losing patience, has gained fighting strength—and what is no less important, the desire to go forth.

My wife was never homebound, nor do I intend to become a recluse. Perhaps John and Yoko taught us a few things about those dangers as well. We still go abroad together, we still think of ourselves not only as spouses but as comrades-in-arms, in the words of Homer, "Woe to their enemies, / joy to their friends!" But there has been that visible changing of the guard I see mirrored among several of my peers. Again, one must be wary of prescriptions in a matter like this, of presenting as a universal program something that presents itself to some of us as a natural rhythm, a thing yielded to more than adhered to. That said, I can envision as one of several utopias a republican state in which men held council till the age of forty, at which age women began terms of their own. So there would be forums of older women and younger men, a domestic background of older men and younger women—and probably more hanky-panky than the society could bear. But not more rage, perhaps, at least not until the hanky-panky reached a full head of steam.

A man easily given to anger is well served by a wife, also possessed of anger, but possessed as well of the wisdom most often found among mothers whose children are no longer young. I kiss my wife good-bye and watch her drive away to town as once she watched me. Now I know what her worries once were—moose in the headlights, black ice on the road—though there is one worry she no longer has, which is that her husband will get into some fracas that she usually knows how to avoid.

⌒

If women on the whole, regardless of their age, seem more adept at coping with anger than men, we can propose two not mutually exclusive reasons. The first is that something in the psychobiology of women gives them a better grip on this emotion. The second is that women have been socially conditioned to repress their rage. I certainly believe the latter, and I'm not disinclined to believe the former. The problem is that, number one, the anger of women is not my problem, and number two, neither explanation will help me with *my* problem. Even if I felt so inclined, I cannot hope to reduplicate the social training of women or the psychobiology of women in my own more-than-half-lived life. Each of those speculative avenues amounts to a moral dead end for me, similar to those equally fatuous questions we find in the Gospels, the ones that Jesus never answers directly—Will few be saved? Who is my neighbor?—not because he's evading the question, but because the question itself is an attempt to evade responsibility.

There is, however, a third explanation, less common but no less plausible than the other two: Perhaps the nature of traditional "woman's work" serves as an antidote to the forces that make men enraged. Needless to say, it can also enrage women, especially when it is done without relief, assistance, or appreciation. But that only serves as another compelling reason why men ought to ponder it.

The chief characteristics of traditional domestic work are these: It must be tended to every day, often several times a day; it is usually simple and often mundane; it is often an act of service performed for others; and finally, as the adage says, it is never done. Change the context, and one could list those same characteristics in a beginner's manual on prayer. Many a man could profit from saying to his wife or lover what the disciples say to Jesus: "Teach us to pray." One assumes that in the disciples' case the question arose from observing how prayer seemed to enrich the life of their master. Likewise, a man in a traditional domestic arrangement might do well to observe what "woman's work" does for his mate.

First of all, a domestic chore can serve as a pause, and often as a reprieve, in one's schedule. The problem with traditional men's work—as in "I take care of the outside of the house, and she takes care of the inside"—is that unless the outside is a barnyard or the path of an approaching tornado, it allows more latitude in scheduling than the inside does. You can always put the lawn off till Saturday. But if it's your job to make supper and have it on the table by a certain hour, then no matter what else you're doing, you have to stop and get busy in the kitchen. This can be frustrating for anyone compelled to integrate domestic work with other work, even with other domestic work. A woman doing her spring cleaning has to halt three times in the process to feed whoever happens to be underfoot.

On the other hand, this halt can be an oasis for someone who's paying too much attention to an abstract problem or a simmering grievance. One of the more memorable scenes from the cartoon series *The Simpsons* has the usually placid Marge Simpson about to blow her stack. "Sometimes this family makes me so . . ." she starts to exclaim. All at once, she relaxes her rigid body and sighs, "I guess I'll go start supper now." It's a pathetically comic moment for Marge, which might amount to a wonderfully healing prescription for Homer. Of course, you can still nurse a grievance or chew on a problem while mixing the ingredients for the sauce. But unless you want an inedible disaster, the work calls for a certain degree of attention. And any act of attention grounds us in the present moment.

Domestic work is also manual; it has to do with matter. There's no such thing as virtual cooking, unless you're satisfied with virtual eating. Making supper puts us in touch with concrete stuff: ingredients instead of factors, carefully regulated fire instead of unchecked speculations, distinct flavors in the mouth instead of vague feelings in the gut. We have already spent some time discussing the mentality and unreality of anger, of how it distorts proportion, imputes motives, imagines inconceivable dangers and unspeakable retributions. Domestic labor calls us back to the real, created world of food, fire, and loved ones that anger in its worst manifestations calls us away from. The Good Shepherd, whose voice the sheep all know, can sometimes call our names in the guise of The Good Cook. Should that come as any surprise to people who remember him and even worship him as bread and wine?

Third, domestic work is done for others. It is a daily reminder that others exist. (As drudgery, it can become the daily insinuation that you, the server, do not exist.) To make supper is to feed the people you love directly; to earn wages is to do the same thing once removed, which is to say one step closer to abstraction and the distraction that comes with it. In my own wage-work, I have often found that I am the most unreasonable, the most inclined to let frustration give way to anger, when I forget that I am doing the work to support myself and those I love. That "materialistic" objective has been the basis for some of my most "spiritual" work. Ironically, it was when I saw myself teaching entirely for the good of the human race, or when I wrote exclusively as an artist, that I became the greatest obstacle to goodness and the worst enemy of art. To cook supper, to use money to buy flour, and to make flour into real bread is to be based in the real world.

A man who elects to cook supper will often experience it as a liberation. He begins to anticipate the happiness of his wife at seeing it done, the fascination of his children (or their chagrin) in regard to what Daddy did differently from Mommy. Because in our culture men get to choose this chore more often than women, who have it thrust upon them as their duty, even housework can amount to a privilege. We tend to regard the image of the domesticated hubby as evidence of a feminist accomplishment; in many cases, it merely confirms the tenaciousness of patriarchal culture. A woman's duty remains a man's prerogative. Like a nobleman dismounting his horse in order to help the serfs pitch hay, a man sets the table, does the laundry. What a surprise, what a fine fellow the baron is, say the villeins. And as the smiling baron once again mounts his high horse, he thinks, What a lark!

But by making the chore a lark, the baron deprives himself of the fourth benefit, which is that of knowing the chore as a discipline. If it remains forever in the domain of whim—if I cook supper only when I feel the need, or have the time, or hope to curry someone's favor, then I will not cook supper when I don't feel a need, which is precisely when my need may be the greatest. We should always remember that emotional ailments, including anger, differ from their physical counterparts in that the impetus for seeking a cure is actually least when our suffering is greatest. A person having a heart attack knows quite poignantly that he needs a doctor; an attack of anger, on the other hand, obscures every need but the urge to vent.

But to choose a saner course we must first believe that choice is even possible, which may require a greater leap of faith than we suppose. Our modern lives are full of opportunities to make superficial decisions—even as the most important decisions are increasingly made for us. This in itself is probably a major cause of rage in our culture: a sense of limitless self-determination repeatedly undercut by the experience of almost complete powerlessness. My computer allows me scores of choices as to font styles and type sizes, but whether I can belong to the human race without having two thousand dollars' worth of ugly humming junk plugged into my wall is increasingly not a choice. Nevertheless, one sphere that still remains within our power—perhaps the last sphere that remains in our power—is the arrangement of our own households, the division of labor there, the rotation of the watch, the balancing of different needs. Sometimes the last of these amounts to the acknowledgment of reciprocal needs between woman and man.

There is a delightful Japanese myth, which I had the good fortune to hear in my adolescence, when it was bound to make the greatest impression, about the first woman meeting the first man. He complained to her, "I have a part on my body that is overfull." She replied, "I have a part on my body that needs filling." So they got their parts together.

In terms of domestic labor, man and woman are sometimes angry because—to reverse the myth—she has a part that is overfull and he has a part that needs filling. The solution works the same as in the myth. Not only does that solution make sense; it makes love.

ANGER
IN THE
CHURCH

They that are whole have no need of
the physician, but they that are sick.

Jesus

THEY THAT
ARE SICK

When my daughter was young, her mother and I enrolled her in a nonsectarian preschool that met in the basement of a church. I can scarcely think of less propitious words with which to begin this chapter than "the basement of a church," that place where charitable impulses and niggling proprietorship join like the ingredients of a witch's brew: eye of newt and toe of frog, nose of fussbudget and thumb of priest, "double, double toil and trouble." Though my wife and I were young in those days, I can't claim that we were innocent. We'd been in church basements before.

The preschool had no affiliation with the church other than the free use of its basement. We were told that some in the congregation were uneasy with the fact that religion played no part in the school curriculum—perhaps a euphemistic way of saying that they were uneasy at having the curriculum taught by a Jew. In what I could only surmise was an attempt to have us practice what they preached, our benefactors put forth a proposal: Every year, the church held a banquet in its fellowship space. Perhaps the parents of the students would like to . . . no, not come and sup with the congregation, but rather wait on their tables? It would be "a nice gesture." I never asked whether the gesture included girding ourselves with towels to wash the congregation's feet. Instead I angrily uttered a word that is as serviceable in the church as the word *amen:* "Sick."

Books tend to be informed by whatever crises their authors were going through at the time of composition. Mine is no different. One of my crises at this time, aside from the ongoing and by now obvious challenge of managing my own anger, has to do with confronting the difficult truth of how a religion founded by an itinerant healer should make so many of its members ill. Or at least fail so miserably to make them well. Granted, Jesus said that he had not come to call the righteous but sinners to repentance. So we shouldn't be surprised to find a number of unhealthy people in churches. My father was fond of saying that the church was "not a clubhouse for saints, but a hospital for sinners." But it turns out that hospitals can be incubators for the very infections they exist to cure. This is in fact the main reason for that much-lamented practice of "booting people out the door" as soon after surgery as possible: The odds in favor of their recovery are generally higher at home. It is almost irresistible to draw an analogy to the church. Check in if you like, but linger to your peril. If you're inclined to ask what any of this has to do with anger, I'm inclined to ask how long it's been since you attended church.

Perhaps I'm being disingenuous. Isn't the question of why there is so little health in the church merely the Christian form of a far more encompassing dilemma, something more catholic than the church universal itself? Why is there so little graciousness in the so-called hospitality industry, for instance, such superstitious dogmatism among scientists, such latent misogyny among feminists, such a weakness for insurrectionary rhetoric among conservatives, such boorish and prideful ignorance among educators, such a wanton disregard for the natural and human resources of a nation among its self-styled patriots, such elitism and haughtiness among those vocally committed to equality, such cynical disregard for truth and justice among practitioners of the law, such a lack of nurture, joy, and faith in family life, such an obsession with pain and bondage among those who claim to pursue pleasure and freedom as their highest goods? Oscar Wilde said that "Each man kills the thing he loves," so why shouldn't the church kill Christ? In other words, why should Christians be any different from everybody else? The answer comes back on the Pentecostal wind, "Because they're called to be."

My opening example of the preschool dinner has to do with the relationship between a church and outsiders, and is therefore relatively mild. The really pathological stuff takes place inside the church. I confess that although I attend a church and in fact have served for quite a while as its vicar, I know little of that pathology firsthand. My lack of clerical credentials and the solidarity of my family-sized parish, part of it made up of grateful refugees from other churches, have combined to give me the ecclesiastical equivalent of a charmed life. But I have listened to the harrowing tales of the refugees, and I have from time to time encountered that peregrinating mischief that makes its way from church to church like a bigamist blazing his trail of aggrieved wives. Nothing makes malevolence rub its hands together like the sight of a tranquil parish or a happy priest.

Essentially, we've circled back to a question we asked once before: How can "home" turn out to be so dangerous? How can we know such anger with people we're supposed to love? Here too the question is dangerous, because one of its plausible answers begs for the abolition of home itself. More specifically, when we ask what makes the church so sick, we risk the possibility that, beyond citing the various corruptions of "authentic Christianity," we shall be forced to conclude that authentic Christianity is itself corrupt. George Orwell quoted Nietzsche as saying, you don't need to be told that the religion is sick; if you have any health in yourself, you can smell it. If this is true, holding your nose will not count as keeping your faith.

⌐

One obvious reason for the sickness of Christian churches is the contamination of Christian teaching. This may derive partially from the sacramental nature of Christianity itself, with its ability to take the flesh of different cultural influences, and to take it so effectively that we're not always sure which came first, the divine commandment or the dopey cliché. A good example is the much-touted ethic of being "nonjudgmental," which appears to have originated with a statement in the Sermon on the Mount, been distilled in the vats of pop psychology, and then fed back to us in a form that Jesus himself could hardly have swallowed. The ethic not only allows but actually invites people to act out every creepy scenario that enters their heads, secure in the knowledge that what would get them fired, committed, or publicly horsewhipped anyplace else will get them nothing but sympathetic attention within the church. I suppose that some would say, "That's how it should be!" I suspect that Jesus would not be among them. We read of any number of times where Jesus said, "Take up your bed and walk" but not a single occasion where he said, "Throw yourself down on your bed, and I will lie down beside you and empathize." Healing presupposes that there's something to heal—a "judgmental" assumption if ever there was one.

On a deeper level, what we're looking at here is the presumed equation of religion with subjectivity, an equation that has been several centuries in the making, and which—though it may seem like an appropriate reaction to the radical objectivity of science—is actually the opposite of the covenant theology of the Bible. A covenant, like a word, is something set between "me and thee" that anchors our relationship in a place outside us both. Neither party can claim exclusive ownership of the agreement. Certainly the covenant is subject to our interpretation, but we too are subject to it as the agreed-upon reference point for all our dealings. That means we are also accountable to each other. A covenant is something like the large stone that shepherds in the time of Jacob placed on the mouth of a well to ensure that none of them could water his sheep until all were present to lift it.

The radical subjectivity that masquerades these days as "spirituality," however, is an entirely different sort of stone, a crystal amulet that each of us wears about his own neck for his own reasons. It means, as the wearers will readily tell you, anything you want it to mean. So if you say, "Please pass the salt," I can say to you, "When you say pass the salt, *I feel as though* you're getting ready to rub salt in my wounds." An appeal to the everyday meaning of "salt" or to the well-established custom of asking one's dining companions to pass food around the table is completely out of bounds; it amounts to "making a judgment" on the value of another person's "feelings," which should never be judged and most certainly can never be wrong. Basically, we're dealing with a form of fundamentalism, except that the fundamental value here is not the inerrant letter of Scripture, but the inerrant flutter of gut sensation. Neither approach has much use for history, analysis, or correction. At bottom, what it says is that no such thing as common life exists. Given what we have already said about anger as a thing in the head, we can readily see the potential for anger in churches organized as loose confederations of subjective sovereign states.

Of course, trivializing the gospel will involve trivializing our language; that is certainly the case in much of the church. A single church convention would suffice to make Orwell feel he had died and gone to hell. The communication in much of church life amounts to a vocabulary of code, a jargon for initiates, where no one says exactly what he means. Of course, the ancient church also spoke in code, as in the book of Revelation, in order to elude detection by the authorities. We seem to have continued the habit in order to elude detection by one another. We disguise ourselves in cues and cant, all because no one wants to say words like *money, sex,* or *tripe.* How many times someone has said to me, "I'm so glad we're not like the Catholics—all they talk about is money!" I have sometimes replied, "That's what we're usually talking about, too, except we say things like 'discernment' and 'models of ministry.'" I suppose that I sound very judgmental.

T. S. Eliot once wrote that the problem with most devotional poetry is that poets write what they think they're supposed to feel instead of what they really feel. The same may be true of the day-to-day discourse of the church—and the duplicity may actually begin with our prayers. We tend not to talk about money, sex, or tripe there either. More than once I have said in a sermon that if there is anything we enjoy for which we cannot give heartfelt thanks, it means that we are either heretics or thieves. We must either change our theology or relinquish our delights. The kingdom of God has not come until we are capable of thanking every person of the Holy Trinity for the incomparable glory of a buck naked behind. Nor will Christians be capable of speaking honestly with each other unless they first learn to speak honestly with their God. I suspect that a part of that honesty may have to do with acknowledging how truly angry some of us are—at one another, at God, and at the frustration of being called to believe that impossible things are possible.

⌒

Some of the sickness of the church may derive from the incomplete digestion of power within a body that counts "powers and principalities" among the works of darkness. If someone were to ask, "In twenty-five words or less, what is the church all about?" we could do worse than to say, "It is an attempt to build a human organization in defiance of those very principles on which most human organizations are built." Jesus defines the paradox of that enterprise when he says, "You know that among the Gentiles those whom they recognize as their rulers lord it over them, and their great ones are tyrants over them. But it is not so among you; but whoever wishes to become great among you must be your servant, and whoever wishes to be first among you must be slave of all." That is a provocative vision, and whenever I'm tempted to grow discouraged or cynical about the church, I try to remember the unique thing we're attempting to do. The peevish customer's question of "Who's in charge here?" has no simple answer in the church.

Unfortunately, the same tendencies toward cant that inform the church's discussions of money also inform its discussions of power. "Why, God is in charge. Who else?" Usually the person who says that. You will even hear people in the church say that the goal of the gospel is to "eliminate hierarchy," though Jesus did not say that no one should lead, but rather that the one who leads should serve. He seems to be describing the transformation of hierarchy more than its abolition. Of course, there is more to our cant than the oversimplification of his ideas. Have you ever noticed how those who inveigh against hierarchy are almost always intelligent, educated, articulate—able to spell *hierarchy* without looking it up—in short, reasonably confident that in the absence of any hierarchy they'll be in charge? Samuel Johnson said something similar: "How is it that we hear the loudest yelps for liberty from the drivers of Negroes?" So-called hierarchy is sometimes the only protection that people on the margins have against the self-serving agendas of their self-styled betters. As more and more congregations become unable to make their budgets, and as the Monday-through-Saturday lives of their members become busier, many churches develop significant power vacuums. Sometimes those most eager to fill the vacuums are those with dangerous vacuums within themselves. Sometimes the blind not only lead the blind; they lead the sighted too.

At the risk of making too easy a generalization, we might say that churches have two kinds of members. The first type consists of people who look to the church to sanctify their busy lives. The second type consists of people who look to the church to give them a life. Both types are necessary, both have a contribution to make, and both have definite limitations. But beyond any shadow of a doubt, power tends to flow toward the second type. Sometimes this is for the good of the church, sometimes it is for the good of the individual, but often it is to the detriment of both.

Churches provide a powerful distraction from the very ailments that, one would hope, churches exist to cure. In some ways, they can work like the bars and lodges of the last century's television sitcoms: They're where you go after supper to hide from the people you can't seem to figure out, much less love and serve. Optimistically, we might hope that the macho men doing dishes at the big prayer breakfast will perform the same office for their domestic partners, as will the women hugging fifty people to the point of hyperventilation at the spiritual "retreat," but one tends to fear that certain forms of charity neither begin nor end at home.

I suppose someone could counter by saying, "Isn't this also part of the gospel?" Remember how Jesus says, with his mother and brothers standing outside, that his true family was there beside him in the form of "anyone who hears the will of God and does it." Sometimes I wish he had said, "And who is my mother? Obviously she is that careworn woman over there with the varicose veins." I only wish it sometimes (and in St. John's account of the passion, I more or less get my wish), because I sense that Christian families are better off than they might otherwise have been had Jesus spoken with less ambivalence in their favor. We have mentioned elsewhere the dangers that come of making our loved ones into absolutes. By leaving home, and by defining discipleship as a willingness to "hate" one's home, Jesus left the home in peace. At its best, the celibacy enjoined on Roman Catholic clergy is a continuation of that legacy. We know what it is at its worst.

That said, I wonder if all the recent "family values" rhetoric is only superficially (albeit viciously) an attack on gays, lesbians, and single parents—if essentially it is a reaction against an idea rooted in the New Testament and achieving full flower in the medieval Church, that if you appreciate your parents or get along with your kids or happen to enjoy spending time with your spouse, you are probably not as good a Christian as a celibate "religious," and you are definitely not a saint. In other words, the rhetoric may amount to the catastrophic reaction of the Reformation still emanating through theological space, like energy from the big bang.

⌒

If people are so easily distracted from the things that make them sick, can it mean that some of them don't really wish to get well? I think it does, and I think we dig deeper into the problem when we pose that question. Side by side with the healing stories of the gospel, we have in certain strains of Christianity what amounts to a mystique of sickness, of pain and filth and debilitation as the hallmarks of genuine holiness. In that connection a close friend of mine whose wife was recently diagnosed with cancer sent me the following riddle:

There are a number of explanations that Christian people give for disease, among them the following: Sickness is God's punishment for our sins. Sickness is God's testing. Sickness is God's will. Sickness is a way to make us stronger. Sickness is all in the mind. What do all of these explanations have in common? Jesus never said a single one of them.

And he added: "I think that any one of them would have made Jesus angry. I think there's more authentic Christianity in the most secular medical practice, or for that matter in the most lunatic faith healer, than in three-quarters of what passes for 'pastoral consolation' in the mainstream church." I can agree with that answer, but I'm not sure it suffices to explain our attitudes toward sickness and our sometimes perverse unwillingness to seek mental and social health. I begin to wonder how neatly we can separate the sickness of the church from the purity of the gospel, placing the malady on one side and the antidote on the other. We have perhaps been sick for too long to pretend that the disease is not a part of us.

After all, the gospel is not only about blind men seeing and lame men walking; it is also about one man suffering and dying for the sins of humankind. It is impossible for Christians, perhaps impossible for anyone in the entire Western world, not to invest his own anguish with a certain romanticism in the light of that narrative. This is not necessarily a bad thing: Romanticism is a form of meaning. But to find meaning in suffering can also amount to finding cause for suspicion in health. Even the notion of a healthy environment seems to give some of us doctrinal jitters; on some level, it's more reassuring to believe that the whole world's falling apart than that human beings can, in accordance with the laws of God's creation, restore it to wholeness.

In view of this ambivalence, it may be difficult to relocate the theme of healing that lies at the very core of the gospel proclamation without also locating the original anger of Christ. You may recall that painting by Orozco in which Christ chops down his own cross. You may recall that there is only one time in all four Gospels where he is explicitly said to be angry: He is about to heal a man with a withered hand, and the religious authorities want him to wait until the Sabbath is over. He won't.

It ain't me, babe.

Bob Dylan

PASSION PLAYS

Christians in the past and some in the present have been scandalized to learn that the story of their Lord's death and resurrection appears to be but one form—and a relatively late form at that—of an archetype found in other myths. Osiris, Dionysus, Tammuz all die and rise and are even mourned by faithful women, just as Jesus is. I should think that the pattern might be as reassuring as it is troublesome: One might infer from the mythological echoes that the Christian story speaks to some primal need within the human psyche, or even—if one chooses to go so far—that Christ fulfills the archetypes of the collective unconscious no less than he is said to fulfill the messianic prophecies of Isaiah. Still, the importance as well as the historical uniqueness that Christians attach to their story is bound to make them a bit jealous of any comparisons. This is not necessarily a bad thing. It is only a bad thing when it moves from passion to prejudice. Believers are lovers, and lovers are not known to be universalists. Making love to every woman in the world is generally the fantasy of men who spend most nights making love to themselves.

It is interesting, though, that the jealousy with which many Christians guard their story against comparison does not prevent them from repeating that story, over and over, with any person willing to be cast in the role of scapegoat. Often the person is a member of the clergy. And often the drama that results is, like the Passion Narrative on which it is based, a tale about anger and resentment turned on a former object of adoration. Sometimes too it is the story of the god-man's own anger, or at least his anguish, at being used in this way.

In any case, it is impossible to talk about anger in the church without talking about the clergyman or -woman as an object of anger and frequently as the star of a passion play. Of course, this pattern is no more unique to the Christian church than a dying god is unique to the Christian story. Get a conversation going among a hillside's worth of crucified ministers, and you hear a story that resonates for any number of their secular counterparts, be they CEOs or celebrities, first lieutenants or second wives. After playing the leading role in one or two of these scenarios, you begin to know the pattern. It looks something like this:

Your predecessor is damned. You hear story after story about what an incompetent or uncaring jerk he was. True or not, the stories can be seductively reassuring. One wants to believe he *was* a jerk. Nevertheless, there are few instances where the commandment to love one's neighbor as oneself has a more practical application than in loving one's predecessor as one-self. That is because, at least as far as these stories of woe are concerned, your neighbor *is* yourself. The story in which your flatterers rehearse your predecessor's faults may well be the story in which they prophesy your doom. The year-king who drinks a toast from the skull of the queen's last husband is not necessarily drinking to his own health. The wisest kings seem to have understood this. Claudius punished the assassins of Caligula, though he might very well have rewarded them and been praised for doing so. The message was obvious. But it's hard for most of us to send such a message with so many messages of congratulation coming our way. Granted, these messages are not necessarily insincere. But it is good to remember that one is not necessarily better than the person one succeeds, just younger to the job.

You get more credit than you deserve, or at least more than you need. More than once, Jesus says to someone he has healed: "Go your way. Your faith has saved you." Your faith, not my power. I suppose one can say that he's being humble. I would also say that he's being consistent with his own advice: "Be ye wise as serpents, and harmless as doves." Wisdom is the ability to see the hollowness of most acclaim and the injustice of much disfavor. Sometimes I wonder if this is all that wisdom means.

You find yourself doing more and more of what others might do for themselves. We protest ever so demurely that we are not the lords of rain and thunder, but we still run around watering everyone's garden and washing their cars. Not the lords of rain and thunder, but we aim to please. Where Jesus would have said, "Take up your bed and walk," we offer to carry the bed, or at least to change the sheets. Of course, with every inch we add to our haloes we must stretch our arms higher to keep them bright. The higher the stretch, the greater the strain—the shorter the fuse.

So far, we have been sketching this familiar scenario from the point of view of the scapegoat; we can look at it from the other side, too. Most of us have played it both ways. The crowd arrayed against the scapegoat invariably contains people who are extremely angry, and of these at least some qualify as former followers of the victim. An analysis of their anger comes close to naming the themes of the play.

These people are angry, first of all, because they have invested faith in someone who seems to have let them down. Their faith may have been misplaced, or the object of their faith misunderstood, but in either case the outraged disciple experiences that terribly annihilating sense of adoration turning into humiliation. Judas betrays Jesus with a kiss, but to understand that kiss we have to imagine all the times that he kissed Jesus before that, plus all the times that he received Jesus' kiss on his cheek, perhaps with more excitement than he wanted to feel, perhaps with more acquiescence than he wanted to show. Judas betrays Jesus because, I am convinced, he believes that Jesus has betrayed him, and underneath that sense of betrayal is the gnawing self-accusation that Judas has been betraying himself. The latter thought is the more insufferable. True loyalty is found most often among those who never entirely surrender to those they love, or who only surrender gradually. The disciple Thomas, the last to believe that Jesus had risen from the dead, would also have been the last, not counting Mary Magdalene, to give him up to the cross. "Where your treasure is, there will your heart be also," said Jesus, but when your heart is broken, your tendency is to throw all of your treasure away.

There is a still darker side to the emotional investment we make in our leaders and our heroes. Faith is equivocal; were it absolutely convinced, it would not be faith. So part of us believes that "This is indeed the savior, who has come into the world"—into our pulpit, into our business, into our bed. "He's so wonderful. He's perfect. He's what I was waiting for." But the other part believes from the start that he's going to screw up, that he's not going to deliver on the promises he makes, or on the promises that we hasten to infer from his arrival in our lives. What is more, this other part may want him to screw up. In this case, the adoration we invest in the hero amounts to the prepaid justification for nailing him to the wall when he fails to come through with the goods. "I trusted you completely." It's a lie, of course. But I told myself that lie, and I told it to you, wanting both of us to believe it at the time, but also knowing I could unmask your frailty and unleash my wrath when the ugly truth inevitably came out. I have a right to slap your face; I paid for it when I kissed your hand. And to be honest (if one can be so honest), I knew what I was buying at the time of purchase.

There is a verse in the Gospel of John that never shows up in the three-year cycle of the lectionary used now in most mainline churches; it's a pity that it doesn't. It goes like this (quoted from the King James Version in which it made its first impression upon me): "But Jesus did not commit himself unto them, because he knew all men, and needed not that any should testify of man: for he knew what was in man." To know the same thing ourselves is a step toward recognizing our own part with those who shout, "Crucify him, crucify him."

It may not be a step toward preventing our own crucifixions, however. If Jesus truly understood the dark dynamics of hero worship, the passions that led to the passion, and could not avoid his fate, our prospects are not necessarily brighter. Still, we can try, as Jesus did, to avoid drinking the bitter cup for as long as we can. As an old priest once told me when I was still a young man: "You can only be crucified once. So you had better make sure it's necessary whenever you're ready to think it is."

One way to pass the cup is to pass on the extra helpings of adoration. "Why do you call me good?" Jesus says to the rich young ruler who addresses him. "No one is good, save God." The saying has wreaked some havoc with theologians of the Trinity, but it's one of the best I know for the homelier theology of getting through an eight-to-five day in one piece. We have a parallel in the life of the Buddha, who at an assembly of his monks invited them to name any faults, "whether in word or in deed," that they had observed in their teacher. One of his favorite pupils responded with fulsome praise.

> "Such faith have I, Lord, that I think there never was nor will be nor is now any other greater or wiser than the Blessed One."
> The Buddha replied: "Of course, Sariputta, you have known all the Buddhas of the past."
> "No, Lord."
> "Well then, you know those of the future?"
> "No, Lord."
> "Then at least you know me and have penetrated my mind thoroughly?"
> "Not even that, Lord."
> "Then why, Sariputta, are your words so grand and bold?"

Another way to preempt these passion plays is by refusing

to wear our conscience on our sleeves. Quite often the nasty drama I've described begins with some attempt to manipulate the scapegoat's conscience, often by insinuating that "You don't really care." The insinuation is assumed to be so devastating because the scapegoat is constantly telegraphing the message that he does care, really care, so very much. In the Sermon on the Mount, Jesus says, "When you give alms, sound no trumpet before you." In contrast to his command, we sometimes discover that the heroic caregiver is investing at least as much energy in the appearance of compassion as in being compassionate. I can think of few goals I would rather attain at this point in my life than that of being kinder than I seem, of seeming less compassionate than I am. Giving alms in secret is not only a prescription for preventing a big head, it can also be a way of avoiding the big part in *The Greatest Story Ever Told,* which is not all that great when you're playing the lead.

⌒

Finally, one can avoid the role by permitting herself to be angry and by permitting her anger to show. Jesus told his followers to hide their acts of piety; he did not tell them to hide their emotions. In fact, we sometimes hide our emotions for the same reason that we make a show of our piety: out of a wish to seem more perfect than we are. How many times do we hear people say that they refuse to raise their voices, not for fear of intimidating their opponents, but out of a refusal "to sink to their level"? A rather smug form of equanimity, in my view. It occurs to me that if Jesus were to "sink to our level" once again and repeat his act of cleansing the temple, he would run a serious risk of knocking over certain plaster images of himself. I'm not sure he would regard that as a great cause for worry. In any case, though we do well to curb our anger, it can serve us in curbing the misplaced adulation of our peers, which must always turn to anger in the end.

⌒

Most Christian communities gather for worship on Sunday in observation of Easter, the day Christ rose from the dead. I think that in many ways, however, the Sundays of the church more closely resemble the first Sunday of Passion Week, so-called Palm Sunday, when people sing their hosannas and wave their palms and get their voices in good shape to cry out for somebody's blood by the end of the week. Even the appearance of a typical church service looks more to me like Palm Sunday than Easter. On Palm Sunday, we know the principal actors. The leading man is on the donkey. The soldiers are on guard. The crowd is on edge. The choir is on the same page. Everybody is *on*.

Easter is quieter, more mysterious. The leading man appears for a bite to eat, then vanishes. He meets travelers on the road; he calls to fishermen at the end of their shift. He does not even seem to be performing the role of a leading man. He allows himself to be examined, but not embraced. He doesn't stay put, not in the tomb, not in anyone's definition or devotion. He moves. He "goes on before you."

I'm not sure the church has gotten to Easter yet. I'm not sure it has gotten to Easter in its forms of ministry, and in its structures of hierarchy. I'm not sure it has gotten to Easter in the consciousness of its individual members. I think that in some ways we're still stuck in Passion Week, that beautiful but incomplete story, as in the groove of a scratched record, repeating the words, distorting the song. And that may be one of the reasons for our anger. We're still thinking of our faith as a drama, with all of a drama's histrionics. We're still thinking of Jesus as a conventional hero, and of our ministers as surrogate Christs, and of ourselves as inferior Christs.

And that brings us as close as I know how to come to the crux of the matter. One of the perennial questions of practical Christian theology is whether to think of Jesus as our exemplar or our savior. Undoubtedly, we must think of him in both ways, though rationality has always been biased toward the first. Thomas Jefferson, for example, was convinced that if we could just get rid of the savior part, the blood-sacrifice part, the atonement-for-sins part, the St. Paul part, we would be left with the words and example of a sublime moral teacher, and with a healthier form of religion. I can find this an appealing point of view.

What I also find, however, is that many of the forms of religious neuroticism *also* tend to the rational side; that is, they favor the theology of Christ as exemplar instead of Christ as savior. The only difference is that instead of seeing Jesus as the exemplar of moral conduct, as Jefferson did, they see him as the exemplar of redemptive suffering, of undeserved persecution, of the nails and the thorns, the spittle and the blood —in other words, of martyrdom. This view also has its appeal. Throw it out, and we must throw out Dietrich Bonhoeffer and Martin Luther King Jr., not to mention what Jesus himself said about taking up one's cross to follow him.

But I'm writing here about our obsessive need to make martyrs of ourselves and of those we idealize. I'm writing about the anger that arises with and in response to those obsessions. And in that regard, I find myself wanting to recover the good news of Christ as savior, not so much in the evangelical sense of "Christendom" as in the existential sense of my own crisis. It is a theology that reaches back to what we mistakenly call "the sacrifice of Isaac," who, as it turns out, did not need to be sacrificed after all. An emphasis on Christ as savior is a de-emphasis on the need to drive nails into our own flesh as a way of earning our salvation. It is a de-emphasis on the heroic, the masochistic, and even the tragic. It is a healthy de-emphasis, I think. The great church father Athanasius is supposed to have said that in Christ, "God became man that man might become divine." Without meaning to contradict Athanasius, I would say that God became human so that human beings might become human too. If even God would be a human being, why should we disdain our humanity? Why should we need to make holy wrecks of ourselves and heroic scapegoats of our sisters and brothers?

One does not have to be a Christian to have a Christ complex. The universal archetype of the dying and reviving god tells us that too. It may be, though, that a Christian has some advantage in overcoming the malady. More than the right to drink vodka, eat pork, or weep unashamedly during performances of Handel's *Messiah*, the privilege of being a Christian is that of being able to say, whether to the multitudes or to the mirror: "I am not Christ."

I do not, finally, want the mother to embrace the tormentor who let his dogs tear her son to pieces! She dare not forgive him! Let her forgive him for herself, if she wants to . . . but she has no right to forgive the suffering of her child. . . .

Fyodor Dostoevsky, *The Brothers Karamazov*

FORGIVENESS

Two days ago as I write, I heard this story from "the new South Africa": A white woman living in an affluent township had aroused the hostility of her neighbors by running a business that drew a number of black customers from other locations. One night a gang of white men set upon her, beat her, raped her, and carved the letter *K* for kaffir (Afrikaans for "nigger") into the flesh of her breast.

And thus begins the sequence of hideous associations that such stories always effect in me. As I scrape old paint from the clapboards on my house, I recall a passage from Susan Brownmiller's book *Against Our Will* about another gang of men who raped a woman in her house while her husband, recovering in bed from brain surgery, watched and wept in utter helplessness. I think of it again, getting into my own bed at night. Making a pot of coffee in the postnightmare dawn, my mind is thrown back to a passage I remember from the writings of Ho Chi Minh, about a French army officer who filled a Vietnamese woman's genitals with liquid rubber because she had refused to give herself to his dog. It was a good twenty-five years ago that I read this, and probably a good half-century since it happened, yet it remains vivid in my memory. And it hadn't happened to me. What if it had?

Beyond the anger and outrage one feels over the crimes themselves, there is for the Christian, or at least for this Christian, an additional source of anger and outrage: The mere suggestion that any person who has suffered such a thing ought to *forgive* the persons who inflicted it. When the Mongols conquered Afghanistan in the thirteenth century, they dug up and destroyed an elaborate tiled system of underground irrigation channels that had been centuries in the making. Pastoral nomads, the Mongols thought of greener pastures in terms of sparser populations. Imagine being forced at sword point to do that demolition, too terrified to resist the taskmaster, yet feeling the horror of your own parched throat at the aridness of the coming centuries. One is tempted to give thanks that the conquered were not Christians. Had they been, should they have prayed, "Father, forgive them, for they know not what they do"? They *did* know what they were doing. So did the men who carved the letter *K* into their neighbor's breast. It took three slices to carve it, three different angles of incision, and pity did not catch up with their hands after the first, or after the second, or after the third. And now, is the woman compelled to forgive them, in addition to whatever else she was forced to do?

Before grappling with an awful question like this, one needs to sift out every consideration that is not awful. To dismiss all forgiveness in the name of the most unforgivable crimes is in some ways to recapitulate the thoughts of those who committed them. You can be almost certain that at least one man in that South African gang recalled some atrocity from the war against apartheid and summoned it up as a way of steeling his nerves, like one of those anti-Semitic fables about Jewish landlords evicting helpless children into the streets that the Nazis used to justify the deportations and death camps. If the glory of human intelligence consists of being able to make associations, metaphors, and symbols, then the perversion of that intelligence consists of false associations and spurious analogies—of vengeance that is not even proper vengeance. The same goes for moral indignation. Should I forbear to forgive someone for stealing my car because at some point in history one people stole another people's freedom? In the deceiving stream of consciousness that flows between the news on the radio and the incivility of the highway, between history and a hangnail, we make these false associations. They leap in sparks of anger from one thought to another, and they make us too much like the things we hate.

So much for qualification. Why are we asked to forgive? How can we even begin to forgive in a world like this one? The questions remain. And anger stands in faithful attendance upon them, if for no other reason than that, for many of us, the definition of forgiveness has something to do with the cessation of anger.

⌒

"To err is human, to forgive divine." So wrote Alexander Pope, coining a cliché and at the same time telling us how not to make a cliché out of forgiveness. To say that forgiveness is "divine" might suggest that human forgiveness can amount to an act of hubris. It is certainly so when we presume to forgive someone for causing someone else to suffer. This amounts to taking a poor man to dinner and then leaving the check for the owner of the restaurant. But forgiveness can be hubris even when we pretend to forgive someone who has wronged us, whom we are simply and truly unable to forgive.

If forgiveness is divine, then it is not an act of willpower but an operation of grace. It can only be as natural as the offense that is to be forgiven. In other words, in certain extreme cases it must be either supernatural or impossible. When in my work as a pastor wounded people come to me with the confession that they cannot forgive, I do not tell them to "try harder" or to "move forward." I ask them if they are able to pray for the grace to forgive. And if not, if they are at least willing to pray for the grace to say that other prayer. And if even that is too difficult, if they are willing to express their refusal to God. At that very basic level, but only at that level, am I able to assert that free will exists.

But before asking God for the grace to forgive, a person might think to give thanks for the grace to be angry. Anger in the face of injury is a mechanism for survival, no less than the clotting of our blood. Forgiveness is the scar, and it comes later. Anger comes first, and like all created things, it is good.

If we choose to look at this as a theological problem, it exists for Christians partly because most of us hold a heretical doctrine of the Trinity. According to orthodox Christianity, the persons of the Trinity are coequal and coeternal, but most of us have trouble holding to that idea. In our misunderstanding, the persons exist in a hierarchy, with God the Father at the top, and the Son under him, and the Holy Spirit somewhere that we can never seem to locate. In terms of the *operations* of these persons, however, almost the exact reverse is true: The whims we glibly interpret as "movements of the Spirit" are uppermost, the teachings and devotions we associate with the heroic Son come next, and the creation we associate exclusively with God the Father (also heretically, because creation is supposed to be the work of the one God in all three persons) we hold dead last. So I attach the greatest importance to divining the best date (cutest clothing, nicest cleric, and so on) for my child's baptism, the next greatest importance to the baptismal service itself, and virtually no importance at all to the water that I waste and pollute throughout the party that comes afterward. When Junior makes his first Communion, I'll buy him a Jet Ski.

Likewise, though we are fully prepared to grant that to forgive is divine, we are a bit reluctant to grant that to rage—as opposed to despairing or destroying oneself—can also be divine. Our reluctance is nothing else but a failure in faith, a devaluing of creation that amounts to a demotion of the Creator. Refusing to think of ourselves as garbage—is that not a gift of grace as well? In the face of extreme degradation, most of us cannot maintain our sense of self through reason alone, any more than we can manage excruciating pain through self-hypnosis, or extraordinary courage, or the "right attitude"; we require adrenaline, we require hormones, we require rage.

And if there is such a thing as a higher gift, a better way, we have no right to ask for it if we are not humble enough to give thanks for the lesser gift already received.

⌒

One of the things that makes forgiveness difficult for Christians is how they hear the commandment to forgive. For one thing, it makes them feel like hostages, not only of their oppressors but of Christ himself. "Forgive us our trespasses *as* we forgive those who trespass against us." Praying that prayer can feel like signing the ransom note that describes the dreadful consequences of not paying your own ransom.

The commandment to forgive also makes us feel as though we occupy a less favored place in God's regard than the person who wronged us. Certainly some of the parables of Jesus can contribute to that impression: God loves the thief, the slacker, the prodigal son, and show-up-late worker. On the other hand, the faithful elder son, the hospitable elder sister, the Pharisee who cannot lay claim to anything quite so glamorous as extorting money from his neighbors or prostituting himself with donkey drivers—God has little regard for them except for saying that they should be better sports. So the kingdom of God is like unto a third-grade class in which a bully with fine clothes and lunch money to spare rips my shirt and spits on my sandwich—and smirks in my face as the teacher says we are to shake hands and "make up" and *both* say we're sorry. At this point, the third grader may find that he is angrier with the teacher than with the bully.

There are, however, several things we may fail to recognize about the Teacher and his teaching. The first has to do with that troublesome conjunction in the petition from the Lord's Prayer: "Forgive us our trespasses *as* we forgive those who trespass against us." Certainly it means what it says. Other lines from the gospel support the sense that God's forgiveness of our trespasses is indeed conditional on our forgiveness of others. What we may not see so readily is the extent to which our failed attempts to do so are redeemed by the love of God. We may not recognize that even our tentative forgiveness is precious to God and might be a key to understanding God.

Jesus sometimes made use of a rabbinical formula that proceeds in this way: "If it is so in a little thing, how much more so in a greater thing." Perhaps the best-known example has to do with his teaching on prayer. "Is there anyone among you who, if your child asks for a fish, will give a snake instead of a fish? Or if the child asks for an egg, will give a scorpion? If you then, who are evil, know how to give good gifts to your children, how much more will the heavenly Father give the Holy Spirit to those who ask him!" *You who are evil*—at first we wince at the words. They almost seem not to belong in the mouth of Jesus. But they are among the most comfortable words in the gospel. The person who falters saying the Lord's Prayer, knowing that she cannot begin to forgive others as she herself would hope to be forgiven, might exclaim in anger: "I cannot do it, all right? So I guess I'm a bad person. No forgiveness for me. I am positively *evil!*" To which the voice of the gospel replies: "Yes, you are. And yet, even in your evil, don't you cut people slack? Don't you sometimes say, 'What I ought to do to that guy . . . What I could do to that guy . . .' and then refuse to do it? Don't you sometimes say, 'That's just my mother. That's the way she is. There's no point in castigating her.' So if you who are evil are capable of even that much forgiveness, if you can hold back the hand of retribution or the word of recrimination that far, how much more will a perfect God extend forgiveness to you?" The *as* that we find so intimidating may hold more encouragement than we think.

As for the parables and the infuriating impression they give us of God's infinite patience with "the other guy," his unfailing preference for rascals, and his unrelenting disappointment with us, here too we may be missing the point. A few points actually. The first and most obvious is that all of us have the right to identify with "the other guy." That we may feel a stronger connection to the elder brother than to the prodigal son, to Martha than to Mary, to the Pharisee than to the publican, is perhaps instructive but not definitive. We are always both characters in every pair, though we might not be both characters at the same time. As the situation varies, so does our role. The prodigal son, in the depths of his penury, was ready to eat swill; his elder brother, in his refusal to attend the homecoming feast, was ready to eat worms. He too was in misery; he too was in exile; he too was missed at home.

If we look closely at the stories in which we imagine ourselves vicariously rejected, what we also notice is the tone of affection—which in some cases is even a tone of complicity—between the "God" character and the one rebuked. "Martha, Martha, you are troubled about many things," Jesus says to the sister who, after all, was the one to invite him to dinner in the first place. Martha, not Mary, had reached out her hand in hospitality. Jesus does not criticize her overwrought hospitality until she herself confesses it to be a burden, and then he speaks to her in the tone of a peer. We read that her sister, Mary, sat at Jesus' feet, listening to his teaching, but Martha stands as it were at his elbow, hearing the gentle admonition of a friend.

That is the word that the landowner in the parable of the Laborers uses for those who complain about his standard of payment. He has paid those who worked only an hour the same as those who worked the entire day. But his address to the latter is "friend," if the latter can but hear it. He has paid him as he promised; he has merely pitied the latecomer, who would otherwise have had to find a night's lodging with only an hour's wage. In the same way, the father in the parable of the Prodigal Son says to the indignant elder brother, "Son, you are always with me, and everything that I have is yours." I take that to mean that little brother has already gotten his share and done with it as he chose. The father puts love above fairness, but he has not forgotten fairness. Nor has he forgotten his elder son, though the son probably thinks so. "You are always with me, and everything I have is yours." What is a night's homecoming party compared to that? In my imagined sequel to the story, the younger son comes home for about three months, mooches a little more money, and hits the road again. If he came back, the father would still receive him; that is what love does. Therefore—if we might indulge in some rabbinical rhetoric of our own—if the father so loves his younger son, who breaks his heart at every turn, how much more will he love the elder, who plugs along as faithfully as he can and lacks only a little merriment to be complete? He complains to his father, "You never gave me so much as a kid that I might make merry with my friends." You can bet that he never asked.

It would follow, then, that forgiveness is enjoined on us at least as much for our benefit as for the offender's. Just because we hear it as a statement of preference for our enemies, or as an attempt to make us even more abject than we already feel, does not mean that it is intended in that spirit. Forgiveness is not some second phase in our humiliation, whereby the persecutor's designs find fulfillment; it is the cauterization of our wounds.

Alexander the Great is supposed to have gone to the philosopher Diogenes, whom he greatly admired, with an offer to grant Diogenes any favor he might name. He found Diogenes sunbathing. "Ask for whatever you desire," said Alexander, "and I will grant it." Diogenes replied, "Stand out of the way of the sun." If I had any wish to Christianize the story, I would have Diogenes say, "I forgive you." But not only have I no wish to Christianize the story, I have no need—it is sufficiently Christian as it is. What Diogenes says to Alexander is that he refuses to have even a moment of sunshine obscured by the conqueror of the world. Forgiveness can amount to the same refusal. Forgiveness is both solidarity and separation: solidarity, in the sense that we admit our own lack of innocence, our complicity in the broad web of human injustice; separation, in the sense that we assert our willingness to cut away some of the strands.

The French have a saying, *Tout comprendre c'est tout pardonner:* "To understand all is to forgive all." Isaac Newton's formulas with the blueprints of Monticello thrown in for good measure do not come as close as that one sentence to expressing the spirit of rationalism, both its enlightening brilliance and its sulphurous darkness. On the one hand, it calls us to use our intellects as keys to compassion. Could a Christian take exception to that? Would Jesus himself have taken exception to that? Look for the causes of the crime, and you will see the criminal more clearly. You will likely see that he is not a different sort of person from you, only a person shaped by different circumstances. "There but for the grace of God go I." Sometimes grace is nothing more than the ability to say that and mean it.

Nevertheless, this approach can in some cases be more absurdly preferential than the most radical reversals of the gospel narratives. In this school the bullies not only teach their victims cruel and demeaning lessons; they assign them homework besides. "For tomorrow I want you to write a theme titled, 'Now I Understand Everything.' Make sure it's neat, written on only one side of the paper—to symbolize the absolute one-sidedness of this exercise—and remember to put your name on it." So as the blinded survivors grope among the smoking rubble for a few grains of barley to eat, a few severed limbs to bury in memory of their butchered children, they must also rummage among the details of Genghis Khan's biography to discover what made him such a nasty boy.

You may find this a bit exaggerated; tell me, then, what you find in your own heart that contradicts it. The cruelest barb of the worst injuries we receive is the sense of obligation —which can amount to a neurotic obsession—that we must "understand" our oppressor in order at last to be free of him. In other words, we can never feel right again until we can admit that he was actually never wrong—or wrong only because wronged himself—and not merely admit it, but comprehend it and believe it. Intellectually, of course, we know that understanding is not always the same thing as forgiveness, but they become almost indistinguishable whenever forgiveness is seen as an operation of intelligence alone. In that case, the *K* for kaffir carved in the woman's breast becomes the first letter of a new alphabet, an obscure language with an impossibly complicated etymology, which she must study for the rest of her life. I see her standing at the blackboard in her torn and bloody clothing. I see the smugly grinning schoolmaster of humanistic rationalism tapping the board with a pointer. And I see Christ, in one of his familiar poses, as he stands outside the door and knocks. All at once the woman erases everything on the blackboard in one furious, sweeping motion, shatters the chalk on the floor, and walks out of the schoolroom. "Truancy!" cries the teacher. "Forgiveness," says the One at the door.

The Gospels draw an explicit connection between forgiveness and resurrection. When the risen Christ appears to the faithful women, he asks that they inform his disciples "and Peter," thus affirming that in spite of Peter's denial that he even knew Jesus, Jesus continues to know Peter. In one of John's accounts of the resurrection, Jesus actually gives Peter three consecutive opportunities to say that he loves him, as if to undo each of the three times he denied knowing who he was.

By associating forgiveness and resurrection, the writers of the Gospels imply at least two things. First, they note the supernatural quality of forgiveness; it does not come naturally any more than a dead man rises naturally. Second, they note that forgiveness belongs to the realm of faith; forgiveness affirms that some things cannot be seen, cannot be known. Comprehending everything can never lead to pardoning everything, for the simple reason that we will never comprehend everything. To forgive requires faith no less than to believe that "the strife is o'er, the battle done. The victory of life is won."

In an earlier chapter, I also drew a connection between resurrection and anger, suggesting that in some ways the resurrection of Christ can be seen as the most sublime expression of the wrath of God. I based that understanding on our experience of anger as an emotion that enables frustration to give way to action. Of course, our ultimate frustration is with death.

In the same way, we might wonder if there is some connection between anger and forgiveness. We have already noted that anger often precedes forgiveness and ought not to be despised in the name of forgiveness. Now we come to a new question: Is forgiveness really the cessation of anger, or its transformation? Can anger not only give way to love but *become* love as the ultimate expression of our desire to break the bonds that hold us? The injuries we suffer almost always involve constraint and diminishment; they confine us in a prison of fear, of hatred, of self-loathing. Anger arises from the desire to break free of that confinement. Anger shows itself as an impulse to knock down walls. As forgiveness, it walks through walls—as the resurrected Christ is also said to have done.

It is tempting to close there. But it is said in addition that although Christ was no longer subject to the grave, nor apparently to the laws of the physical universe, he still had the holes in his hands and his side. Neither his resurrection nor his forgiveness required that he hide the evidence of his hurt. Quite the contrary. We have no idea how it will be in heaven. But he has shown us something important about how it is on earth.

But I say to you that listen, Love your enemies, do good to those who hate you, bless those who curse you, pray for those who abuse you.

Jesus, Sermon on the Mount

LOVING
THE ENEMY

I go trout fishing with a friend who, whenever we clean our catch, likes to find out what the fish have been eating. I watch as he slits open a stomach to release a tangled black and brown lump of gnats and hellgrammites, centipedes, worms, and now and again some creeping thing that neither of us has seen before. Cut to the pit of Christian meekness, and a similar bait-ball spills onto the ground: a matted hatch of passive-aggressive insults dutifully swallowed by the mouthful, filtered like plankton through the teeth of forced smiles —not to forget the words of angry protest that never made it past the throat, now half-digested lumps indistinguishable from lies.

"Love your enemies"—isn't that what Christ commands, and isn't that why we have such a mess in our stomachs? We may be abashed to realize that we have swallowed so many creeping things not in an effort to follow the Sermon on the Mount but in the belief that we could somehow avoid it altogether. That is, we could avoid having to love our enemies simply by refusing to make any. No need to be so magnanimous if you can just manage to be nice.

A careful reading of the gospel exposes the folly of that approach. No one could follow even a third of the instructions put forth there without making an enemy. Loving self-sacrifice set loose in a world of "enlightened self-interest" is bound to cause trouble, not least of all in our own households and in our own houses of worship. Jesus explicitly predicts the first:

> Do not think that I have come to bring peace to the earth; I have not come to bring peace, but a sword. For I have come to set a man against his father, and a daughter against her mother, and a daughter-in-law against her mother-in-law; and one's foes will be members of one's own household.

He illustrates the second throughout his own short life.

Taken separately, Jesus' prediction of familial strife and his commandment to love our enemies are among the most troubling sentences in the gospel; taken together, they reassure us in a bittersweet way. That is, we come to realize that we are enjoined to love the very people we would most hope to love anyway. We hear "love your enemies," and we automatically conjure up images of mutant cannibal marauders on chopped Harley-Davidsons. More often, the commandment means love your mother-in-law, who in spite of any resemblance she may bear to the marauders is at least family. Nevertheless, as Jesus pointedly reminds us, family is often the foe.

The first logical step toward loving an enemy is admitting that you have one. Like the first logical step toward forgiveness—that of acknowledging that you have something to forgive, that you have been wronged—this step comes as something of a liberation. "You will know the truth, and the truth will make you free." If the word *enemy* seems too grotesque, then the liberation consists of putting your hostile thoughts into some kind of perspective. Lillian is not your "enemy"; she's just a nosy pain in the neck who sits at the computer next to yours. On the other hand, if the name fits, the liberation comes from saying something true to oneself—possibly as a prelude to saying something true to the enemy. In either case, the liberation of naming the enemy can also be a partial liberation from anger. That is because anger itself has helped liberate us from our denial. Spent in a worthy cause, anger becomes less necessary.

The act of naming will certainly make us hesitate. The word *enemy* is so strident, so devoid of the irony that we postmoderns take as a form of spiritual consolation. *Enemy* is a suspicious word to about the same extent, and for some of the same reasons, that *friend* has become such a debased word. It makes sense that in a society where half the people we know count as "friends," no one we know should ever count as an enemy. Aristotle may have been too doctrinaire when he said, "He who has friends has no friend," but he may have been closer to the truth than many people ever come to friendship. Perhaps he ought to have said, "He who has no enemy probably has no friend either."

For a religious person, naming the enemy may come about as a result of praying on the enemy's behalf. This may well be one of the reasons Jesus enjoins the practice on his followers. Praying for an enemy *as* an enemy amounts to an admission, to oneself no less than to God, that one is seriously at odds with another human being. Having confronted the truth before God, one is in a better position to confront it with the enemy.

Of course, it would be sweet to think that a confrontation of this kind always leads to dialogue, resolution, closure. The truth is that where people have reduced the social intercourse of human beings to the cant phrases of "dialogue," "resolution," and "closure," confrontation will in all likelihood lead to no such thing. Telling someone he is my enemy is more likely to elicit amusement, a pretense of incredulity, a supercilious show of concern. "I'm sorry that you feel that way. I'm sorry that you have this problem."

The person who tries to call antagonism by its proper name is likely to be treated as a spoilsport. This is progress, however. Spoilsports do just as they're called: They spoil the sport; they wreck the game. The wicked fun of many forms of adult harassment rests upon the pretense that "everything's cool here," that "we're all friends in this place," that "we all want the same thing and are all working toward the same goal." The harasser's implied challenge says, Would you dare destroy these illusions? Would you dare call my actions by name? Would you dare risk so heinous a charge as that of lacking a sense of humor? You cannot begin to love an enemy without answering each of the questions above with an emphatic "I would."

In some cases, though, naming the enemy amounts to making him realize a situation of which he himself was only vaguely aware. This is especially common where the injured party has been trying hard to comport herself with Christian gentleness. There are people who simply cannot resist testing that sort of demeanor, especially if they sense that different energies lie underneath it. In the same way that certain people are sexually aroused by rubbing up against a vow of celibacy, others are stimulated by pricking a code of kindness. While this can be deliberately cruel, it is more often the result of impulses that are probably best understood by studying the behaviors of toddlers and certain animals—or better yet, of toddlers *with* certain animals. I'm not sure that it's pure viciousness that pulls the kitty's tail, or that prompts the kitty herself to toy with the mouse; it's that mixture of curiosity and boredom that finds expression in all the lesser forms of torment. "What will it do if I do this?"

Sometimes it will bite. And of course the Christian who bites will often feel like a great failure, just as the person who intentionally provokes the bite may feel as though he has unmasked some great sham he always suspected was there. This dynamic is also a game, one that pits mock sanctity against smug mockery, with nothing gained for either side. When the prisoner under interrogation is finally made to cry out in pain, what has he proved or his tormentor disproved but the respective humanity of each? Anyone who deliberately sets about to prove that I'm only human can in no way disprove that I am a Christian.

Only I can do that. And I am most likely to do so when naming my enemy succeeds in disarming him—that is, when I seem on the verge of a real breakthrough in our relations. In that event I may find it difficult to disarm myself. Loaded for bear, we sometimes cannot resist discharging our weapon, even when the bear turns out to be dead or a cub. The most flagrant violation of the commandment to love our enemy may be a willingness to forgive him every trespass but that of repentance. We would almost do better to hate our enemies forever than to love them only to the point where they respond to our love.

⌇⌇

Once we have named our enemy in prayer and even to the enemy's own face, what then? If honesty does not effect peace, then it can lead only to war. And although an open declaration may be preferable to the covert raids of daily hostility, it does make the Sermon on the Mount seem even more lofty and unattainable. How exactly does one pray for an enemy who is not instantly disarmed by being named as one?

We know the obvious answers. We pray to be protected from the enemy. We pray for the enemy's change of heart. Barring that, we pray for the enemy's defeat. In the fullest possession of ourselves, we pray not to forget that we too are imperfect and need to remember the values that transcend our own need to win.

But if that were all we had to pray for, then Jesus' commandment to "Pray for those who abuse you" would be too banal for comment. Surely each of those petitions, at least those for protection and victory, formed the stuff of "war prayers" for thousands of years before Jesus was born. Obviously, he intends something more radical, and probably more disturbing.

The problem is exacerbated by what follows the verb *pray* in his commandment; we are to "pray for *those who abuse you.*" Telling us to pray for our enemies is, at the very least, a call to humility. But telling us to pray for those who abuse us sounds almost like a call to humiliation. Like the commandment to forgive all who trespass against us, it seems to make us collaborators in the abuse. It sounds like a recipe for self-destruction, masochism, pseudomartyrdom; at the very least, it sounds like a good reason for avoiding prayer.

There is, however, a way in which praying for the enemy or the abuser constitutes a more militant and healthy stance. I can pray for God to defend my enemy. I can ask that God will not allow my enemy to be subdued beyond the point of total defeat, that is, to the point of utter despair. And why would I ask this? Because, loving him as I love myself, I intend to do everything in my power to oppose him. I intend to prevent his abuse from destroying us both. In a sense, I am coming to his rescue by refusing to use my own meekness to ensnare him in his own wickedness. To my mind, this has always been the dark side of pacifism: giving the foe enough rope to hang himself. My prayer for my abuser, like my fight against him, is a refusal to make peace with his damnation. Whatever charges he may one day have laid on his soul, I am not interested in being the reason for a single one of them. I will help him fight the rap, and I will do so by fighting him.

One of the stock threats in our vernacular is "God help you." God help you, because I'm coming at you with everything I've got. Said in the right spirit, this can be a form of prayer "for those who abuse you." And it can be a terrible and dreadful prayer to say. It means that my outrage and determination have reached a point where I am willing to enlist the aid of God for the person who is hurting me. On some level, it means that I am angry enough, resolved enough, even to work *in opposition* to God, should he answer my prayer.

Of course, that is a dangerous place to be, and as good a place as any for asking if some possibility of peace still exists. Perhaps only the most resolute warriors are capable of praying for their enemies. At the close of Homer's *Odyssey*, when Odysseus is about to slaughter the kinsmen of the suitors he has lately slain, Athena appears and halts him in his tracks:

"Son of Laertes and the gods of old,
Odysseus, master of land ways and sea ways,
command yourself. Call off this battle now,
or Zeus who views the wide world may be angry."
He yielded to her, and his heart was glad.

His heart is glad because, after years of adventuring and fighting, he has performed his most heroic feat, which is self-mastery. We must not forget, however, that at this transcendent moment in the story, the spoilers of his house are already dead, and their fathers are already on the run. Earlier in the narrative, when he stands to fight in his own great hall, Athena is there to cheer him on. He is not the kind of man to pray for his enemies, but with the goddess for an ally, he could have afforded to. The prayer would have been the highest expression of confidence, and a fairly high expression of humanity as well.

When we meditate on the commandment to love our enemies, we invariably think of the great heroes of nonviolent resistance, as well we should. The teachings of Gandhi are like so many green technologies: We have the need and the know-how; we just haven't mustered the will or the market. We delay doing so to our peril.

And yet an exclusive admiration of nonviolent heroes seems a bit like an exclusive admiration of Platonic love. It is akin to the sensibility that dogmatizes the perpetual virginity of Mary and then refers to her, her spouse, and her miraculously conceived child as "the Holy Family." The implication is that other more naturally constituted households are unholy. The problem of the Holy Family is at bottom a problem of the Holy Trinity: We see the Holy Spirit at work in the incarnation and forget about her movement over the primeval waters of creation and of our own mothers' wombs. Likewise, we fail to see that the love of our enemies may not be entirely incompatible with armed conflict. If one of the great nonviolent heroes of the Sermon on the Mount was a non-Christian, some of its violent heroes have been non-Christian too.

On at least two occasions in history, we find them arrayed against "our side" in some of the most brutal conflicts our side has known: the Crusades and the Indian Wars of the American frontier. To read in any depth about either conflict is to risk losing all faith in any possible redemption for the human race. Their chronicles could serve as the Old and New Testaments of a religion that worshiped the atomic bomb. The Franks, as their Muslim enemies called them, not only slaughtered "infidels" without respect to age and gender, they are on record—their own record—as eating them. They are also on record for roasting Christian babies, though I do not recall whether they ate them or not. In Constantinople they raped Orthodox nuns with abandon; on Cyprus they cut off the noses of all the Orthodox priests. It is small wonder that when Constantinople was besieged by the Turks some two centuries later, many in the city felt that a conquest by Muslims was preferable to an alliance with Christians farther west.

In the midst of this dismal, disheartening history, we come upon Saladin, a fierce adversary of the Crusaders and, by their own accounts, a merciful one as well. When he learned that the son of his enemy had just been married inside a fortress that his troops held under siege, the sultan sent emissaries to inquire in what part of the castle the honeymoon was being held. He then gave orders that the bombardment be directed elsewhere for the space of a night. We can dismiss such a gesture as mere chivalry between the powerful, but Saladin's humanity extended to the powerless as well. Not only did he allow Christian captives to buy their freedom, he freed numbers of those unable to pay. I have not looked deeply enough into his legend to discover those things that might have marred it, but his legendary status in the Christian world— where the official doctrine for centuries was that Saladin and his coreligionists were eternally damned—speaks eloquently of the man he must have been.

The same can be said for the Shawnee chief Tecumseh, who attempted to build a Native American alliance capable of halting westward expansion. Handsome, charismatic, and fearless, he was known even among his foes for his hatred of cruelty. I have already recounted in another chapter how he stopped his braves from scalping American prisoners with the cry, "Are there no men here?"—perhaps the best example I know of someone unwittingly answering his own question. His compassion first showed itself when he was only a youth. While a Shawnee war party burned a white settler at the stake, the young man rose in indignation and delivered an oration that is reported to have put the older warriors to shame. In his own lifetime, when many truly believed that the only good Indian was a dead Indian, and assiduously practiced what they preached, Tecumseh filled his enemies with admiration.

Neither Tecumseh nor Saladin was without anger—quite the contrary. At least one parley with the chief ended abruptly when he drew his tomahawk in a white heat. The sultan wore a sword, of course, and he drew it with similar rage to decapitate a particularly odious prisoner, Reynald of Châtillon (the father of the bridegroom for whom he had shown such extraordinary consideration, also the man responsible for the rape of Christian Cyprus). After bringing his prisoners refreshments, Saladin had charged the crusader with his many atrocities and been met with an impertinent reply. When the other prisoners saw the ingrate's head drop from his still-standing body, they began to grow pale and tremble, but Saladin assured them that he meant to treat them well; only "that man had gone too far."

Such violence and anger, even more than religious differences, will prevent many from seeing Tecumseh and Saladin as proper exemplars of Christian teaching. I tend to see them in terms of the incarnation. The Word is made flesh and dwells among us. The Word comes to us where we are, and at least to some degree, as we are. Krishna appears to Arjuna as a charioteer on a battlefield, and I am not sure that Christ couldn't appear in the same guise. That possibility gives us another way to think of loving the enemy. We're usually inclined to say that only love is capable of turning an enemy into a friend. True enough. It may also be, however, that it is only through the love of mutual enemies that some people can acknowledge love at all.

I have a vivid recollection of what may have been the first time I heard the name of Malcolm X. I was around ten years old. My father and I were sitting together in the same room. I was playing on the rug; he was reading a magazine. All at once, he held up a picture for me and said, "That's Malcolm X." I can't remember if I asked "What's he doing?" before he said, "He's letting the Black Muslims know that if they come after him, he's ready."

The photo was the famous *Life* magazine shot of Malcolm X standing in front of the parted curtains of his home, rifle in hand. At the time I was not sure who he was or even who the Black Muslims were, though a schoolmate had told me a terrifying story of their mutilating a boy our age in the lavatory of an amusement park. And now they were coming to get this Malcolm.

The tone in my father's voice was not one of glee or contempt. It did not have to do with anticipated retribution, with the chickens coming home to roost. Curiously, it was one of admiration. I could recognize that at the time, but I could not really understand it. There weren't too many people in *Life* magazine who elicited that response from my father, and not many of these were black militants. In several years' time, probably one of his greatest fears was that I would become a militant too.

I had to grow older before I realized that his tone of admiration was essentially one of identification. My father also saw himself as a man standing guard, prepared to defend his family against all comers, Black Muslims included, by any means necessary. In the picture of Malcolm X brandishing his gun for all to see, making a point of telling reporters that he had instructed his wife, Betty, in its lethal use, my father saw something that other white Americans would better see in Martin Luther King Jr. He saw his brother.

I believe that when we get more distance from our present time, we will recognize how many men and women found the same thing in the same place. Dr. King told his fellow Americans, we are all equal. None of us is better than any other. But at the same time, and in spite of himself, he was saying that he was better than the bunch of us. It was hard for him not to impart that message, for one simple reason. He *was* better.

Malcolm X told us something different. He said, I'm no better than you are, and that is why you had better beware. "I'm the man you think you are," he said in one of his speeches. "If you want to know what I'll do, figure out what you'll do. I'll do the same thing—only more of it." These words have never moved me to tears as the great speeches of Dr. King have done more than once. But they moved a number of people who might have remained unmoved by King.

Malcolm X called himself "the angriest man in America," quite a claim in any age, and a staggering superlative in his. Yet his anger remains something of a paradox. He is not known to have lost his temper in a single act of violence. His anger was never without a certain civility, a certain humor, a certain innocence even—not to forget a definite power. He was more formidable in his white shirt and narrow tie than an army of "gangsta" rappers in leather and chains. But then their message is different from his; they seem to be saying, "We're even nastier than you think we are," not "I'm the man you think you are." After his pilgrimage to Mecca, Malcolm also showed us that anger could change its mind, just as Dr. King showed us more than once that love could hold its ground.

Even after Mecca, Malcolm X maintained that violence was an option. We might be surprised to learn that Gandhi maintained the same thing. Violence, he said, was always preferable to cowardice. Malcolm X never ceased to be the man who stood by the parted curtains, rifle in readiness. But paranoia does not publicize itself in this way. Paranoia lurks and broods; love warns and hopes that its warning will be heeded. "I taught you not to bite," a Hindu sage is supposed to have told a cobra, "but I never said you couldn't hiss."

Were I to design a monument to Malcolm X, I would portray him with a sword, but in the process of sheathing or unsheathing it, and I would instruct the sculptor to make neither the sword nor the scabbard more prominent. I would have a double inscription, one ascribed to Jesus that read, "Think not that I have come to bring peace, but a sword," and another ascribed to no one, but obviously applied to Malcolm, "Think not that he came to bring a sword, but peace." And every year I would take some flowers to lay at its feet, for my father and for me.

But God said to Jonah, "Is it right for you to be angry about the bush?" And he said, "Yes, angry enough to die."

Jonah

ANGER
AT GOD

Inevitably, people of faith get angry at God. As we have already noted, even the profanities that we utter in times of stress can amount to spontaneous confessions of faith that God not only exists but is in charge of existence. "God damn it" means that God made it. God controls it. And if God does, we're likely to blame God when things go wrong, meaning for the most part when things go wrong for us.

Anger at God, or at least irritation with God, has a long and honored place in the Judeo-Christian tradition. Job is perhaps the most famous example, cursing the day he was born, though he stops short of cursing his Creator. That is what his wife urges him to do in a passage as ironic as it is poignant. "Curse God and die," she says, hoping to cut short her husband's misery. But if living an upright life has not guaranteed

Job's safety, why should blasphemy guarantee his doom? Job is no martyr; Job is also no fool.

He answers his wife, "Shall we receive good at the hand of God, and shall we not receive evil?" Turn that around and it reads: Should we praise God for all the blessings of our lives and not complain to him about the bad? Job is aware of that proposition, too. And he does complain to God, magnificently:

> I loathe my life; I would not live forever.
> Let me alone, for my days are a breath.
> What are human beings, that you make so much of
>   them,
>   that you set your mind on them,
> visit them every morning,
>   test them every moment?
> Will you not look away from me for a while,
>   let me alone until I swallow my spittle?
> If I sin, what do I do to you, you watcher of humanity?
>   Why have you made me your target?
>   Why have I become a burden to you?
> Why do you not pardon my transgression
>   and take away my iniquity?
> For now I shall lie in the earth;
>   you will seek me, but I shall not be.

I have quoted from Job at such length not to preface any commentary but rather to describe the domain where all commentary is moot. At the extremes of mortal experience, anger at God is not so much a right to be exercised or a problem to be resolved as it is a truth to be lived, an existential crisis in which one either finds or loses his faith. You can perhaps discern the degree of your own anger at God, assuming you're angry at God, by examining your expectations for this chapter. If you were hoping for some esoteric map to lead you out of the predicament, a friend with easy answers, then you do not sit on the same ash heap where Job sits. If you did, you would instantly have been insulted by the mere suggestion that I could offer any counsel whatsoever.

~~

There is another kind of religious anger, both less magnificent and more prevalent than Job's, which comes of sitting not on an ash heap but in a pew. This is the anger of the soul in rebellion against the constraints of religion. Sometimes this kind of anger expresses itself as a grievance against God; at other times the rebel feels that God is on her side—though perhaps that is the rarer experience. I spoke with a man once who had recently left a religious cult. Though he was ostensibly "free to go," the psychological pressure exerted by other members of the community made his departure feel like an escape. He fled with his family, like Lot with his, taking little more than the clothes on their backs. And all the way down the road, he told me later, he was overcome with the dreadful sensation that God was about to kill him.

Perhaps the best literary expression of religious anger appears in a poem by the seventeenth-century English poet George Herbert. It is called "The Collar," probably a pun on "choler" but not, as some suppose, an allusion to a clergy collar. Herbert was in fact a priest, but the practice of wearing clergy collars came long after his death. It is not a priest's collar he

has in mind, but a dog's, a prisoner's, and he wants to rip
it off.

I struck the board, and cry'd, No more.
I will abroad.
What? shall I ever sigh and pine?
My lines and life are free; free as the rode,
Loose as the winde, as large as store.
Shall I be still in suit?
Have I no harvest but a thorn
To let me bloud, and not restore
What I have lost with cordiall fruit?
Sure there was wine
Before my sighs did drie it: there was corn
Before my tears did drown it.
Is the yeare onely lost to me?
Have I no bayes to crown it?
No flowers, no garlands gay? all blasted?
All wasted?
Not so, my heart: but there is fruit,
And thou hast hands.
Recover all thy sigh-blown age
On double pleasures: leave thy cold dispute
Of what is fit, and not. Forsake thy cage,
Thy rope of sands,
Which pettie thoughts have made, and made to thee
Good cable to enforce and draw,
And be thy law,
While thou didst wink and wouldst not see.
Away, take heed:
I will abroad.

Call in thy deaths head there; tie up thy fears.
    He that forbears
    To suit and serve his need,
    Deserves his load.
But as I rav'd and grew more fierce and wilde
    At every word,
Me thoughts I heard one calling, *Child!*
    And I reply'd, *My Lord.*

What person of strict religion could read "The Collar" and not feel that it struck some chord within him? Not only a person of strict religion—a person of any strictness whatsoever, any self-imposed restraint, any integrity even, must sometimes feel the urge to break free. And although Herbert's rebellion is apparently quelled by the voice of his Lord, there are times when such a rebellion is of greater duration, tenacity, and substance than the poet's. Before assuming that every rebellion against religion is a rebellion against God, we would do well to recall how many religions began in revolt: Buddha's against Brahmanism, Christ's against Pharisaic Judaism, the Baal Shem Tov's against a later version of the same, Luther's against Catholicism, George Fox's against Anglicanism, Roger Williams and Anne Hutchinson's against Puritanism, Muhammad's against amoral animism, Hiawatha's against the more brutal forms of tribalism, Malcolm X's against the Nation of Islam. In the biographies of these figures and others like them, we often come to a place where the budding founder "struck the board, and cried, 'No more.'" Or we can imagine such a place. Not every revolt will open up a new direction, or a happy one—fanatics have revolted too—but we should not be too quick to regard every "choler" as a sin. Anger can be the color of the Holy Spirit shining through history, just as light is given color coming through stained glass. We sometimes forget that Moses meets God in the wilderness after killing an Egyptian taskmaster who was beating a Hebrew slave. When God says to Moses from the burning bush, "I have heard the cry of my people," he is speaking to someone who has also heard the cry.

Religious anger is perhaps most trustworthy when it comes in response to the plight of those excluded or shortchanged by tradition. It is useful to remember, for example, what part of the temple Christ cleansed. The tables of the money changers were not set up next to the altar of the holy of holies. In that case, the high priest would have wielded a scourge also. The marketplace that Jesus disrupted was in the outer temple courtyard; in terms of the geography of the temple, it was little different from the church lawn. So to many of his contemporaries, the action Jesus took must have seemed completely unwarranted, hysterical, mad. But the courtyard had another purpose; it was the place allowed for the "God-fearers," that is, for righteous Gentiles drawn to the teachings of Judaism though they were not Jews. The "zeal for your house" that the disciples noted in Jesus' violent act was at least partially a zeal for those on the doorstep of that house. The Father's house was intended "as a house of prayer," and in fact, while Jesus was flinging around furniture, all kinds of prayers were being offered in the inner sanctuaries. But how could the God-fearers be expected to pray in the bustle of a livestock market? The little Lord Jesus had been born in a stable, but apparently he had few sentimental notions about people having to worship in one—a characteristic he shares with others born in similar circumstances.

His ire would be happily recapitulated in a church that continues to be absorbed by its own in-house debates—many of them over the most "relevant" issues of diversity and justice, of course—while outside on the street people are harassed and helpless and hungry, like sheep without a shepherd. The academic academy grew up in the cloisters of the church, and now the church has come of age behaving very much like an academic academy, which debates what books ought to be in the literary canon while people who never learned how to read serve crackers and cheese to the debaters. Oh, for some prophet to kick the legs off those tables!

But there are so many tables, with resolutions, name tags, the wares of seminaries and technology vendors. Had I a talent for painting, I would depict the cleansing of the temple with Jesus fallen to one knee, in the pose of a station of the cross, amidst a score of overturned tables. He hangs his head, he is exhausted. Behind him, stretching back as far as the vanishing point, would be a numberless host of tables, as yet unturned, each one stacked a yard high with position papers, convention materials, and casserole dishes. And I would title the painting after that verse in Isaiah: "Whom shall I send, and who will go for us?" Who will finish the job?

⌁

Herbert's anger in "The Collar" is not so much directed at the shortcomings of religious institutions, however, as at the repression arising from religious life. We could say that his anger is personal. He wants to give freer rein to his passions, and it makes him angry with himself—and perhaps with God—that he has not done so. It has often been noted how libertines make the most devout converts; the reverse is no less true. Beware the choler of those who finally break their collars.

Sometimes I wonder if I am more choleric than I have to be because of the Christian imperative to control my temper. In other words, I wonder if controlling my anger also makes me angry. Trying to see everyone's point of view, trying to be patient beyond reason, trying to remember that the other person is also a child of God, that I am also a sinner—how far do you go with all this before you explode from accumulated grievance? And at least to some extent, I believe this is a fair question to ask. I said once to a friend that reconciliation often works for me like a weird version of the Heimlich maneuver: I frantically assist someone in disgorging the hat that I rammed down his throat when he failed to respect me for approaching him with my hat in my hand. After a while I begin to wonder if approaching someone in that way, given the risks, is not meekness at all but a form of treachery. Wouldn't it be more charitable to approach people with my hat on my head, more formally and with more reserve, wise as the serpent and harmless as the dove—instead of like a dove with six-inch retractable fangs? I do think so, and I am trying.

There's another question I have, though, and it takes me in a somewhat different direction. Am I really angry because Christianity puts insufferable restraints on my true self, or because I am denying that Christianity is an integral part of my true self? In other words, am I seething because of repression or because of cowardice? For which reason am I most often angry: the stifling of my natural self, or the disguising of my supernatural self? It seems like a somewhat abstract question, but it could easily be made more concrete through an experiment.

Take a week, I tell myself, and be as uninhibited, as shamelessly abrasive as you dare to be within the law. Don't fake, but don't fret either. Forget the kingdom of God. Most of all, forget that other people have feelings. Act on *your* feelings. Be a savage. Then take another week, and consciously attempt to be as religious as you know how to be. Show the same indifference for other people's secular prejudices as you showed for their feelings the week before. Don't be pious, but live the gospel in as bold a way as your imagination allows. Be a mensch. Be a meshuggener even. (Too bad the early church fathers had to rely on Greek; they'd have done better with Yiddish.) At the end of those two weeks, ask yourself, Which approach to life made me the more angry? Which gave me the greater peace with myself?

I have yet to try the experiment. To be honest, I suspect I already know the outcome. *Both* approaches would make me less angry than I am now. Both would give me more peace. And perhaps I would find more common ground between the two than I imagine. Perhaps the best instruction I can give to myself right now is not "Be less angry" but "Be more deliberate." Be more awake.

⌒

We cannot talk about anger at God or in the church without a parting word or two about the biblical book of Jonah. My wife and I have friends who like to play a few games of "Desert Island" after dinner: Which three record albums would you want to have, which five books, if you were a castaway? We've never played it with books of the Bible, but Jonah would certainly be in the running for me.

The book of Jonah tells the story of a prophet whom God calls to deliver a message of doom to the wicked people of Nineveh. Jonah doesn't want to do it. So he takes a ship headed in the opposite direction, in fact to the very edge of the known world, a place where every angry man or woman dreams of going at one time or another. When a storm blows up, Jonah attributes it to divine retribution and urges the pagan sailors to throw him into the ocean. The pagan sailors respond as pagans often do, with a sense of right and wrong that puts People of the Book to shame. They keep rowing. But Jonah eventually prevails on them to toss him over—I sometimes wonder if this is altruism or depression—and the sea is calmed. As everyone knows, Jonah is then swallowed by a "great fish," which popular legend holds to be a whale. In the belly of the fish, Jonah undergoes something of a conversion: We know that because he praises God in a neat little psalm and because, like converts the world over, he cannot resist a few condescending remarks about "those who worship vain idols," in spite of the fact that a few of that sort tried their best to keep him out of the drink. No sooner is the psalm over than the author has the whale vomit Jonah onto the shore, perhaps as a subtle comment on some of the sentiments expressed in the psalm, perhaps not.

So Jonah goes to Nineveh, as he should have done from the start. The Ninevites repent, and in many people's minds this is how the story ends. But this is precisely where the real story begins. God *also* repents of his destructive designs upon Nineveh, and Jonah is furious. "O Lord! Is not this what I said while I was still in my own country? That is why I fled to Tarshish at the beginning; for I knew that you are a gracious God and merciful, slow to anger, and abounding in steadfast love, and ready to relent from punishing." We may have thought that he fled to Tarshish because of the harshness of the message he was told to deliver, but now we learn that this was not the case! He fled because he suspected all along that God was not going to follow through on it. "And now, O Lord, please take my life from me, for it is better for me to die than to live."

There are only seven verses left to the book, and they are surely among the loveliest in the Bible. It would be a shame not to give them here in full:

> And the Lord said, "Is it right for you to be angry?" Then Jonah went out of the city and sat down east of the city, and made a booth for himself there. He sat under it in the shade, waiting to see what would become of the city.
>
> The Lord God appointed a bush, and made it come up over Jonah, to give shade over his head, to save him from his discomfort; so Jonah was very happy about the bush. But when dawn came up the next day, God appointed a worm that attacked the bush, so that it withered. When the sun rose, God prepared a sultry east wind, and the sun beat down on the head of Jonah, so that he was faint and asked that he might die. He said, "It is better for me to die than to live."
>
> But God said to Jonah, "Is it right for you to be angry about the bush?" And he said, "Yes, angry enough to die." Then the Lord said, "You are concerned about the bush, for which you did not labor and which you did not grow; it came into being in a

night and perished in a night. And should I not be concerned about Nineveh, that great city, in which there are more than a hundred and twenty thousand persons who do not know their right hand from their left, and also many animals?"

The story of Jonah contains at least two insights into anger, both rather striking. The first is that all the events that trouble Jonah, that frustrate him and infuriate him, are intended as part of his education. What a lot of trouble God takes with the lesson plan! We read that "the Lord hurled a great wind upon the sea," "the Lord provided a large fish," "the Lord God spoke to the fish," "the Lord God appointed a bush," "the Lord appointed a worm," "God prepared a sultry east wind." The story reads like the account of a six-course dinner put on by the most careful and attentive hostess—little pickles and dainty forks, sheltering bushes and sultry east winds—all so that Jonah can come to a place where he is able to see a city full of people and animals as God sees it. You can say that the theology here is naïve and anthropocentric. Fine. And yet, how many of those who would call it so harbor the belief that the source of all their frustrations is some malevolent force, some cosmic harpy with no better design than to befoul their picnic lunch—a view no less naïve or anthropocentric, but somehow more acceptable to their sense of themselves as sophisticated human beings?

The book of Jonah asks us: If we have enough faith to say "God damn it," why do we not also possess the faith to say "God appointed it"? If we can ask, "What have I done to deserve this?" why can't we also ask, "What am I to learn from this?" Granted, neither is an absolutely valid question. In a certain predicament—in a death camp, for instance—both would be utterly absurd. But most of us are not in death camps. We're in what amounts to a depressive funk, where we can believe in God enough to think he might hate us, but not enough to think he might teach us. We are more likely to blame the universe for giving us a brain tumor than to trust it for giving us a brain. Forgetting God for just a moment (because the moment itself proves that God does not forget us), which theory makes more sense from a purely evolutionary point of view: that the human species is being "taught" through its interactions with other creatures and phenomena, or that it's being screwed? Swim with the whales; then give your answer. For that matter, swim with the sharks.

The second of the insights we find in Jonah is both simpler and more startling. The book of Jonah says that the thing that makes us the most angry with God, more angry than droughts and famines, male pattern baldness and cellulite, is God's mercy. That is what really enrages Jonah, and if we're completely honest, it's what enrages us too. The child who dies under the wheels of a car may lead us to wring our hands and even to shake a fist at heaven, but unless the child is our own, what really infuriates us is the fact that the driver lives on to enjoy life, to beget other children, perhaps to find his way toward some kind of redemption. It is mercy—not justice or injustice—that makes us the most angry in the end. When people tell you that the Holocaust makes them angry at God, are they thinking more about slaughtered Jews or aging Nazis? We cannot know beyond a hunch. But I do know there is a difference between what makes us hypothetically angry at God when we're chatting at a dinner party, and what makes us angry when we're on the highway, driving home afterward. Before, it was all about "how a supposedly benevolent God" could allow so many terrible calamities, each one imagined rather calmly over the coffee and cake, but now in the drizzle and the glare of the oncoming lights, it's how God can allow so many reckless idiots to go on breathing in the world. The mercy is what's so maddening.

And maybe this is also the real cause of anger in the church. At bottom, is it really the institution that galls us so, the sad history and bad behavior of "organized religion"? Or is it rather our subconscious disdain for any club that would have us for a member, and our very conscious disgust at the outrageous suggestion that God actually cares and cares intensely for these misfits who kneel and mumble in the pews beside us?

ANGER
IN THE
WORLD

Persistent depression is only too clearly the sign that a man is living contrary to his vocation.

José Ortega y Gasset, *The Dehumanization of Art*

WORK

When I look for people who have their anger under control—I don't say people who never get angry—what I find most often are men and women who love their work. Not infrequently, they're men and women who work "for themselves" in their own businesses or at their own trades, sometimes in their own homes. My wife and I buy some of our meat from a butcher whose pleasure in his work is so evident that we would probably go into his shop even if we became vegetarians. I can do without beef; I cannot do without the sight of happiness in action. I could imagine several things that might anger the butcher during the course of his day, but I can't imagine many days that he comes to work angry or goes home in a foul mood.

Persistent anger, perhaps even more than persistent depression, is the sign of someone living contrary to his or her vocation. That is not necessarily the same thing as saying that an angry woman or man is in the wrong line of work, though that may be the case. It could be that an angry woman or man is in the wrong kind of job. Put our butcher in the meat department of a big chain supermarket, and a meat cleaver might turn from a favorite tool to a dangerous temptation. In a case like that, the work is fine, but the conditions of the job make the work impossible to perform or to enjoy. (This is the other side of a no-less-common predicament: that of the individual with the "perfect job," where everything is ideal except the nature of the work itself.) In fact, the person who feels truly called to a certain work is the one most likely to be enraged by a job that frustrates his or her vocation. Find the angriest physicians at a dysfunctional hospital and you will probably be able to divide them into two groups: a minority who never should have become doctors in the first place, and a majority who could never dream of being anything else. Those in the middle will probably find it easier to make some accommodation—one reason we should never be too disdainful of those in the middle. Perhaps there are people called to have no discernible calling but their own unshakeable decency.

But all of us are called to do work in the world. One of my repeated prayers whenever I visit the sick is "Give your servant her work and the means to do it." I say this almost as often as "Give your servant healing"—though I have met people who seem to think of work and sickness as little more than different forms of the same mortal woe. Many of them mistake this for a biblical idea: that God curses Adam and Eve with work. This is no different from saying that "the knowledge of good and evil" is the knowledge of sex, in other words, that the shame of nakedness is what makes nakedness desirable— that sin is what enables us to be born.

A more careful reading of Genesis dispels both notions. In the second creation story, for example, Adam and Eve are placed in the garden "to keep it," and Eve is created as a "fit helper" ("an help meet" in the King James translation) for her husband. It's hard to see how the pair were supposed to "keep" the garden, or how Eve was to "help" Adam, if there was no work to do (and just as difficult to see how they were supposed to be "fruitful and multiply" if their genitals were on the prelapsarian list of forbidden fruit). Toil, not work, is the punishment of our first parents. Work that enrages us and breaks our spirits—*that* is the curse. Conflating work with toil—or thinking of work purely as a job, as a thing we do for money or not at all—is proof enough that we have fallen.

Work is nothing less than how we make love to the world. I have read that in certain peasant cultures it was customary for a husband and wife to have sexual intercourse in a plowed field before planting it. Beyond the naïve assumptions of sympathetic magic—the fertility of the human couple used to prime the fertility of the soil—the practice speaks strongly to me about the meaning of work. I don't necessarily grasp that meaning in an intellectual way. After all, it is magic that betokens an overintellectualized view of the world, one in which all effects have causes and all causes are formulaic. The meaning I take from the lovers in the field is more evocative, more religious. I imagine them walking hand in hand to the field in moonlight, how their hearts quicken when their feet touch the plowed soil. I imagine the moment when something tells them, or when one whispers to the other, "This is the spot. This is where we lay ourselves down." I think of thighs bared on freshly turned furrows, of knees and buttocks impressing the loosened earth, of the smell of the soil so rank and the sight of the stars so dizzying that the lovers hide their faces in each other's necks. I hear their panting cries in the darkness, perhaps echoing other cries—of nocturnal animals, of other couples in other plowed fields. Imagine the once-a-year holiness of it, the simultaneous privacy and community of it, the hunger in the loins consciously summoned to prevent a hunger in the belly, and perhaps fed by the fear of that other hunger—the act of love both ceremonial and ravenous. Imagine too the man and woman going to plant the field the next day, like two lovers making a bed in the morning, drawing the coverlets up between them, so different now in daylight with their clothes on, how they smile at the memory. And every day, no matter how hot, every storm no matter how drenching, touches their most private flesh like a beloved hand.

Perhaps the total meaning of these images can be understood only in contrast, say to the fabled "quickie" at the office. According to the *Harper's Index,* the most favored place for that kind of encounter is "the boss's desk." A sex act performed on that plane is either an act of power (if the boss is involved) or an act of contempt (if the boss is not); in either case it is performed in defiance of the work, perhaps in defiance of those with whom one works or those one works to support. It is hard to conceive of it as anything other than an act of suppressed rage—a variation on that crude cliché of "taking the job and shoving it."

Anyway, when I think of paradise, I do not think of a naked man and woman on the morning before they eat an apple; I think of a naked man and woman on the night before they plant the corn.

⌒

But we are not in paradise; our anger tells us so. In regard to work, many of us are not in the promised land either. Perhaps the best biblical setting for describing our situation is the land of Egypt, "the house of bondage." Not without reason do the authors of the Torah place its commandments against that background. "I am the Lord your God, who brought you out of the land of Egypt." We tend to read that refrain solely as a statement of obligation: God has delivered his people, so they owe him their obedience. But the refrain can also be read as a statement of analysis: Slavery is the background of, and the alternative to, God's call to an observant life. Existence profaned, work reduced to nothing but toil—those are the primary conditions of a slave.

Work becomes toil, first of all, when the worker fails to enjoy its fruits. This is one of those truths that "everybody knows" but that we seem to keep missing. Either we expect workers to find fruitfulness solely in the work itself (as with public school teachers, for instance, who until very recently were expected to pay for their groceries with idealism), or else we expect wages alone to provide a sense of fruitfulness (as in the case of certain well-paying assembly jobs, where workers have no meaningful connection to the things they produce). Both situations describe the quality of work in the house of bondage.

But fruitless labor can also be the predicament of privileged workers who strive to achieve a standard of living that the work itself revokes. They toil for "a nice house" but are never at home, even and especially when they're under their own roof. Or as Thoreau put it, they make themselves sick in order to pay the doctor. In contrast, the biblical story of creation is about the satisfaction that follows making: "And God saw that it was good." The story of work for many of us is the story of Genesis turned into an apocalypse: The maker may not see "that it is good" until some distant end of time, possibly at the point where he's about to drop dead.

It takes no great intelligence to see that in many ways the rage of those toiling at the top of the social pyramid parallels that of those toiling at the bottom. In both cases, it grows from the frustration of solving an impossible puzzle, either how to make ends meet, or how to meet one's own exalted ends. The hope of the Old Testament is a vision of every one sitting in the shade of his own fig tree, but those without a tree, like those with a sprawling orchard of them, rarely get a chance to sit in that shade. Seen in this way, the anger associated with work is at least as much a political and cultural problem as a psychological one. "Anger management" treated solely as a matter for trainers hired by the personnel department is something like a "war on drugs" treated solely as a matter of law enforcement. Neither approach looks for the social cause of the problem. If anything, the approach runs the risk of exacerbating the problem.

As long as we believe that we can reverse the Fall by abolishing work, either through laborsaving devices or the exploitation of other workers, we shall experience work as a form of punishment and an occasion for rage. Work does not need to be abolished, but redeemed. No civilization ought to call itself advanced until it has embraced the task of that redemption.

~⌒~

Work also becomes toil, and an occasion for rage, when we do not employ our best gifts in doing it. I wouldn't say when our work fails to be "challenging," because I have come to suspect that word, with its sly and managerial insinuation that a human being has to be hassled or perplexed in order to feel alive. But I'm almost as wary of the word *gifts*, which, like the related word *charisma*, has been shanghaied from the Christian gospel in order to serve a very profane agenda.

Our culture tends to define *gift* as something I can do that makes anyone else who tries to do the same thing look sick by comparison. It's Michael Jordan playing basketball; Django Reinhardt playing the guitar. In contrast, the New Testament speaks of gifts as those abilities I can contribute toward making the church—and by extension, the world—whole and well. "There are varieties of gifts, but the same service." My gift may not distinguish me, but it does serve to fulfill me, and it fulfills me by enabling me to serve.

It also fulfills me, though the New Testament doesn't say so, by giving me pleasure. (For that idea, we must turn to Augustine: "Love God and do what you please.") We tend to think of pleasure as something we derive from play, but its greatest use may be in dowsing the wellsprings of our work. Accomplishments alone cannot do this. We cannot always find our pleasure—or the best gifts we have to give—by recognizing our names in a trophy case. More than one person who was judged to be "gifted" as, say, a mathematician or a dancer discovered that the gift she had to give was as a physician or a firefighter.

Admittedly, the work that I enjoy will most often be the work in which others find me the most proficient or the most useful. But what I'm the most good *at* will not always determine what I do the most good *in*. Picasso is quoted as saying "My mother said to me, 'If you are a soldier, you will become

a general. If you are a monk, you will become the Pope.' Instead I was a painter, and became Picasso." Who's to say that,
his gargantuan ego aside, he would not have made a fine pope?
Perhaps there was a priest in his youth who thought so. Pablo,
you could be a great man in the church if you would only put
aside your doodling. Does anyone wish that he had tried?
Had he done so and succeeded, I think one thing more than
any other would have called him back to his palette: the sensation of overwhelming anger, or depression, every time he addressed the crowd in St. Peter's Square. Of course, pleasure
alone is not an infallible indicator of one's calling. Pleasure is
not incompatible with evil, after all, but it does seem virtually
incompatible with rage.

～～

Anger can also arise from giving no pleasure to others in the
work that we do. On the most basic level, that means we can
be angry because of a lack of appreciation in the workplace.
But on another less subjective level, the sense of giving no pleasure can come from divining that the work we do is worthless
or even harmful. What, more than anything else, determines
the demeanor of the man or woman who waits your table
in a restaurant? Beyond factors like personality or working
conditions, the most reliable determiner seems to be the
quality of the food itself. If it's likely to sicken the customer,
it's not likely to gladden the person who brings it. Talk to
anyone who loves his or her work, and invariably you're going
to hear some proud disclosure about where the work goes,
where the product gets shipped, who buys it, who has a use
for it, who can't get enough of it. "And this stuff here goes all

the way out to Tacoma, Washington. They use it to make . . ." What accounts for the profound sadness of those in the sex trade, aside from the degradation of the work itself, but the knowledge of how little pleasure they actually give?

The otherwise laudable Christian tradition of seeing all things as useful "in the service of the King," may blind us to the possibility that certain forms of work are simply not appropriate for a person of faith. The early church certainly thought so, especially in regard to soldiers, though in its eagerness to refute the ceremonial laws of Judaism it probably gave the matter short shrift. (Scholars tell us that at least some of the "sinners" referred to in the Jewish communities of the New Testament were nothing more or less than persons employed in disreputable professions, not only prostitutes and tax collectors but tavern keepers and donkey drivers, as well as their wives. The church may understandably have wanted to avoid such judgments.) One-eighth of the Buddha's Noble Eightfold Path is "right occupation," and the Buddha is supposed to have singled out several as "not right," including those of butcher and brewer. We might do worse than to ask if it is "lawful" to be a developer of strip malls or a purveyor of third-rate pharmaceuticals to the third world. Sometimes rage in one's employment is no different than fever in a case of food poisoning: It's a sign that something is wrong, not just in the culture of the workplace or in the psyche of the worker, but in the moral and spiritual value of the work itself.

This raises a few interesting questions. One is whether certain forms of work call for anger (as opposed to arousing it), and if there are not vocations especially suited to angry people just as there are vocations especially suited to ambidextrous or bilingual ones.

In that regard, I think of the attorney Mitchell Stevens in Russell Banks's novel *The Sweet Hereafter.* "Angry? Yes, I'm angry; I'd be a lousy lawyer if I weren't," he says. Later in the narrative, he adds, "I do it because I'm pissed off, and that's what you get when you mix conviction with rage. It's a very special kind of anger, let's say. So I'm not a victim. Victims get depressed and live in the there and then. I live in the here and now."

But we are likely to be skeptical of "this very special kind of anger." Is it truly aroused by conviction, or is it merely the sublimation of unresolved issues in Stevens's own life? It would seem to be both, in which case the service he does for others may sometimes result in a disservice to himself. His own case never comes to trial.

It is too easy, however, to dismiss the value of such an accommodation to anger simply because it is imperfect. How many of the good offices of art, government, education, and philanthropy were performed by women and men with at least one screw loose? An entirely balanced human being does not often tip the scales of justice for anyone. Sometimes the price of the common good is the sublimated grief of an uncommon individual. But it would be a good idea if such individuals knew the price of their contributions, and I'm not sure they always do.

I recently visited a police officer, who told me that the average age at death for a Vermont state trooper is fifty-six. I was incredulous. Vermont is not often the scene of shoot-outs and hijackings. But as the officer explained to me, it was not violence or high-speed car crashes that shortened the lives of most of his peers, but adrenaline. With each response to a crisis, the body produces an adrenaline rush. But then the body has to do something with the adrenaline—especially when it has produced more than it ultimately needs, as in the case of a false alarm. Over time this biochemical flux takes its toll in terms of heart disease, cancers, and all the other effects of stress. The man who told me this is around my age. It was hard not to wonder, given his job and my predisposition, which of us was more likely to go down first.

⌒

Some of the rage we encounter in work has to do with a loss of connection to the physical world. This statement may seem to make no sense in that we think of anger as arising from frustration, and frustration as arising from the inevitable conflict between our wills and matter. We want "it" to do one thing, and "it" does another. So isn't our connection to the physical world driving us nuts, rather than any loss thereof? The problem is that in many cases we have reduced our frustration with matter at the cost of increasing stress. There is a difference between them. If frustration comes of being stalled, stress often comes of being rushed—of being able to do more in less time, with a higher quota of production and a smaller margin of permissible error. Stress may be harder to bear than frustration because of its inscrutability. A frustrated person can usually tell you why she's frustrated. A person under stress, on the other hand, often cannot tell you precisely why she's starting to come apart. That's because she's usually been moving too fast to keep track. Most of us have had the experience of flying off the handle without knowing exactly why, and of needing to trace the buildup along an intricate path of cause and effect, which, as often as not, involved hurry—not an attempt to overcome matter so much as the dream of cheating time. Of course, that has long been the cherished goal of industrial culture, one hardly modified by the so-called information culture. We fly off the handle because we flew away from anything having a handle a long time ago.

Emerson said, "There is virtue yet in the hoe and the spade, for learned as well as for unlearned hands." Part of this virtue is that it puts us very literally in touch with the elemental resistance of the material creation. The rock in the sod and the root underneath it both remind me that I cannot have everything that I want, and that I cannot have even some of what I want without struggle or a lapse of time. As we become increasingly impatient with even the most refined forms of material resistance (does the PC ever boot up as quickly as it should?), do we not also become more intolerant of resistance in other forms? As I virtually do away with my own body, why not do away with *every* body that opposes my will? Surely the move to gate off communities and to isolate segments of community into various self-defined and self-centered tribes is not unrelated to our desire to abolish the hoe and the spade. As with our fellow men and women, so with the wild creatures, which many of us encounter now as nothing more than momentary bumps under our tires. Direct contact with matter—contact in the bracing sense of a "contact sport"—reminds us of limitation and finitude; it necessitates hesitancy. It demands that thought slow down enough to become reflective. Digging my own grave, I am challenged by the grating of my spade on a stone: "Are you sure this is what you want to do?" it asks.

To redeem work, we must redefine efficiency. The efficiency expert must become more than he already is, which is quite a bit when you think of it: engineer, physicist, accountant. The efficiency expert of the future, however, will also have to be a psychologist, an ethicist, and not least of all an artist. Admittedly, if work can never be better than toil, then pure technology is the best approach to it; then efficiency does indeed consist of doing as much as possible as quickly as possible with the attendant aim of getting the unpleasant business over with as soon as possible. But if work is not entirely fallen —that is, if we would not be entirely puritan—then other considerations come into play, with anger having some part in suggesting what they might be. How can work be made less infuriating, more beautiful, more useful not only in its product but in the actual process itself?

Jesus said, "My yoke is easy, and my burden is light." Might he have meant that we are always making the hard things easy and the easy things hard? Might he have meant to suggest that it is not the yoke itself that makes us slaves, but our own frenetic craziness? We pursue happiness and find her fleet of foot. She turns to chase us, and we snarl over our shoulders, "Two can play that game, you know!" And off we roar in our shiny new machines.

⌐⌐

One last thing that turns work into toil is making an idol out of work. That is certainly a danger in preaching work's "redemption" as I have been doing: By degrees, we come to mistake work for the redeemer. But the danger is already present in the absolute value we assign to jobs and to whatever "gets the job done." The word *job* is as close to "God" as some people come in speaking reverently. If Hitler were alive today, he'd justify the building of Auschwitz on the grounds of how many new jobs it was going to provide. Run over your mother and plead for leniency on the grounds that you were on your way to your job.

Many people fail to realize that the priest and the Levite in the parable of the Good Samaritan are not so much hypocritical as conscientious. They have what we would call a good work ethic. They pass by the wounded man lying in the road because exposure to blood or to a corpse would defile them for duty in the temple. It would interfere with the job. The irony of the parable goes way beyond the fact that a Samaritan proves to be more righteous than the Jew. The main irony is that in passing by the wounded man in order to serve at the temple, the priest and the Levite become idolators. They have made a god out of their work. Within the Old Testament frame of reference, we might say that they have gone back to Egypt, no less than the worshippers of the golden calf had gone back to Egypt. In other words, their frame of mind belongs to slavery. A slave is usually defined as a human being who is owned by another, but a slave is also a person for whom a given function—be it making bricks, playing the lyre, or officiating at sacrifices—is absolute. That function is the reason for the slave's existence. He was not made, in his master's eyes, to "love God and enjoy him forever," as the Presbyterian catechism has it. The slave was made, or at least made a slave, in order to "do the job."

The Bible attempts to check the absolutism of work with the observance of the Sabbath. Of course, the fact that the Sabbath itself can also become an absolute sets the stage for many of the conflicts of the Gospels. Jesus runs afoul of the religious authorities for doing good works on the day of rest.

When I read these stories as a kid growing up in a quasi-Sabbatarian church, I was gleeful at the way that Jesus was willing to lay aside the commandment in order to meet some basic human need, allowing his disciples to pick the grains of wheat as they passed through the fields, healing the sick in the synagogue itself. I loved him for his rebellion. Though still rooting for Jesus, I find that I am much more sympathetic to the scribes and Pharisees than I was as a kid. When I imagine myself in the story now, I'm no longer the cheeky disciple standing at the master's elbow itching for a fight. I find that I'm standing with the geezers these days, not that I love Jesus any less (and some of them loved him too), but that I understand from hard experience how ruthlessly one must guard the sanctuary of rest if there is to be any sanctuary at all. Jesus probably understood this too. Because he allowed his disciples to pluck a few grains of wheat on the Sabbath doesn't mean he would have approved of their harvesting the whole field. Because he healed a man with a withered hand on the day of rest doesn't mean he would have spent its remaining hours listening to his life's story or reading his manuscript.

So we can find a corrective to the idolatry of work in the tradition of the Sabbath, which I believe Christianity needs to reexamine in the worst way, and we might find a powerful antidote to anger in the same place. Like the Syrian captain Naaman, who would have attempted any heroic quest to heal his leprosy but balks when Elisha tells him to bathe in the river, I find that my anger often boils down to nothing more Promethean than the fact that I'm tired. To be honest, and I hope not too irreverent, I've occasionally wondered if some of the testier moments in Jesus' life didn't result from the same thing. "And the crowd came together again, so that they could

not even eat. . . . People were saying, 'He is beside himself.'"
Jesus had something important to tell his contemporaries
about the dangers of rigidity and legalism, but perhaps they
had something important to tell him too. They certainly have
something important to tell us.

So, perhaps, does contemporary feminism. If the feminist
revolution of my generation was in large part a refusal to take
marriage and motherhood as absolutes, it continues by refusing to take work as an absolute either. By insisting on the
right to be both mothers and paid workers, women have
placed both work and parenthood in relative relationship—
that is, under God, indivisible, with liberty and justice for all
(except the underpaid day-care workers). If you wanted to
speak in terms of the Eden myth, you might say that Eve, having eaten the forbidden fruit, continues to chew on the problem, as opposed to Adam, who continues to blame her for his
indigestion. Her assigned sorrow was to be in childbirth, yet
she fought to have Adam come into the birth room, thus reducing some of the alienation that causes *his* sorrows. She
fought to enter the workplace, and now she fights to reenter
her home on different terms. In all these struggles, she addresses not only her own problems but two of the fundamental problems of men—in fact two age-old sources of anger for
men (often imposed by other, more powerful men): their separation from the Mother (as sons, fathers, and worshippers)
and their enslavement to work. I don't wish to overstate the
case. I'm not saying that feminism is the answer to all our
prayers, only that it is a reason for some of my hopes.

My family is not Jewish, but lately on Friday evenings we say the Service of Light in the Episcopal Book of Common Prayer. My wife and daughter light the candles on the table, as would be their office in a kosher home. To see that office as nothing more than a vestige of patriarchy is to lack imagination, as it is to see the Sabbath as a vestige of anything less than our divine origins. When does the God of the Hebrew Bible seem more human, more vulnerably like us, than in his rest? Perhaps only in his wrath. I seek for him in both places.

Like two doomed ships that pass in storm
We had crossed each other's way:
But we made no sign, we said no word,
We had no word to say.

Oscar Wilde, "The Ballad of Reading Gaol"

WORDS

One of the more notable customs of the region I have called my home for almost twenty-five years is that of refusing to talk to someone with whom you are angry. I don't mean avoiding that person, not returning his calls or answering his letters, sitting as far away from him as possible at picnics and wedding receptions, that sort of thing. I mean looking at his physical person from a distance as close as three feet as though he does not exist. I mean greeting his "Good morning"—not even with coldness or indignation but with the pretense of never having heard it. This is not the dirty look we're talking about here, but the you-are-dirt look—with "dirt" referring to nothing more remarkable than an earthy substance under your feet. This local version of the silent treatment works something like shunning among the Amish, except that for the Amish shunning is a communal thing, voted upon by the elders for reasons known by all, including the shunned, and reversible by some public act of contrition. Our type is all the more deadly for being completely informal, personal, and in many cases irreversible. Taboos become more, not less, nasty as they become less tribal.

The first time—and I'm happy to say one of the few times —the ban was imposed on me, I had no clear idea as to why. I had done no more than exchange greetings, and those of a conventionally friendly sort, with the woman who suddenly refused to exchange even a glance with me. To this day I have no certainty as to the reason. My best guess is that the silence had to do with my remarks at a town meeting when certain individuals began to balk at the idea of paying tax dollars for "kids in special ed." The shunner was not one of these individuals, so I hadn't attacked any of her remarks, though it's reasonable to assume that I had attacked her sentiments. I should add for the sake of fairness that the ban is not reserved for spendthrift liberals, friends of "retards," or "flatlanders." I have heard of natives with impeccable pedigrees and respectable IQs who "never spoke a word to each other after that."

As with many peculiar customs, this one both invites and confounds an easy judgment. On the one hand, it strikes me as childish and absurd. You have to see it in action to get the full effect; when you do, you have the distinct impression that you're back in junior high, and the equally distinct impression that the silent individual was never so happy as at that time of his or her life. Certainly the person does not seem happy now. What makes the practice so absurd is that the ill feeling is very likely the result of a breakdown in communication. So with all the self-assurance of a quack doctor bleeding someone to death in order to save his life, the offended person refuses any and all attempts to communicate.

On the other hand, one can't help but wonder if there isn't something rather civilized about this most uncivil treatment. The freeze on all communication is also a freeze on escalation. Tensions can hardly rise when two adversaries are not saying anything to each other. The ban represents a very strict and literal interpretation of that old adage, "If you can't say something nice, don't say anything at all." It also shows a respectful awareness of the relationship between anger and speech. I'm told that in the logging camps that once dotted this region, there were two rules in the cookhouse: prunes at every meal (to keep the bowels open), and no talking at meals (to avoid fights). I think of these rules as a kind of North Woods charm to ward off evil—bowels open and mouth shut.

When we talk about anger, we are never far from talking about language. Words incite anger and express it. If Seneca was correct in saying that anger arises out of a discrepancy between our wishes and the real world, then anger may also arise from the discrepancy between the world of our words and the world as it is. Our world, our language, and our minds —one can imagine them as three circles that overlap but never achieve perfect congruency. We do not say exactly what we mean. We do not hear exactly what was said. We are able to imagine but not to attain the kind of creative power that speaks our wishes into being, "Let there be light," and there is light. So we become angry.

The relationship between language and anger would seem to be most acute at the high and low ends of verbal capacity. The man or woman of words, able to make his or her thoughts "perfectly clear," grows angry when others seem unable to grasp such perfection. To these acutely verbal individuals, the world appears to be teeming with the block-headed and the perverse, which it most certainly is, though verbal competence has never formed a reliable exemption from either category. Once again, the phenomenon of road rage provides us with a metaphor. The greater the horsepower, the greater the potential for acting like a horse's ass. The faster the words come to our mouth, the faster we expect the mountain to come to Muhammad.

On the other hand, anger can arise out of the frustration of not being able to make one's mind known. I remember a broad-shouldered boy in my high school years, who once confided to me, "I don't know what to do with words. Some guy starts throwing words at me—I just hit him." Fortunately for my nose, he never perceived me as throwing any words in his direction. Someone who's worked with a preverbal or nonverbal child knows the tantrums that can arise when the child cannot communicate his needs. These outbursts have their counterpart in adults who grow angry as a way of saying what they cannot otherwise articulate. They may also grow angry because of the consistent success of those who can articulate. People who "know how to talk" also know how to get what they want. After physical attractiveness, the ability to use words may be the most reliable way of achieving one's desires. I find it interesting that one of our regional expressions here in Vermont has the word *ugly* as a synonym for *angry*. *Ugly* accurately describes the effects of anger; perhaps it connotes one of the causes as well. If so, we might also use the word *inarticulate* as another synonym.

Perhaps I tend to look at things too much like a schoolteacher, which I once was and in many ways remain, but it seems to me that genuine "anger management" has a great deal to do with education—and not necessarily with education about anger. If we would inhabit a world with less fury, we should teach all our children to read, write, and speak. And to those who master rhetoric we should teach philosophy—especially those Eastern kinds that set great store on keeping one's mouth shut.

If that isn't simplistic enough, I can go one better: At bottom, much of anger has to do with the concept of a "fair share," and with people getting more or less than their own. Trace anger to the most primal origins imaginable and what do you see but the verbal or physical grab for something that belongs by rights to another, to all, or to none. Take two routes to the understanding of wrath, one through psychology and the other through inequality, and the second will invariably prove the faster and more scenic route. But knowing that also comes down to a matter of education, and what it means in the deepest sense to be an educated human being.

⌐

That said, educated human beings seem to be having as much trouble as anyone else these days with the relationship between anger and language. The common perception of those living outside the American academy is that if any two words appropriately describe the discourse of our intellectuals, these words are *angry* and *linguistic.* One imagines that college professors, not unlike some of my neighbors, are either not talking to one another or else talking about language. "She keeps going around town calling me a tramp. . . . Oh, and now she's saying I'm Eurocentric." Frankly, *language* has become one of those words that I don't much like to hear any more. Someone says "language" and, borrowing a page from my old classmate, I just want to hit him.

That is an unfortunate reaction, of course, the opposite of what it "means in the deepest sense to be an educated human being." It is also a somewhat hackneyed reaction. These days one is almost expected to wrinkle his nose at the mention of "political correctness," in much the same way as one is expected to feign hunger an hour after eating Chinese food. Speech codes and "sensitive" nomenclature are easy to mock because both can degenerate so easily into silliness, and frequently do. Still, I have to say that the guiding principles behind political correctness seem basically sound to me. As I understand them, they go like this:

1. The most interesting, creative, and pleasurable kind of human society is as diverse and inclusive as possible.

2. If a diverse population is to live in peace (that is, to avoid the kind of Balkanization that conservatives claim is the goal and the danger of multiculturalism), it must develop codes of courtesy.

3. In an "age of communication," those codes will largely be linguistic.

To dismiss the logic in the name of good old common sense strikes me as more than a little ironic. The logic is about as commonsense as you get.

The problem with political correctness, however, is that most of us tend to be a good deal more zealous about taking offense than preventing it. This can be self-defeating, to say the least. If instead of becoming more courteous, each of us labors to become more reflexively fastidious, we may wind up being too diverse even to appreciate diversity. We may discover all too soon that there is a carrying capacity for tact as for everything else. But to refute a bad idea for the sake of a foolish application is not to be a critic, just a third-rate curmudgeon. Speech codes, like all codes, are attempts at civilization. Henry Miller is supposed to have said that the final stage of any civilization is to reject civilization itself. I for one am not averse to postponing the final stage for awhile, even if the stopgaps include a few awkward pronouns.

Nevertheless, the speech code that interests me the most is my own. I don't have to listen to someone else's offensive speech if I don't want to, but unfortunately I do have to listen to mine. What is more, I have to live with it, in consequence and memory. The phrase "foot in mouth" is meant to suggest an image of extreme awkwardness; it might just as easily be taken as an image of extreme self-punishment, when "foot in rear" doesn't go far enough. A reader might wonder why I haven't included a chapter entitled "Anger at Oneself"—you're reading it now, if you're reading between the lines. Were I to write such a chapter from a purely anecdotal standpoint, about three-quarters of the material would pertain to violations of my own code of speech. I suspect I am no different from most people. I suspect that most of us are struggling with our own speech codes more than with any other moral dilemma. No wonder we jump at the promise of a respite, such as the largely academic controversy over political correctness: speech code as spectator sport. Anyway, in its present version, my code looks roughly like this:

1. Speak less. Treat speech in the same way as your doctor has advised you to treat food. "Try to leave the table one-third less than full."

2. Make your needs known. Never be upset for failing to receive what you never asked for.

3. Complain for the sake of change, or for the sake of camaraderie, but never to get attention or to put on airs. Complaints are not credentials.

4. Never take offense—or give it—over matters of taste. Speak of your own passions, but do not denigrate another's passions. When there is nothing in the world left to disagree over, then let us have at one another over music, cuisine, and movies. Let us fight in the streets over style.

5. Speak nothing but the truth, but seldom all of the truth. "Telling it all" is tedious in small matters and cruel in large. Will God ever tell us all the truth about ourselves? Who could bear it?

6. Speak your heart only to those dear to your heart. "Cast not your pearls before swine."

7. Listen as though it were a sacred obligation. Take careful note of the correlation between your attentiveness to others and your aptitude for prayer. Grace for the one never exists without grace for the other.

8. Coax the quiet and the shy, but do not badger them. Have an eye out for those who look for an invitation to speak, and give them one. But do not cater to those who coyly wait for repeated invitations.

9. Ask more questions than you answer. Refuse questions that are impertinent or that tempt you to appear more knowledgeable or convinced than you are.

10. Call no one by an epithet. "Whosoever shall say, Thou fool, shall be in danger of hell fire." Names are sacred.

11. Say nothing about another person that you would not admit in that person's presence. It will probably find its way to his ears anyway.

12. Explain yourself to the degree that others wish to understand, not to the degree that you wish to be understood. The wish to be understood absolutely is a violation of the first commandment: "Thou shalt have no other gods before me." Only God understands us completely.

13. Never use knowledge or vocabulary to exclude another person. This is no different from eating bread in the presence of the hungry.

14. Waste no time with people who deliberately misunderstand you, who caricature what you say in order to attack it more easily. Pick on someone your own size.

15. Use or abstain from offensive language with an eye to etymology and connotation. *Shit* is a fine old word for an indispensable thing. *Fuck* is a violent word for a beautiful thing.

16. Be wary of prescribing commandments. Break any code for the sake of unsentimental compassion. A noble silence is not always the opposite of noise. Nor is hatred always the opposite of love. Sometimes dogma is.

It's interesting that we use the word *profanity* to refer almost exclusively to language. Surely we can be profane in other, nonverbal ways, but we tend to think of profanity as linguistic. It makes sense to me. In some ways, language seems the most profaned of all human activities, that is, the most careless, the most taken for granted. I have met only a few persons who behaved like perfect atheists, but I have known a number who spoke as if they were. Language, with which we make metaphor, is itself a metaphor of our sins. We gab the way we drink; extemporize the way men womanize; abuse words the way we pollute air and water: in the confidence of an endless supply and in the presumption that anything free for the taking is to be taken without thanks. Maybe that is the reason Jesus says (in verses no writer loves to hear): "I tell you, on the day of judgment you will have to give an account for every careless word you utter; for by your words you will be justified, and by your words you will be condemned." The word *account* suggests that words are no less part of the economy of creation than are any other resource. They are there to be used, but to be used with care, to be used in such a way that they might be used again, by someone else, and where possible to be made more beautiful than we found them. In short, they are not to be wasted.

Of course, waste comes in various forms: Things "go bad" because they are abused and ruined; they also go bad because they are hoarded and spoil. A wasted word is not only a misspoken word; it can be a word left unsaid. It can be a damned shame in either case. The word usually translated as "hell" in the Gospels is *Gehenna,* the name of the refuse dump outside of Jerusalem. Here where worshipers of the Canaanite deity Moloch once brought their children for sacrifice, the Judeans of a more enlightened age burned their garbage. Hell is about waste. Angry words and angry silence—profanity in all its forms—often burn down to nothing more or less than the sinful wasting of our lives.

I remember from my days as a teacher how my students would often say that "life" was the theme of some story or the meaning of some symbol that they had been asked to interpret. "It's about life," they'd say. To which I'd reply, "Well, it's *all* about life. You have to be a little more specific than that." And in the study of literature, I suppose you do. Still, I wish that before coaxing my students to a different answer, I had paid more homage to the one they gave. Yes, people, "it is about life." Every word, every action requiring a single breath, is about that finite experience we call life. You may say it is about the loss of academic standards, or the encroachment of state government on the rights of local municipalities, or exactly how long it takes one waitress to bring out two cups of coffee, but it is about life. It would make sense to get angry over forgetting that, but for the most part we get angry simply because we forget.

⌒⌒

The ban of silence imposed by one neighbor on another in a small New England town has its counterpart in the silences of even more intimate relationships. One type of silence amounts to a game that might be called "Guess Why I'm Angry." The other more subtle type might be called "Guess What It Takes to Please Me." Both kinds have to do with the hypertrophied mentality we have discussed before: When my head becomes the whole world, I expect that everyone in the world ought to know what's in my head. In Robert Browning's poem "My Last Duchess," a Renaissance duke explains to a visitor why he had his last wife put to death. Though she had done nothing dishonorable, he found her too indiscriminate in her attentions and too liberal in her gratitude toward others besides the duke. As the duke goes on to explain, the problem did not lie in her willful disregard of her husband's jealousy; it lay rather in her innocence of it, and in his resolute refusal to enlighten her.

> Even had you skill
> In speech—which I have not—to make your will
> Quite clear to such an one, and say, "Just this
> Or that in you disgusts me; here you miss,
> Or there exceed the mark"—and if she let
> Herself be lessened so, nor plainly set
> Her wits to yours, forsooth, and made excuse,
> —E'en then would be some stooping; and I choose
> Never to stoop.

So much for the confessions of one who has no "skill in speech." Beyond the pettiness of the duke's jealousy, one is appalled at the pride of his reticence. One is more appalled to think of what he might have learned about another person's heart, or what reassurance he might have found for his own, had he made some attempt to share his insecurity with his wife. But in his eyes that would be "stooping." Apparently, having her murdered was not. The whole situation strikes us as the extremity of evil—yet most of us have probably acted in our own versions of the same drama. Someone "ought to have known" what angered us, and we would not stoop to tell him.

But we would stoop, perhaps, to some form of ostracism or vengeance.

Of course, reticence is not always the result of pride—and Browning's poem hints at that too. Sometimes the things that anger or otherwise hurt us seem too strange for words. They do not strike us as worthy of mention. Along with codes of acceptable speech, society maintains a code of acceptable pain—a code that pain seldom honors. I spoke with a psychiatrist once who told me of a woman he knew who was plunged into a profound depression because she had broken her grandmother's hairbrush. Psychiatrists will hear confessions of that sort, and sometimes priests, but how does one tell such a thing to a husband or sister? Even if they heard you with all the sympathy they possessed, how would they understand that sensation of a fissure opening in reality itself merely because a hairbrush lies broken on the floor? People lose their children —of what consequence is a hairbrush? Of course, it is precisely the insignificance of the accident that gives it its power to mock and to maim. Mourn a child and the angels mourn with you; mourn a hairbrush and your dearest friends shake their heads.

If my own meager experience as a priest has taught me anything, it is these two principles: First, more people are in pain than you can imagine; and second, the causes of the pain are also unimaginable. In speech and in silence, in the experience of my anger and in my experience of the anger of others, I try as best as I am able to remember those principles. Even if the neighbor giving me the silent treatment were to speak, she could or would not tell me everything that's wrong. She may not even know it herself, and some of what she knows she would find impossible to confess. Nor could she tell me everything she "heard" when I offended her. This is not a reason to refrain from speaking my mind in her presence. I am willing to stoop in ways that Browning's duke disdained, but I will not stoop to be governed by another's subjectivity. The worst tyranny imaginable is a state where everyone is entitled to file a grievance and no one is required to give an explanation. I will try to remember, though, that I always exist in the presence of the ineffable and the invisible, which, after all, is the essence of religion. I am in the world like a rescue worker. My work requires me to move the debris of Eden using the tools of language. But with each movement, I must not forget the survivors who may lie hidden underneath the debris. And when I happen to be among the injured, I must not be too proud to announce my presence with a cry.

I cannot praise a fugitive and cloistered virtue . . . that never sallies out to see her adversary. . . .

John Milton, *Areopagitica*

VENTURING
OUT

G iven the regenerative power of work, and the various pit-
falls of speech, I am constantly tempted to believe that
immersion in the first and withdrawal from the second are
the best ways for someone like me to avoid anger. Do your
work, keep quietly to yourself, and you will do less harm into
the bargain. You will also be less vulnerable to harm from
others. You will come as close as possible to peace.

I make these resolutions at the same time as I recognize
that the offensiveness that causes many people to withdraw
from human society is partially the result of that very withdrawal. Perhaps "the barbarians are at the gates" for no better
reason than that the rest of us no longer wish to sit there. We
may protest that this is so because the gates have been over-
run by the barbarians, but the matter is more complicated

than that. The so-called crisis of our public schools is in some ways a microcosm of this same dilemma. Whenever we pull back from our neighbors in anger or disgust, we hasten the decline of our neighborhood. The moral dangers of reclusiveness are well-known and, I think for most of us, deeply felt. They can be all the more serious when we withdraw for an allegedly moral purpose, such as controlling our anger. Milton's argument against censorship of the press can also be applied to the attempt to self-censor our daily impressions. "I cannot praise a fugitive and cloistered virtue, unexercised and unbreathed, that never sallies out and sees her adversary, but slinks out of the race where that immortal garland is to be run for, not without dust and heat."

But the argument I keep having with myself, and that any person who has read this far is likely to have also, cannot be settled by a few words from Milton or a few verses from the Bible. Especially not the Bible, where those who would be "God's people" are intermittently challenged with the call to "come out" (from Sodom, Egypt, Babylon) and the call to "go forth" (to Canaan, to Nineveh, to "all the world"). The one call does not cancel out the other. And neither call can be dismissed as a mere temptation.

Without a doubt, we can spare ourselves some anger by choosing to control some of our stimuli. Refusing to do so is every bit as childish as trying to control them all. A good part of adulthood, it seems to me, consists of exercising the privileges of selective association and occupation that childhood denies us. With apologies to St. Paul, we might state those privileges like this: When I was a child I ate as I child, I threw up as a child, I hadn't the foggiest sense of my own digestion as a child, but when I became a man I put away those things that make me sick. I learned a long time ago, for example, that the anger I felt at inconsiderate behavior in a movie theater was equal to or greater than any pleasure I might take from a film, so I see almost all my movies at home now. Once in a while, I do go to an "arts theater," but the behavior there is not always better than at the popular cinema down the street from it. The bad manners of the cultured are not all that different from the bad manners of the young: Both amount to an irrepressible indignation at the thought that an audience would find anything more fascinating than the bad-mannered individuals themselves. So the one type throws around its candy, and the other throws around its cant.

But unless we intend to become complete hermits—and the experience of the Desert Fathers reminds us that absolute isolation is not a foolproof cure for rage—we cannot always avoid the circumstances that annoy us. I can cut down on the time that I spend "out there," but I still have to go to town sometimes. There too I have tried to make a conscious discrimination between the places where I'm likely to feel comfortable and the places where I'm likely to get annoyed, avoiding the latter as much as possible. But there's no fast rule with these things.

The other day, for example, I came perilously close to stepping over the line in a small drugstore of which I'm very fond. I think of the pharmacy as an oasis—which might actually have contributed to my anger, since a provocation there was more likely to enrage me than a provocation somewhere else. The pharmacist is a wonderful man who walks his little dog to work with him every morning and hangs portraits of the entire graduating class of the town high school in his display windows every May. Behind the counter he has these two gregarious women, posted at the register like coanchors on the morning news, so it's like the Jane and Judy show every time you go in, and I love the show. Because the store is on the main street, they get a lot of walk-ins, poor folk and elderly who come to get their prescriptions filled and perhaps to get a little medical advice on the cheap. I sometimes wonder if the patience they find there isn't a medicine in itself.

To be honest, I wasn't feeling so well on the day this happened, or I guess I should say "almost happened." I knew it too, and in the end the knowledge may have helped me restrain myself. I had just turned around in a parking lot where some jerk in an obscenely large SUV was giving the horn to an old woman too timid to break into the flow of traffic. The two adjoining stores were a discount grocery and a liquor outlet, so of course I immediately had the SUV guy pegged as a cheapskate or a drunk, probably both.

A few minutes later, I went to pull into the space in front of the drugstore and came upon a small child walking off the curb to get into his mother's car, which made it impossible to see him from the street. Fortunately, I was driving with a lot less belligerence than Mr. SUV, who doubtless would have plowed the kid into the storefront before he could have located the reflex to blast him into paralysis with his handy little horn. And where was Mother while her son was about to walk through the valley of the shadow of death, that is, off the curb and into the blind spot of her parked car? She was sitting obliviously in the driver's seat, wearing what Emerson once referred to as "the gentlest asinine expression," as she gabbed away with another woman on the curb. And immediately I had her pegged, too (what is the wicked impulse that makes us glance at the driver of a car we pass or that passes us except to stereotype the driver?): college-educated, vaguely New Age, militantly concerned about radiated vegetables and secondhand smoke, and utterly unconcerned that her little boy was walking into an oncoming car. "How to Improve Your Parenting in Just Two Easy Steps": Shut up for five seconds and pay attention.

I smiled at the kid. At least I had the grace to do that. And not to tell the woman about the two steps toward better parenting—I suppose that was a grace also.

Inside the store I waited for the clerks to find my prescription. At the same time a smirking middle-aged man stood beside the counter and asked the other woman about a new drug he'd heard advertised as "a female Viagra." He went on and on about it. The women seemed at turns mildly amused and tense. The man was obviously not a stranger to them, but he was just as obviously not some poor soul who'd lost his keeper or his mind. Like the woman in the car, he seemed bright, middle class, almost professorial. He looked something like Norman Mailer might after an all-night poker game, with his shirt pulled out in anticipation of betting it on one last losing hand before deciding to fold instead. I left the store in disgust, got into my car, got out of my car, and headed back in. I reentered the store to find that the man had followed one of the clerks behind the counter—the pharmacist was away for some reason—where he continued his witless dissertation about the female Viagra. I asked the other woman, "Is this guy bothering you?" "No, no," she whispered. "It's all right. We're used to him." A few days later she thanked me profusely for my concern and was a bit more candid about the difficulties of being "used to him." I pointedly suggested that she didn't need to be used to anybody like that.

Truthfully, I wish that she had given me some pretext for grabbing, say, a portable commode off the shelf and beating him about the head with it. Maybe she would have been more inclined to accept my assistance if she hadn't sensed how close to the line I was standing. Why was I so enraged? The poor taste of the man's remarks was not even the biggest reason. Mainly it was his smug awareness that the women were captive to their customer, that they couldn't just leave the store, nor did they have much power to make him leave it. What nearly lost Clarence Thomas his confirmation as a Supreme Court justice wouldn't have lost him the time of day as a retail customer. It's something I try not to think about whenever I leave a tip; it makes me want to hand my wallet to the waitress.

But it *is* something we should try to think about whenever we're inclined to prescribe easy rules for the avoidance of anger. We should remember those men and women whose skills and bills place them in continual contact with the almighty public. The argument over how far to withdraw from the world is to some extent an argument of privilege. That said, I wonder if it's an argument that any person, however privileged, ever wins.

So what would I do to be less angry with the world and less at odds with myself when I am in it? Two things come to mind.

The first has to do with recognizing my brother or my sister in another angry person. Though this clearly wasn't the case at the drugstore, sometimes the people who enrage us are themselves enraged. We grow angry at them, in part, for failing to see a reflection of ourselves—or perhaps because we *do* see a reflection of ourselves, at some level, and don't like what we see. We get confused between the demon we're fighting in our heads and another person who's fighting the same demon. In other words, we mistake the person *for* the demon. If we could cultivate the discipline of saying, "That is my brother; that is my spitting, fuming image," we might find, if not more peace, then at least more patience. We might also find the courage to take one of those extraordinary steps that are sometimes the most effective antidote to anger. So instead of muttering to ourselves, "What's his problem?" we might answer our own question by saying, "Whatever it is, it approximates *my* problem," and by going on to say out loud, "I have days just like the one you're having, friend. You should see me when I'm mad. Can I help you out?" We might get nothing but contempt in return—but I'd rather get a fist in my eye than seem contemptible to my eye.

I would hate to say anything so trite as "Cultivate a more positive attitude"—but then I think what I find most trite about that sentence is not the word *attitude* but the word *positive*, with all its connotations of self-hypnosis and playacting. I'm at least willing to say, Cultivate a more *generous* attitude, a more liberal heart. Instead of thinking, "I have to go to the store this afternoon, so God preserve me from the idiots," I might think, or even pray, "I'm going to the store this afternoon. God, help me to recognize my siblings and bless them." Maybe this is the best way to interpret "the mark of Cain" that we read about in Genesis. We sometimes forget that a mark was placed on the first murderer so that those who found him would *not* kill him, and I wonder if the mark is nothing other than the predilection toward rage that makes murder possible and the danger of violence recognizable. If we sons and daughters of Cain have to wander the earth anyway, what better way to pass the journey than to look for others with the same mark and to make them know that they are not alone and need not despair?

The second approach has to do with opening our eyes not only to the rage that mirrors our own, but to the mercy and kindness that reduce all rage to shame. This may be one reason that some religions enjoin pilgrimage on their members: Going to see the relics of the saints, we meet their flesh and blood descendants on the road.

Recently some friends of mine, a husband and wife with two young children, a toddler and a nursing infant, drove from northeastern Vermont to Georgia in order to attend a wedding there. They did not have the greatest car. The first time it broke down, a Puerto Rican tractor trailer driver pulled off the road to help them. Under the hood, in need of a sharp-edged tool, he took out a knife and grinned at the father. "What good's a Puerto Rican without a knife?" he joked. He followed the family through three states, delaying his own deliveries and his own homecoming, stopping for four or five additional breakdowns. Though my friends must have experienced any number of occasions for road rage on such a long trip, what effect could those occasions have had so long as a diesel-driving angel flew behind them? They made it to their wedding. May their guardian also come safely to the Marriage Fiesta.

Of course, we don't have to leave home in order to recognize how often what we take for danger turns out to be grace. The reversals that happen in literature or in strange places can also happen in our own backyards. Wherever they happen, they serve to remind us that anger often comes of premature conclusions. The old advice about "counting to ten" has as much to do with letting all the data come in as with keeping all of our bile from spewing out. One summer afternoon when my wife and I were new to the Northeast Kingdom, she saw from the porch of our second-floor apartment a delivery truck go lumbering down our side street, where the driver tossed what seemed to be a handful of litter out his window. My wife hates litter with a passion, as do I, and she was immediately angry. But in the same split second that it took for her mind to form the words "You slob," she noticed that the truck was a candy truck, and the litter was candy. Her epiphany closed with the fingers of several children standing on the sidewalk, who caught it in midair at the same instant as she "got it" in midcurse.

Anger is often nothing more than a hasty judgment registered as a nasty emotion. Anger can result from a failure to acknowledge the full narrative sweep of life, how events unfold, how characters develop, how interpretations fail. One of my favorite parables outside those of the gospel has to do with a friend of my wife who probed a single mystery among the many that formed her small rural community. What she found, in the end, was simply more mystery.

The friend was living way out in Victory, Vermont, a remote township with the double distinction of being perched above a bog and of being the last place in the state to receive electricity. During the course of earning her master's degree, this friend found it necessary to commute several times a week from Victory to the state university in Burlington, a good hundred miles away. Coming home late at night, she would see an old man sitting by the side of her road. He was always there, in subzero temperatures, in stormy weather, no matter how late she returned. He made no acknowledgment of her passing. The snow settled on his cap and shoulders as if he were merely another gnarled old tree.

She often wondered what brought him to that same spot every evening—what stubborn habit, private grief, or mental disorder. I wonder if she didn't sometimes begin to doubt her senses, or believe in ghosts.

Finally, she asked a neighbor of hers, "Have you ever seen an old man who sits by the road late at night?"

"Oh, yes," said her neighbor, "many times."

"Is he . . . a little touched upstairs? Does he ever go home?"

"He's no more touched than you or me," her neighbor laughed. "And he goes right home after you do. You see, he doesn't like the idea of you driving by yourself out late all alone on these back roads, so every night he walks out to wait for you. When he sees your taillights disappear around the bend, and he knows you're okay, he goes home to bed."

I can think of several ridiculous places to take a story like this. Perhaps the most ridiculous is to deny the possibility that the man we see at the side of a road is a serial killer. All we can say in the light of this story and of the several that precede it is that folly comes of pretending to know the world better than it can actually be known. Anger can be one form of that folly. Anger can amount to a bitter certainty that admits to no surprise. Anger is like a young man who takes every flirtation as evidence that women are laughing at him. To expect no surprises is to give no quarter, show no faith, have no fun.

✐

Side by side, then, with the tempting resolution to stay home and stay focused, I would place this corollary: that I go out deliberately with the aim of claiming kinship with my angry brothers and sisters and with the additional aim of developing a richer heart. "It is not good for the man to be alone," God says in Genesis, and in Isaiah tells us "not to hide yourself from your own flesh."

Samuel Johnson, an irascible man easily susceptible to annoyances, once said that "There is nothing which has yet been contrived by man by which so much happiness is produced as by a good tavern or inn." A man who not only got mad but was also afraid of going mad, Johnson realized how important human company could be in saving the mind from its own delusions. Avoiding those places and situations that are bound to enrage us is one thing, but withdrawing from all human contact is like attempting to avoid food poisoning by going without food. Sometimes we need to eat out almost as much as we need to eat.

I love to eat where the customers know one another and the proprietor knows the customers, where a little background noise buys a lot of intimacy, where the cooks and servers have names, and dishes may even have nicknames. I know a restaurant where there's a waitress who's outlasted at least four different owners. I'm probably not the only person who thinks of the place as belonging to her, though it does not. She's friendly, extremely efficient, and as my wife likes to say, "full of beans." I remember one lunchtime when a lanky working man asked her with the bright-eyed eagerness of a small boy, "What can you tell me about that pot roast with gravy?"—one of the specials chalked on the board. "Well," she said placing one plump hand on her hip and tossing her hair back, "it's a pot roast . . . and it comes with gravy." She let loose a merry shriek. He smiled sheepishly and ordered the pot roast.

Change the setting and you have a fine little Zen *mondo* there: "A monk once came to Hui-neng and inquired, 'What can you tell me about the pot roast with gravy?' The master roared with laughter and said . . ." Isn't the master also laughing at our petulance? As a purely cerebral condition, as the bodyguard of our *pre*conditions—a mastiff ready to bite when all the worst things we have imagined come to pass—anger can exist as a denial of contradictory evidence, of mystery, of experience itself. And the fear of anger can lead to this very same denial. "I might get mad, so I'd better stay home. I'd better play it safe."

A more abundant life, on the other hand, belongs to those who remain brave enough to try the daily special. It cannot be tasted through an explanation or processed through any one emotion. It's a pot roast, and it comes with gravy.

It was as if that great rush of anger
had washed me clean. . . .

Albert Camus, *The Stranger*

NAPOLEON'S
TEST

According to an apocryphal story, a woman once came before Napoleon and accused one of his officers of rape. Imagining himself a late Solomon, the emperor handed the woman a sword and commanded her to insert it into a scabbard as he moved it back and forth in front of her. When she failed, he acquitted the officer. His point was as obvious as his analogy was anatomically ridiculous: There is no such thing as rape.

I have imagined this scene many times: the supercilious emperor wiggling his scabbard; the woman at first grimly and then frantically attempting to bring the sword point to the opening; the other officers, very probably including her rapist, mocking her efforts, inflating the little man's vanity with their laughter. The sword grows heavy in her hand; it loses altitude, prompting one of the regimental wits to charge her with a lack of ardor. Perhaps the woman's mind begins to be violated by the inadmissible suggestion that she has not told the truth, that she was not raped after all. She reddens, she sweats, she redoubles her efforts. But with each vain thrust, with each new burst of laughter, the monstrous insinuation pushes itself further into her conscience, even as everything she knows and has experienced resists it.

A part of what makes this scene so horrible to contemplate is the proximity of her vindication. The solution to Napoleon's absurd puzzle is literally *in her hand*. If only she would raise the point to his neck and say, "Hold still, bitch."

The story makes us angry, or it ought to, but Napoleon's test might also serve as a parable about anger itself. The story represents the terms of a game that all of us have played, in one form or another, until overcome by failure and fury. Perhaps we drop the sword and run weeping from the room. Perhaps we use it to cut our own throats or, in a gesture that leads inevitably to the same outcome, we thrust it into the emperor's bowels.

The endings vary, but the beginning is the same: We are appointed some test that promises vindication. It will exonerate us, prove us, set us above reproach. It will show that we are sincere believers, genuine heroes, true friends, real women or men. Invariably, it is a false test based on false premises and spurious analogies. Still, we play. We hold out the sword, we aim for the shifting aperture that is supposed to represent us or a part of us. We hold justice in our hands, but we are unable to see it as anything else but a game piece given to us by the designer of the game. One more thrust, we think, just a bit more effort and concentration, and we shall prevail. Our determination is at least as great as our tormentor's amusement. Like the woman, we know that we can do it, for the simple reason that we know something like "it" was done to us. After all, truth is on our side. But we have already forsaken the truth by accepting the terms of the lie that has been foisted upon us. In other words, we lost at the very moment that we allowed ourselves to be convinced that our predicament was a game we could win.

The answer to this moral riddle will vary from life to life. I cannot claim even to know all the ways it answers in my own. But I think I know how to pose the relevant questions. What is the false test I have accepted? What do I hope to prove by taking it? And is there a sword that has been placed in my hand as part of that very test, by which the test might be destroyed?

⌒

A woman asked me what I was writing these days, and then she asked what I knew was coming next, "Why anger?"

I gave her my stock reply. It is an emotion I know well, I said, an emotion with which I have struggled. And the struggle is made poignant by certain beliefs that I hold as a Christian, a humanist, and "a progressive" in my politics if not in my bets. I gave a fair answer to her question. But I can take her question further. When exactly did I first start writing about this emotion and why? I discover that I can give a specific answer, an exact set of coordinates that locate the origins of the project. Granted, I have always had a temper. I have never been a laid-back type. But there was a recent period in my life when I was angrier than usual, and angry more often. At least two things were making that so.

For one thing, I had become a supervisor of other workers, something I had never anticipated becoming. I had worked for seven years as a high school English teacher. I was considered a fairly good one, and I think that I was, if not quite so good as I was reputed to be. Without any changes in the job or in my approach to it, I probably would have bowed out or burned out in a few years. There was simply no way to do right by a hundred students according to their needs and my standards and still have a life outside of school. I had always believed, and I had always hoped, that I was there for the short term.

Then my department head, who had also become my friend, died of cancer. I was with her throughout the last months of her life, and it was during that time that she told me I could probably fill her position if I wanted it. She gave me some advice, and she gave me her blessing. After her death I was indeed offered the position, and I accepted. It felt like a legacy that I ought not refuse. It also felt like the provisional solution to a perennial problem: With fewer classes to teach, I could do a better job teaching—and I could be a halfway decent father and husband too. In exchange for a little more responsibility, a little more stress, I could "achieve balance." In other words, I could get the sword into the scabbard.

To some extent, I suppose that I was able to manage—the schedule, but not the stress. Suddenly I was called upon to solve problems that were not of my making, along with the usual problems that were. Often caught at what seemed like an impossible juncture of con artistry, dysfunction, and pride —the student's, the system's, and mine, respectively—I was forever trying to prove what could not be proven, to fix what could not be fixed. I assumed that if the world really worked, if I really worked, then there had to be some formula by which education, equality, excellence, and ego could all assert their rightful claims, with yours truly as the arbiter. It was mad.

It was also ironic. I had become a teacher out of a love for reading and writing, in addition to an appreciation for young people and a preference for working on my own in my own space. And there I was, without time to read and write, a distracted mentor to the children I taught and frequently an official adversary of the children I didn't, as well as a team captain who had never even wanted to be on a team. Of course, we can chalk up that kind of irony to what Samuel Johnson called "the vanity of human wishes" and the writer of Ecclesiastes simply called "vanity." In other words, we can point to a principle of futility that operates in most human endeavors. But notice how we use *vanity* to denote both that futility and the pride of our hearts. How much of what we do in vain is done because we are vain?

So it was the job that was making me so angry, but only in part. This was not my only "problem with school." At the same time, I watched with increasing despair as my own daughter was jostled about in an overcrowded elementary school taught by overloaded teachers and populated by undernurtured kids. Behind the scenes was an underpaid, undereducated community that I seldom met—our village having not so much as a general store—except on those occasions when they massed in the town hall to hack apart a school budget. I found it as hard to direct my anger as to manage it. I was never sure whom to blame. For the first time since graduate school, I discovered that there were people I despised. I can remember hearing the commandment "Love your neighbor as yourself" as though it had been written to mock me.

Of course, we were all being mocked in one way or another. The favorite practical joke of deprivation is to make enemies out of people who ought to form a united front. And schools contain enough mockery of their own: cruelty, boredom, purposelessness beyond imagining. Have you ever played the mental game of going one worse than the worst; for example, what could be worse than slave labor? Answer: slave labor that does not even benefit the master. Slave labor that is debased beyond exploitation. Picking cotton and carrying it to the dump. Doing homework that no one sees, writing papers that no one reads, taking exams that no one reviews with you. Drowning by degrees in the presence of lifeguards who think their primary job is to make a little mark every time your head goes under water. Critics of education mount the most swaybacked of high horses when they accuse "the educational establishment" of teaching selfish values, crass materialism, blind conformity. I'd take any one of these over the didacticism of despair, the idea that work is meaningless except as dues for the right to play. The best thing that many schools teach is resignation, the grim hope that comes of learning that "this too shall pass." Critics complain that too few graduates are prepared for life, but they might at least give the devil his due by acknowledging how well many of them have been prepared for death.

Then one day I heard my daughter tell her mother: "I'm not good at anything." This when I was working twelve to fourteen hours a day so that other people's kids could discover that they were good at some things and be able to feel good about themselves into the bargain. But could I be certain that I had not made at least a few of them feel exactly the same way? Something broke with those words. I asked for a year's unpaid leave, bought a bunch of books, and told the state office of education that my daughter would be spending her sixth-grade year at home.

I have to be honest and say that I did this as much to save my own soul as to rescue my kid. I did what I did because I was being consumed by anger. I suppose I have anger to thank, along with God and the liberal laws of the state of Vermont, for one of the happiest years of my life. Part of what distinguishes that year is how free it was of anger. It was certainly full of challenge. I was the superintendent, teacher, bus driver, nurse, and cook of my own school. And this wasn't one of those you-go-be-creative-while-I write-my-novel setups; I could account for every minute. I did my lesson plans as always, hour blocks of "traditional" school in the morning, hands-on projects in the afternoon. We did a simulated archeological dig at the site of an abandoned farmhouse in the woods. We took over an upscale restaurant for an evening, with our own menu, our own cooking, and my daughter's friends helping out as waitresses. We visited fossilized coral reefs and interviewed farmers, scientists, and state troopers. My daughter scrubbed up and assisted a pediatrician in examining a baby thirteen hours old. We played Handel, chess, and hooky. At the end of the year, she returned to the classroom (though we did manage an encore between the eighth and ninth grades). Her father did not.

The experience taught me a few things about anger, about myself, about my fellow human beings. I needed merely to mention what I was doing, for example, to put certain people immediately on the defensive. "I'd be very concerned by the lack of socialization," they'd tell me. Sometimes I would explain that we had addressed their concern by seeing that my daughter had art and music at the town school, and by involving her peers in some of our projects. At other times I merely quipped that there had been socialization at Alcatraz too. Homeschooling, like other forms of abstinence, tends to be interpreted as an accusation by those who do not abstain. The teetotaler, the vegetarian, and the virgin are invariably heard as shouting, "Drunkard!" "Butcher!" and "Slut!" even if all they have actually said is, "No, thank you." Another part of the anatomy of anger, I guess: anger as guilt.

I was more sympathetic to parents who told me, often in the tone of someone making a confession, that they lacked the training, the money, or the patience to take such a radical step. To these I would say, "Maybe you also lack a good reason." Why do it if you don't have to? The experience of teaching my own child at home was so valuable for me precisely because, inveterate moralizer that I am, I could extract so few morals from it. In some sense, it solved nothing, not even for us. Seen from a practical perspective, it was reckless and irresponsible. For what it cost our household in income, we could have paid for a year's tuition at Harvard. Seen from another perspective, it was tantamount to an admission of defeat. A sword had been placed in my hand with which I was supposed to slay all the dragons of ignorance (without giving any one of them so much as a scratch, of course), and I used it instead to come to my own child's defense. Hardly an altruistic decision. I didn't care. The question of "What if everybody did it?" had no meaning for me. Everybody did not do it, everybody could not do it, everybody did not need to do it. I did, I could, and I felt that I had to.

In an earlier chapter, I characterized the anger of men like Agamemnon and Saul as growing out of a fatalistic conception of life, the "shit happens" philosophy on a grand scale. In some sense, it was happening to me—the shit and the philosophy both—and in some ways I had been cooperating with the process. Agamemnon holding the sacrificial knife over his daughter is not all that different from Napoleon's suppliant trying to get the sword into his wiggling scabbard: The disgrace that they believe will come of "just walking away" is already assured. They will be disgraced no matter what they do. That is not to say that they have lost all freedom. It's only to say that sometimes the offer you can't refuse turns out to be the one offer that you can.

I have spent a good part of this book looking at occasions when I have been angry, hoping that the reader might do the same, if that seemed useful. But it is every bit as important, perhaps more important, to identify those occasions when we have not been angry at all, when we might have been but weren't. Or when we began in anger, and then rose to something else. That was certainly the experience I had in homeschooling. Anger sometimes works like the first stage of a rocket. Without it, you'll have a hard time getting off the ground. But if you cannot at some point let it go, it will only pull you back to the ground once its fuel is spent. You will rise a ways only to crash. So it is never enough merely to ask, When did I blast off in some rage only to burn out before I got anywhere? It is also good to ask, When have I blasted off only to find myself in a whole different orbit?

Not long ago as I write, the state of Vermont became the first in the nation to legalize the covenants of gay and lesbian couples. The bill provided for the formation of *civil unions,* a term intended to make a distinction from marriage, though couples so joined could count on nearly all the rights and benefits that married couples do.

The reaction here in the Northeast Kingdom of Vermont was not so ugly as it might have been, but against the backdrop of hate crimes elsewhere in the nation, it was scary enough. Identical placards, black lettering on white, began to appear on the roadsides, nailed to barns and houses, and in bumper sticker form on the backs of cars and pickups: "Take Back Vermont." A few of the signs appeared, literally, in the treetops. The slogan was purported to cover several grievances, including school funding and land use laws, but no one doubted that the central issue, the straw that broke the camel's back, was civil unions. Some of the protests were not so subtle: Another usually smaller bumper sticker read: "Instead of a Deer, Kill a Queer."

After decades of my daydreaming about a grassroots revolt in the hinterlands, this was the form it took. Steal our farms, freeze our wages, stunt the growth of our children, poison our lakes and streams—and what finally mobilizes the masses? Two sixty-year-old lesbians joining hands on a cake knife. Any populist bone left in my body broke there. I knew from experience that some of those who posted the signs would have given their lives to protect those women from attack, but their willingness to throw in their lot with the rest was not reassuring. And what was even more depressing than the revolt was the relatively limp response to it. There were almost no signs challenging the others. I may have counted two or three "Vermont: Keep It Civil" signs on front lawns. I did not see one sign of that sort affixed to a house, nor did I have any intention of affixing one to my own. A few people wrote letters to the local newspapers urging tolerance, but these were easily outnumbered by the weekly succession of diatribes—many adorned with a full complement of biblical quotations—that sometimes enlarged the letters-to-the-editor section to several full pages.

It was evident to me that people were afraid, that I was afraid, to identify my house as belonging to a queer-sympathizer. And I think that some of those who put up the "Take Back Vermont" signs could smell that fear and were invigorated by it far more than they were inspired by any homophobia. Disenfranchised rednecks, many of them, often those standing in stony silence at the backs of town meeting halls, now *they* were the vocal majority. The liberals were the tongue-tied ones for a change. One could sense the heady thrill of it, what I imagine it was like to loot the houses of your "betters" in company with other Brown Shirts.

I began to wonder how long it would be before some gay kid was found beaten to death in a roadside ditch. I began to anticipate my own remorse at having said nothing. (I did manage to deliver a sermon on the issue, which was not exactly preaching to the choir, but close. Our bishop had already endorsed civil unions.) And I began to grow angry, not only at the imaginary sight of that young man's body being pulled from the ditch, or even at the very real sight of "Take Back Vermont" signs posted ever-so-indignantly on the front lawns of individuals known to be wife beaters or pedophiles, but at the bother and the time it would cost me to do my duty as a writer and a priest in my community. Truthfully, when I imagine participating in the Underground Railroad, I can hear my voice muttering angrily in the shadows of the lantern light, outraged at slavery not only because of the misery it has brought to my fellow human beings but also because of the extra chore it has given to me. One more goddamn thing I'm supposed to do.

Anyway, a few weeks before the election, I delivered a letter to the local newspaper. I drove it to the office, about fifteen miles away, and when I came home, my wife met me in the driveway with the portable phone. The editor had read the letter—she must have read fast, or I must have driven slow, for it was thousands of words above their stated length limit— and she was printing it entire. My wife later confided to me that although she had resolved not to pressure me to write on the subject, she was relieved that I had decided to do so on my own. "I think there were people expecting to hear from you," she said.

I guess there were. Within hours after the paper (a weekly) came out, I began to hear from some of them—all in praise of what I had written. It was as if I had lanced a sore. A woman from my parish whom I thought might never speak to me again called to say that "we needed a different perspective." Another parishioner had phoned an hour before to tell about her two gay relatives, both of them news to me. A farmer's wife called and described how she had read the letter to her husband while he worked on the barn roof; a tolerant man, he had not tumbled off. A former student wrote to tell me how he and two of his companions had read the piece aloud on a truck trip to deliver maple syrup to New York. "Kick-ass writing!" one of them had exclaimed—the best review I ever got. Two Quakers, parents of former students, wrote me separate letters of appreciation, sealed in the same envelope, like the homely metaphor for a marriage. An older gay couple e-mailed the newspaper to say that they would "make Mr. Keizer's article required reading—if we believed in such a thing as required reading."

But the response that moved me most came from a gentle-voiced young man who called and would only identify himself as "Brian." Sometimes you intuit things in the same mystical way as you intuit them in dreams, and I knew almost immediately that Brian was the young man whose battered body had tormented my waking thoughts—not that my letter had saved him (would his attackers have even bothered to read my three-thousand-word epistle, much less allowed themselves to be swayed by it?) but that my vision had been of a real person, now met briefly over the phone.

The story of my letter does not end with that catharsis, however. And there is something I should like my Quaker friends to know. My waking nightmares of Brian had been dreamed side by side with waking nightmares of an attack on my own house, of bullets fired through my living room windows, or someone setting fire to our barn. Even before my letter was published, I went and purchased a lightweight, cut-down, pump action, rapid-cycling, twelve-gauge shotgun. It was not my first gun, but it represented the loss of my last illusion about owning one. No one uses a weapon like that for target practice. No one hunts with it either. It has one purpose—or, I guess, two cross-purposes: to kill someone, or to convince him that you will. And yes, I could imagine all the earnest voices asking me, "What would Jesus say?" Well, according to tradition, Moses said that two men lying together is an abomination. Funny, isn't it, how quickly liberals become biblical literalists when it suits their argument.

Or how quickly Christians turn aside from the gospel

when it doesn't suit their fear. I had some hard questions to face. I had arrayed myself against the majority of Christians in my neck of the woods with my letter, and I would certainly have alienated most of the remainder with my gun. What kind of a Christian was I—what kind of a person even? Perhaps no one has given a better answer than my first-grade teacher, who wrote on my very first report card: "He *worries* so!" But then, if I did not worry so, or act on my worries, I would not have written on behalf of Brian.

The main point of all this is how far I had traveled from being angry. As soon as I put pen to paper, my anger began to disappear. In fact, most of those who praised my letter cited its lack of rancor—even as I compared the "Take Back Vermont" signs to the *Nicht Juden* signs posted outside German villages in the late 1930s—its humor, its attempt to understand some of the frustrations of my opponents. By the time I test-fired the gun, which plowed out a great trough of snow in front of me, I felt nothing but a dreadful sense of compassion, not just for the victims of bigotry this time, but for the bigots too. I wanted no harm to come to any of them. Is this what it means to love your enemy? I wondered. And are we best able to love our neighbors as ourselves when we have at last recognized how much we resemble them?

For it was glaringly obvious to me then; I suddenly saw the gun in my hand for what it was: incontrovertible proof that I was a redneck too, armed and dangerous. Political differences aside, I inhabited the same mental landscape of outrage and perceived threat. Opposing a group of people with words, and prepared to oppose them, if necessary, with deadly force, I discovered that I resembled them more closely than I did many of "my own kind." Failing to fit my heart into the

wiggling scabbards of "biblical morality" and nonviolent resistance, I found out what I really was, which turned out to be
nothing more than what my religion had always said I was: a
sinner, and of a rather undistinguished regional variety. I am
neither dismayed nor encouraged by that thought. I am simply
humbled by it, humbled, you might say, at a point beyond
rage. "Just as I am . . . O Lamb of God, I come."

The refusal to take Napoleon's test is a refusal to justify yourself on someone else's terms. It may also be an acceptance of
one's place in history. As glib as the statement may sound, I
invite anyone to test it against experience. A truly contemporary
man or woman is seldom angry in a seething, self-destructive
way. He or she may be intensely angry—but no more intensely
than purposefully. The anger has some point, and some
threshold beyond which it is able to become something else.

One of the larger tasks for any thoughtful person who is
also a religious person is that of discerning the grace of his or
her generation. To ask, What is the unique opportunity of my
time? We know people who are adept at noting the follies of
their times; this too is a gift, but not the greatest or most useful. Likewise, we know people who have an unerring sense of
"what's new" and of catching every wave as soon as it crests.
This may be a gift as well, providing that some resilience comes
with it. New waves will leave us high and dry otherwise. But
what I'm talking about here is something else, a combination
of insight and appreciation that sees more in the moment
than the latest "shit happening."

It seems to me that one grace of our era is the chance to achieve personal honesty at a fairly sophisticated level. The reason is not that we have become less prone to conformity than our predecessors, but that the currents to be conformed to are presently so numerous and complex that in the end you can't be something you're not for the one simple reason that you can't even figure out what that something is. And even if you succeeded, there are others so needy to establish their own identities that they feel compelled to deny the authenticity of yours. You may *think* you're a real environmentalist, a real feminist, a real black man (what's an unreal one look like, do you suppose?), but you're not. I'm describing an epiphany that might occur at the moment when all the officers in Napoleon's entourage also take out their scabbards and wave them in front of your face or when, seized by sympathy or malice, they all take your right hand at the same time, but with varying angles of perception, and attempt to guide the sword into the emperor's scabbard. It's the moment when you simply have to give up the game. A certain degree of frustration departs with that decision, and a certain degree of peace takes it place. I'm reminded of a quote by Andrea Dworkin (which I sent to a school principal I know, who now carries it in his wallet): "On one level I suffer terribly from the disdain that much of my work has met. On another, deeper level, I don't give a fuck."

Sometimes the grace of our era is made flesh in the struggles of a particular group. If that holds true for the present time, then I think the gay and lesbian experience of "coming out" most nearly embodies the grace I'm trying to describe. It is the grace of giving up the pretense of fitting into an "unnatural" —that is, unnatural for you—set of expectations. I'm not sure

that we in the straight world have fully reckoned how courageous and how political an act this is. We think of it as political only in the sense that yet another disenfranchised group
is standing up to be counted. But coming out strikes me as of
the very essence of what it means to be political: It's not an
example; it's practically the definition. A "love that dares not
speak its name" can also be a cozy love, within certain bounds,
a rather safe love. Anonymity brings immunity and, in the
most furtive way, a community of refuge. But the decision to
"come out" is also a decision to *come in* to the larger circle,
and to do so as no one but your undisguised self. It may require some anger to take that step. But it also involves a for-
saking of anger, the renunciation of the Napoleonic test with
all of its attendant frustrations. Perhaps it may best be understood as a recapitulation of the divine revelation, where God
identifies himself to Moses with the words "I Am Who I Am."
The Lord is finally "out" in the burning bush, and calls his
people "out" too—out of Egypt, out of the closet of historical
obscurity.

   Writing this book has been an experience of coming out for
me, out as a Christian, out also as a man with "un-Christian"
thoughts and with emotions that are not easy to own. I worry
about how these ruminations will be received, by the critics
I hope to impress, by the editors of publications for which I
hope to keep writing, by the members of a religious community
to which I hope always to belong. But then there comes that
point of release, beyond anxiety or anger, when I find myself
repeating the last words of Camus's character Meursault just
before his execution. (And publishing a book has always felt
to me like an execution, just as writing it feels like the heady
flight of a fugitive.) Meursault becomes angry, perhaps for

the first time in his passive life, when a priest comes to his jail cell to comfort and convert him. Finally, Meursault is forced to assert who he is, and who he is not. He is "out," in other words. And although what he takes to be "the benign indifference of the universe" I worship as benignity of a different sort, I feel very close to him now as I near my own final chapter.

> It was as if that great rush of anger had washed me clean, emptied me of hope, and, gazing up at the dark sky spangled with its signs and stars, for the first time, the first, I laid my heart open to the benign indifference of the universe. To feel it so like myself, indeed, so brotherly, made me realize that I'd been happy, and that I was happy still. For all to be accomplished, for me to feel less lonely, all that remained to hope was that on the day of my execution there should be a huge crowd of spectators and that they should greet me with howls of execration.

I have now spent fifty five years in resolving, having from the earliest time almost that I can remember been forming schemes of a better life. I have done nothing; the need of doing therefore is pressing, since the time of doing is short.

Samuel Johnson, September 18, 1764
About six in the evening

SOMEDAY
YOU WILL

I have a friend, a retired professor, who relieved some of the poverty of his postgraduate years by working as a night watchman on the Harvard campus. Books were a luxury for him then, and the kind of big book that comes off the scholarly presses in limited hardcover editions was way over his budget. So for a few minutes of each shift, he went into the library, searched with his flashlight for the volume containing Samuel Johnson's journal, carried it to the photocopier, and reproduced several pages. Then he resumed his watch. Eventually he had the whole volume, which means he also had the quotation on the page facing this one.

He would have had a number of other entries much like it, usually penned on Johnson's birthday or on the first day of the new year, or on the anniversary of his wife's death. Each one laments the failure of his previous resolutions; each one professes his intention to resolve again. It moves me to think, not only of Johnson resolving and resolving, year after year, just as I do, but of my friend assembling his photocopied pages like the fragments of a treasure map, matching his dark nights to Johnson's, his poverty, his tenuous hopes to those of the writer. I love to conjure up that image even more than I love to conjure up the image of him shocking his dinner guests one evening not long ago by noting that he detected "a good deal of anger in our friend Garret." Not Garret surely! "Oh, yes," he averred. "That's a very angry boy."

Perhaps I would have been offended by the comment, which I was not present to hear, except that my friend confided it to me. He was not needling me, either—I had told him what I was writing, and then he told me what he had said. He meant that I knew the material. He meant to say, and by way of reassurance, that I may have fooled others, but I had not fooled him. There is a distinct comfort in being known, is there not? I shake my head whenever I hear some well-meaning cleric argue for removing still more of the penitential language from the Book of Common Prayer: "Why do we have to keep beating people over the heads with the idea that they're bad?" she will say. Because, I reply, they already know they're bad and thus can take comfort from the acknowledgment. The only thing more painful than the remorse of feeling wicked is the loneliness of being told that you're good. All that "I'm okay, you're okay" means to me is "I'm completely oblivious, and you're completely alone." Praise me for nothing but my struggle.

And there was my consolation: If my friend could sense my anger, then perhaps he sensed my struggle as well. What had led him, after all, to photocopy those pages—not of *Rasselas* or *The Rambler, The Lives of the Poets,* or even Boswell's entertaining *Life,* but the journals—if not his profound appreciation of Johnson as one who took stock of himself in the night, the better to soldier on in the morning. (Or I guess it would have to be the afternoon—Johnson had a notoriously hard time getting out of bed in the morning.) Every so often some purveyor of reheated iconoclasm attempts to get our attention by claiming that the hero of Boswell's biography might not have been such a nice man. He was *not* a nice man. Even Boswell knew that. He was a good man, and if you really want to get a rise out of people nowadays, try suggesting that the two things are not necessarily the same. In fact, I suspect they are very rarely the same.

And yet isn't it wicked to believe that they are *never* the same? How many forms of self-righteousness are based on just that belief? Which brings us to what I think was the essence of Johnson's inner struggle: the effort to avoid all the self-swindling—the "cant" as he liked to call its verbal form—that inevitably results, depending on one's predisposition, in either a "nice" hypocrite or a shallow curmudgeon.

Johnson seemed born to struggle, and not only with his petulance, though that is the main reason for celebrating him here. He was partially blind, partially deaf, possessed of various nervous tics and peculiar mannerisms as well as an appearance that many found ugly (a childhood infection with scrofula having scarred his face). He suffered bouts of depression so severe that at one point he seems to have bought a lock and chain in anticipation of his being carted off to the madhouse. Recalling one such period of "melancholy" that had seized him in his youth, he said that he could stare at the church clock in his hometown for the better part of a morning without being able to tell the time.

He also struggled for much of his life with poverty—sometimes walking the streets of London all night because he had no place to sleep—and even his harshest critics have never denied his lifelong concern for the poor. For years he maintained a household of quarrelsome dependents that included a blind woman poet, a tentatively reformed prostitute, a freed African slave (and in time, his dependents), and a doctor whose indigent patients paid him, when they paid at all, with free drinks he did not have the heart to turn down. ("Perhaps the only man," Johnson noted, "who ever became intoxicated through motives of prudence.") At its best, Johnson's anger, like all the best forms of anger, was aroused by any show of callousness toward human misery. His famously scathing review of a book suggesting that human beings were the unwitting playthings of superior powers is but one example. His rebuke of the fastidious Mrs. Thrale when she turned up her nose at the foul odors coming from the cookshops of a poor neighborhood is another. "Hundreds of your fellow-creatures, dear Lady, turn another way, that they may not be tempted by the luxuries of Porridge-Island to wish for gratifications they are not able to obtain."

But not all of his retorts were so philanthropic. Some of his more choleric remarks are painful for an admirer to read; on occasion they also seem to have been painful for Johnson, who would go out of his way to make amends when he judged himself to have spoken too harshly. Several of his put-downs have taken on the patina of legend—"I have found you an argument; I am not obliged to find you an understanding"—but for the person who was their object, they may have taken on the patina of a permanent scar. A lot of Johnson's anger strikes one as the result of a seething impatience, a kind of intellectual road rage that flared up at the slow pace of the traffic, the sly detours and self-serving maneuvers of the other drivers. "The woman's a whore, and there's an end on it," he growled during a conversation about a certain lady's marital adventures. I wonder if he was talking mainly about the woman, or if he was merely challenging the others to say what they really meant. In either case, the man who once carried a passed-out prostitute home on his broad back, and whose powers of association seem virtually unmatched by any English speaker on record, could not have uttered such a remark without instantly recalling the savior who supped with "harlots and publicans." He could not easily have reproached others without suffering reproach from himself.

The inner struggles of Johnson boil down in many cases to the plight of a man who was a Christian by conviction, but not by disposition. Or we might rather say, who was a Christian by settled conviction much less than by a desperate existential faith. Johnson's convictions, I think, were more classical, and perhaps more agnostic than those of most saints. He would have found the company of Seneca more congenial than that of St. Francis. Before his death he hastily destroyed a section of his journals that some of his biographers have suggested may have pertained to misgivings he had in regard to religion. The conjecture seems very plausible to me. The journal entries that we do have suggest that the simple act of attending church was often more than Johnson could bear; he repeatedly chides himself for his "neglect of services." Johnson's life is of great interest to me, not only because of a similar tension between my own temperament and my religion, but because I believe that the religion itself is based on a certain inner tension—and I think that Johnson grasped that latter tension at its very best.

In Johnson we see a simultaneous insistence on the sinful

state of humanity and on the duty of human beings to be better than they are. He is neither an optimist nor a pessimist; he is what you get when you cross a humanist and a realist with no dominance given to either set of genes. Though the eighteenth century has sometimes been called the Age of Johnson, he stands opposed to many of its more optimistic assumptions, including those that led the century to also be dubbed the Age of Reason. As one of the characters in his short novel *Rasselas* says: "There are a thousand familiar disputes which reason can never decide, questions that elude investigation and make logic ridiculous, cases where something must be done, and where little can be said." He sounds very modern, almost *post*modern there. Once in a gathering of forward-looking, educated white men proud in their rejection of the "superstitious" past and confident in the promise of an "enlightened" future, Johnson raised his glass and said, "Here's to the next insurrection of the Negroes in the West Indies!" I doubt that the rising up of the Negroes offended the men so much as the implicit putting down of their imperial achievements.

Still, you cannot believe in uprisings without believing in some possibility of positive change, and you cannot believe in positive change without believing that some things are morally preferable to others. In other words, for all his pessimism about the human condition, Johnson refuses to despair of it. He refuses to retreat into cynicism or nihilism. Those poignant resolutions in his journal—"to avoid idleness. . . . To go to Church every Sunday. . . . *To keep a journal*" [my italics, his irony]—are all doggedly progressive in their belief that "something must be done," and *can* be done. That was the achievement of Johnson, no less than any other of his many literary accomplishments. He continued to struggle, as all of us must, with minimal gains but with optimal faith.

Of course, the relevant application of these struggles is to anger. Some of Johnson's last words before dying speak of the tentative balance he had achieved between the fierce man he had necessarily to remain and the kinder man he had struggled to become. To one of his visitors he said, *"Iam Moriturus,"* "I who am about to die," the salute of Roman gladiators before fighting in the arena. And to a young woman visitor, he spoke what may have been his last words: "God bless you, my dear."

That beautiful combination of gladiator and godfather is also found in the story of Johnson and two young friends who decided, after a night on the town, to pay the older man a call. They showed up at his door in the wee hours of the morning and began pounding on it. Believing he was about to be set upon by robbers, Johnson took up the stout walking stick he was in the habit of carrying. He appeared at the door in his nightclothes ready to crack a head or two. But when he saw the two young men (and can't you see them as well?—hats on cockeyed, smiles slightly awry), he responded in a way that sets him forever apart from Agamemnon, Saul, and those other figures of Olympian rage to whom he bears a superficial resemblance. "What, is it you, you dogs?" he said. "I'll have a frisk with you."

And so Johnson dressed himself, and the three men spent what remained of darkness drinking and conversing in their favorite pubs. At dawn, when the grocers were setting up their stands, Johnson thought it a good idea to help. Not meeting with much welcome there, the three revelers found a boat and went out rowing on the Thames until the two young men excused themselves to keep a breakfast date with some young women. Imagine how far they might have rowed otherwise.

That image of Johnson roused from his bed in the middle of the night is one of the images I try to keep always before me. There he is, both armed and hospitable, as ready to frisk with a young dog as to brain a mad one; not the best man who ever lived, but an example of the best that a man like me might manage to become. How I wish I could have sat down with him, if only for an hour.

⤙

"Someday you will." So says the woman I love, having read the preceding words—she who has tried twice now to read my favorite biography of the great man and found it too much of a slog, even for my sake. She whose faith is so far from being worn on her sleeve that she would sooner go sleeveless in January than say a table grace out loud. Women in Afghanistan do not veil their faces any more than she veils her faith, yet it shines on me always, and even after so many years of living together, it continues to amaze me. "Someday you will"—as if to say, "Did you ever doubt it?"

Before this book had a title, I usually told people it was about anger and faith. At other times I said only that it was about anger. But without faith of the kind my wife possesses, I would have no subject. I would have anger, but I would have no subject. I could write about faith by itself, but what point would there be in writing about anger by itself?

For the premise behind the book—a premise I cannot claim to prove in its pages, or demonstrate reliably in my life—is that anger can be redeemed. The belief behind everything I have said is that anger can be controlled without being destroyed, and expressed without necessarily leading to destruction. "A bruised reed he will not break, and a dimly-burning wick he will not quench," says the prophet Isaiah. I can read that two ways. First, that God herself stands as proof that wrath and mercy can coexist. The One who breaks the rocks does not break the bruised reed. And second, that the Consuming Fire Who Is God allows us our own fire, however much it fumes and stinks at times. We are permitted our share of honest fury. This is my faith, and like all faith, it falls as far short of certainty as it goes beyond mere speculation. On the one hand, it proves nothing. But on the other hand, it determines the way I spend my money, cast my votes, and read the signs of my times.

I am writing this just weeks after the terrorist attacks on the World Trade Center Towers and the Pentagon. By the time you read these words, the United States may be at war. We may have suffered an even more devastating attack. We may have devastated other nations. It is tempting to say that anger no longer has a place in such a world at such a time, and there are those who do say it, just as there are those who say that in view of the suffering brought upon us by religious fanatics, religious faith has no place in the world either. But statements like these also strike me as fanatical—for what is fanaticism, after all, but a war against faith, a campaign to replace faith with unbending certainties and the fallible humanity God created with a perfect creature of our own making. Contrary to conventional wisdom, fanaticism does not demand blind faith; it takes offense at faith. It attempts to abolish faith. And its first step is always to abolish faith in ourselves and our possibilities. Talk to a fundamentalist and tell me if I'm wrong.

Faith comes hard, in trying times as in tranquil ones. Our follies loom so large. But amid so much that dismays me of late, so much sentimentality, self-righteousness, and saber-rattling, I see any number of people trying to arrive at an honest answer to the question, "What should we do?" And part of the question translates as "How should we act on our emotions?" How do we make some kind of peace between anger and hope, between pity and self-preservation? If suicide is the best way to serve God, then perhaps it does not matter if we also kill our own emotions. But if the service of God is life, and abundant life, then emotions matter very much.

What should we do? The question is not separate from asking what we should do with our anger. Denying our anger at a time like this may prove every bit as dangerous as giving it free rein. What difference is there between refusing to acknowledge a child and failing to set him any rules? He comes to the same dead end either way. Besides, I'm not sure it's anger so much as a deadly dispassionateness that is terrorizing and tempting us now. I do not see rage so much as the cold-eyed calculation of patient assassins and "measured" responses. The calmer the rhetoric of the mullahs and the generals, the more nervous I get. The cruelest people I have ever known were nothing if not calm. An angry torturer is a liability; he always botches the job. The art of exquisite torment, like that of mass destruction, comes of the practice of perfect equanimity, whether in a dungeon or a marriage, a secret cavern or a congressional hall. Might it be anger that actually comes to our rescue in the end, like an indignant mother, perhaps in the literal form of indignant mothers, wringing their hands at the heaps of corpses and the dusty lines of refugees and crying out, "Enough, enough, enough!"

"Someday you will." When she said that to me, I felt as if I were looking faith square in the face. It was better than seeing Dr. Johnson. As I imagine it now, that meeting would be beautiful mostly for the delight of hearing her whisper in my ear, "Didn't I tell you?" and remembering all of a sudden that, yes, she did. Against the background of suicide missions and apocalyptic fantasies, one hears acquaintances talking as though the world was now neatly divided between those who believe in a life here and now and those who believe in a paradise to come, as though lovers could similarly be divided between those who believe in tenderness and those who believe in ecstasy. More and more, I believe in the intersection of today and someday; and I don't only mean this in a metaphysical sense. It can be put in the most pedestrian terms. "Someday you will master your anger." Yes, and some days you do.

THE AUTHOR

Garret Keizer is the Episcopal priest of a small rural parish and a former high school English teacher, as well as the author of *God of Beer*, *No Place But Here*, and the critically acclaimed *A Dresser of Sycamore Trees*. His work also appears in *The Christian Century* and *Harper's Magazine*. He lives in northeastern Vermont with his wife and daughter.